THE POISONED CHALICE

THE RISE AND FALL OF THE POST-ISOLATION SPRINGBOK COACHES

GAVIN RICH

Published by Zebra Press
an imprint of Random House Struik (Pty) Ltd
Reg. No. 1966/003153/07
Wembley Square, First Floor, Solan Road, Gardens, Cape Town, 8001
PO Box 1144, Cape Town, 8000, South Africa

www.zebrapress.co.za

First published 2013

1 3 5 7 9 10 8 6 4 2

Publication © Zebra Press 2013
Text © Gavin Rich 2013

Cover images: background image © David Rogers/Gallo Images;
Rudolf Straeuli © Duif du Toit/Gallo Images; André Markgraaff/Getty Images/Gallo Images;
Peter de Villiers © Steve Haag/Gallo Images; Heyneke Meyer © Teaukura Moetaua/
Getty Images/Gallo Images; Kitch Christie © David Rogers/Allsport/Gallo Images;
Jake White © Tertius Pickard/Gallo Images; Nick Mallett © Tertius Pickard/Gallo Images

PUBLISHER: Marlene Fryer
MANAGING EDITOR: Ronel Richter-Herbert
PROOFREADER: Louis Greenberg
INDEXER: Sanet le Roux
COVER DESIGNER: Sean Robertson
TEXT DESIGNER: Jacques Kaiser
TYPESETTER: Monique Cleghorn
PHOTO RESEARCHER: Colette Stott

Set in 11pt on 14.5 pt Garamond

ISBN 978 1 77022 565 7 (print)
ISBN 978 1 77022 566 4 (ePub)
ISBN 978 1 77022 567 1 (PDF)

Contents

To my wife, Anna, and children, Kate and Peter, for putting up with my absence, sometimes for weeks but often for months and occasionally for several times a year since I covered my first Springbok tour in 1992

ACKNOWLEDGEMENTS

I have long felt a need for a book that records the journey the Springboks have travelled over the first two decades since South African rugby was unified, but the idea for a book on the coaches came to me when Peter de Villiers and I were on our book tour after the publication of *Politically Incorrect,* Peter's life story and a book on which we collaborated. So many people asked me if all the Bok coaches' stories were similar to Peter's. My response was that they all had different experiences, but that common threads ran through all of them.

There have been books on the individual coaches, but I resolved to tell the story of the Bok coaches as a collective in the post-isolation era, starting with John Williams, who was appointed in 1992 via a letter that consisted of just one line, through to current coach Heyneke Meyer. I am one of the few rugby writers who travelled on the first tour to France and England who is still on the beat and thus possessed of what someone once referred to as "a long view of the coaches", so I felt I was in a position to write the story. As you will see when you read this book, a lot has changed, but a lot has also stayed the same.

Jake White, who has decided he wants to put his South African chapter behind him and start a new life in Australia, was the only living post-isolation Springbok coach who I did not get to interview, and I am indebted to all those, from Williams through to Meyer, who were able to make the time and were willing to be quizzed by a reporter who some of them, during parts of their reign, must have despised.

It's not easy being a Springbok coach, and much of this book is about the pressures they are confronted with. But while the title suggests sympathy with those who have held down the hottest and most pressured position in South African sport, I agree with those who claim that some coaches have used the obstacles as a convenient excuse for their own poor decisions. So not all the coaches will agree with everything I say about them. But then hopefully that should be an indication that I've done the job I set out to do and that I have been honest. I made a commitment to all of them that I would be fair, and hopefully I've lived up to that.

To those colleagues who were on the beat in 1992 and have joined me in doing the long haul, my thanks for your companionship over these 21 years. Louis de Villiers, Dan Retief and Mark Keohane are the others who have experienced what I have, and although Dan and Mark have spent some of the past few years off the beat, all three of those guys could have written this story. To Mark in particular, who took some flak from some of the coaches in this book, and maybe even from me, my thanks for the friendship and the shared experiences on those occasions, such as the 2007 World Cup, where we travelled together and shared accommodation.

Talking of good guys, Liam del Carme and Mike Greenaway are strong personal friends with whom I have also shared much of the journey, and I thank them both, as I do Stephen Nell. Craig Ray was a good sounding board when I first started thinking about writing this book. Thanks also to Jon Cardinelli, Clinton van den Berg, Zelim Nel, Jacques van der Westhuizen, Ryan Vrede, Kevin McCallum, Brenden Nel, Andrew Koopman and others who have suffered my madness and resolved to tolerate it.

Talking of madness, a special thanks to Simon Borchardt, who supplied me with 50 scrapbooks of newspaper cuttings he had compiled from 1990 to 2000. As a means to jolt my memory, they were particularly invaluable, and if anyone wants to write a book chronicling sport in our changing country over the first decade of transition, you know where to go. In fact, I might go there myself.

Finally, to my editor, Ronel Richter-Herbert, for pointing me in the right direction when I departed from the chronology of the story from time to time, and just for being patient, and to Marlene Fryer for trusting me enough to bring out this book in what in the end was a much quicker time period than maybe it demanded. Some of the coaches warranted much more than the 10 000 to 12 000 words I dedicated to them, so I hope I have done their individual stories justice.

GAVIN RICH

AUTHOR'S NOTE

Readers may notice that 11 Springbok coaches of the post-isolation era are featured, whereas officially there have been 12 since 1992. Initially I did intend featuring Gerrie Sonnekus, but after being asked nicely not to by someone close to his family, and realising that the book was already in danger of getting way too long, I resolved to leave that part of the Bok coaching story out. Gerrie departed the job before he effectively had a chance to experience it. I cover the reason briefly at the start of Chapter 5.

1

Mad Coaches Disease

Nick Mallett loves a good laugh, but, like most people, he doesn't enjoy being the butt of a joke. And as usual, South African rugby was making a laughing stock of itself. That explained the former Springbok coach's irritation when he arrived at a Sandton hotel on a crisp Highveld morning in September 2006 for the meeting that the whole country seemed to be talking about.

Rudolf Straeuli, who had been keeping a low profile while trying to recover his reputation following the infamous events that tarnished the Springboks' 2003 Rugby World Cup campaign, wasn't doing cartwheels of delight either as he flew in from Durban.

As for Ian McIntosh … well, as an early victim but also a long-standing survivor of the weird, confusing and often cruel machinations of South African rugby politics, the wily veteran had seen it all before. He had, in fact, twice before attended meetings similar to the one he was about to take part in now – once when he himself was the Bok coach, when Louis Luyt had summoned 19 different coaches to Ellis Park the week before a Test against England in 1994, and again three years later, when Carel du Plessis was in charge.

Du Plessis was at the meeting too. He had flown in from the Western Cape, as had Harry Viljoen. In fact, the only living former Springbok coaches from the post-isolation era not at the 2006 meeting, which had been called by South African Rugby Union (SARU) president Oregan Hoskins, were Professor John Williams and André Markgraaff.

Williams lived too far away, on a farm near the Limpopo/Botswana border, to make it to Johannesburg, while Markgraaff had turned his back on rugby the year before, after he had challenged the business practices of the then SARU president, Brian van Rooyen. Markgraaff also disliked the incumbent Springbok coach Jake White, as he felt White too often and too naively poked his nose into rugby politics, which he knew nothing about.

1

White was to be the focus of the meeting, which was being held to address a crisis largely of his own making: his team had suffered five consecutive defeats. The 18-34 defeat to the All Blacks at Loftus the previous Saturday was the culmination of the negative momentum that had started with a home defeat to France and then haemorrhaged into a 0-49 annihilation at the hands of Australia. The Springboks had also lost to the Kiwis in New Zealand, and again to the Wallabies, in Sydney.

Sections of the media and a great many South African rugby fans were calling for White's head with a passion and vehemence that in some countries would drive a vote of no-confidence in the national president.

So, as Mallett saw it, the meeting wasn't really being held to deal with White at all, but just to placate the media and public.

As he recalls: "I was irritated by the whole thing. It was absolute nonsense. The meeting was being held so Hoskins and the SA Rugby chairman [Mpumelelo Tshume] could report back that they had done something, but what they were really doing was just covering up the fact that they had no clue what to do."

Hence Mallett's reluctance to get involved, and why it took much persuasion from SARU to get him there. Like McIntosh, Mallett had also attended the 1997 coaches' indaba, which was called to help out Bok coach Carel du Plessis. In Mallett's view, it had not achieved much except to make him, Mallett, unpopular with the then South African Rugby Football Union (SARFU) president, Dr Louis Luyt.

Administrators who "have no clue" have long been the bane of Mallett's existence. They're the reason he has refused to get on the grass and coach in South Africa since losing the Springbok job in 2000. And in 1997, he told Luyt straight out, without pulling any punches, that it was *his* cluelessness that had led to the Boks losing the British & Irish Lions series. After all, *he* had appointed Du Plessis, even though the former "Prince of Wings" had no coaching experience worth mentioning.

"I told Luyt that it was his fault that the Springboks were in the mess they were in, because he had appointed Carel to the job when he had no coaching experience. [My words] nearly came back to bite me when, later in the year, I was up for the Bok job myself."

Heading into a similar meeting nine years later, Mallett didn't want to ruffle feathers again. But as he listened to the coaches who spoke before him, he decided what he was going to say when it was his turn. He wanted the administrators, Hoskins and Tshume, to realise the ridiculousness of the situation. He cleared his throat to speak.

"Listen, you've appointed Jake until the World Cup next year, and he will have his ups and downs, as we have all had as Bok coaches."

He then read out the success rate of the other coaches at the meeting in matches against New Zealand and Australia. He didn't mention his own record, as his success rate was the only one better than White's, which he felt qualified him to raise this point.

"I just wanted to make it quite clear that Jake was actually in a position of strength. His record was far superior to most of the coaches present."

Mallett then proceeded to address each coach in turn.

"Mac, the Boks won only a small percentage of their games during your tenure; André Markgraaff's record in terms of games won and lost wasn't great; Harry and Carel, you were both shocking. So what right do we really have to sit here and judge Jake?"

Mallett was determined to drum home how silly the situation was. "As ex-Bok coaches, all of us had lost the job at some stage, and therefore we were in no position to judge. All we could do for Jake was sympathise with him. I pointed out to Hoskins that having experienced the poisoned chalice ourselves, not one of us sitting around the table would actually want the job.

"What we could do was [empathise] with Jake and what he was going through in the face of the demanding public and media. We had all been through it ourselves, and we knew there had been times when all we'd wanted was some support and a bit of time to get things right. We had all experienced what it was like to be in a situation where the team was struggling, but we felt we had it in our grasp to get it right if we were left to our own devices."

Mallett still thinks the 2006 meeting was a crazy idea, but at least it served some purpose, for Straeuli headed back to his home in Mount Edgecombe feeling far more positive than when he had first arrived.

"It was great to be among people who had shared the same experience and who understood the incredible pressures of the job," he told me. "Looking back, I wish that I had had something like that when I was Bok coach, as one always feels so alone in the job. A lot of positive [input] could come from a group of people who understand what the coach is experiencing, and who can lend a sympathetic ear and operate as a sounding board."

To some extent, McIntosh provided that kind of support to White as his official mentor during White's four years in charge.

"Every Springbok coach reaches a point where the pressure just gets too much and where you need to have friends around you," McIntosh says. "I will never forget Cecil Moss, who coached the Boks during the 1980s, phoning me to congratulate me when I was appointed. He warned me by saying that no one ever knows how lonely the job of Springbok coach is until they've actually experienced it. And it's very true."

But there was only one coach at that particular meeting who was feeling the pinch, and that was White.

Although White described the meeting as just another "unnecessary distraction" in what was the build-up to an important Tri-Nations Test against the All Blacks in Rustenburg, he later recalled it in a more positive light. Like Straeuli, he appreciated the other coaches' empathy.

More importantly, White felt that Hoskins and Tshume now knew that the same complaints he had about the administrators who ran South African rugby had also been voiced by his predecessors. It just showed what little progress had been made in taking Springbok rugby forward.

"I was reassured because the coaches said the things I wanted Hoskins to hear, the things I had been saying all along," White explains in his bestselling autobiography, *In Black and White*. "They were pointing out that we will be inconsistent, that we don't have structures in place, that we worry about the provinces first before Springbok rugby, and that we don't look after the players. The coaches spoke about three-year cycles, and how the team hit the wall in the third year. They said that Hoskins and Tshume could hire any coaches in the world and the situation would remain the same."

The coaches' indaba served another purpose, too: some of what was said during the meeting reinforced White's vision for Springbok rugby and reassured him that he was on the right track.

"Nick Mallett came up with ideas that he thought would be a way forward. I felt better that at least I wasn't going mad. People were seeing things the way I was seeing them."

Ah, there's the word ... "mad". White needed convincing that he wasn't going "mad". That word frequently made it into my media coverage at the time. Two weeks before the Sandton meeting, I even wrote a story for the Saturday editions of the SA Independent Group in which I wondered whether White was succumbing to the same ailment all Springbok coaches suffer from at some stage. I called it "Mad Coaches Disease".

White had been contradicting himself with almost every public utterance he had made in the two months leading up to the Sandton meeting. He seemed a shadow of the man who had dragged Springbok rugby from the brink of despair two and a half years previously, when he first took over as coach.

However, even in those early days, when White seemed so together and unflustered, and when he was shocking everyone by coaching his Springboks into winning matches they were expected to lose, wizened hacks in the media were asking among themselves: "So, when is MCD [Mad Coaches Disease] going to set in? When is the pressure going to start taking its toll?"

Those of us who had been around for the duration of the post-isolation period up till that point had seen plenty of examples of MCD. The symptoms usually included contradictory behaviour, poor selection choices, incomprehensible strategies and odd public statements. Even those who seemed immune to the disease at the start, like Nick Mallett, who set off with a long winning streak, succumbed to MCD eventually.

All the coaches reacted to the pressure in different ways, but at some stage MCD would strike and people would start asking, "Has this guy lost it?" Harry Viljoen, for example, had told his players not to kick the ball before his first Test in charge, and had then gone to the opposite extreme by selecting a team that could *only* kick. MCD even drove him to unexpectedly resign his job, but at least he was honest enough to admit that the pressure from the media and the public was one of the main reasons why he was standing down.

But is it really any mystery that MCD exists in a country where rugby is followed and supported so passionately, and where the Springboks are expected to win every game? Not to mention the other factors at play … For instance, no other rugby-playing country has the divided past of South Africa. It is hard to think of a national team in any sporting code in other countries that had once been as reviled as the Springboks by a majority of their countrymen. And after the apartheid years, rugby was intensely scrutinised during the transformation phase, which made demands many of the coaches were not equipped to deal with.

Even now, with both South African rugby and the country as a whole having made such great progress towards normalisation, there are still constant reminders of an unseen power struggle that underpins the game in this country.

"Maybe I should give the game back to the Afrikaners," South Africa's first black coach, Peter de Villiers, said bitterly when he was threatened with a sex-tape revelation in 2008. De Villiers subsequently apologised for his comment, and made the point that he wasn't referring to Afrikaners per se. But everyone understood what he meant, as rugby had for so long been dominated by the Afrikaner elite. If you look back at the pre-isolation days, how many Afrikaans doctors, lawyers and businessmen were in prominent positions in rugby administration? And a behind-the-scenes struggle for control continues to this day.

Many of the Bok coaches of the last 20-odd years were ordinary, normal people who loved the game but, once they were in the job, discovered that it was about so much more than just rugby. Rugby has come to mean an almost disproportionate amount to a population group that has felt increasingly marginalised and stripped of its identity, and in this environment the coach has assumed a position of tremendous importance. What is expected of the Springbok coach is almost impossible.

In his book, *The Real McCaw*, All Black captain Richie McCaw describes how his coach, Graham Henry, changed their whole approach to the 2011 World Cup on the basis of what he had seen in the Springbok dressing room after a Tri-Nations match in 2009. Henry told his players that he had realised whereas the South Africans played for their country, the All Blacks played for the team. It inspired him to introduce nationalism as a motivational tool for the All Blacks.

Sean Fitzpatrick, another All Black skipper, had said something similar after the 1995 World Cup final, when his disappointment at losing was diffused by the experience of participating in an event that was so much more to the South African nation than a mere sports competition.

That level of emotional investment brings pressure and responsibilities that transcend anything a coach of a national sports team normally experiences. In South Africa, you don't just coach and lead the team; in a sense, you become the leader of a country. It's small wonder then that so few have lived up to the massive expectations.

"It takes a certain type of character to be a Springbok coach, and I don't think I had the character for it, and I don't think most of the coaches who have taken the job have had the right personality for it," reflects André Markgraaff.

As well as being a former Bok mentor himself, for many years Markgraaff also worked on the other side as one of the officials who appointed and selected the coaches. Given his experience in the game and the high-ranking role he played for much of the time, Markgraaff's opinion on how Springbok coaches are selected is damning, and may explain why some of them appeared somewhat out of their depth.

As he explains: "Too often it was just a case of choosing a guy because he appealed to some people in the executive and satisfied some faction. Jake White was the only coach [who was] appointed through a proper professional process where there was a commitment to objectively arrive at the best [man] for the job."

Indeed. It also explains, as Mallett has said, why the journey of the post-isolation Springbok coaches has encountered so much turbulence.

"What was amazing about that 2006 meeting was how many of us had shared the same experiences, encountered the same problems, and yet still, many years later, nothing had been done to redress shortfalls that should have been staring the administrators in the face. For me, half the problem is that people who have made the coaching appointments haven't been qualified to do so."

When Mallett was interviewed for the Springbok job in 1997, he wasn't even asked about his rugby philosophy. Not one of the people who appointed him had played or coached at the highest level. With the exception of 2004, when Markgraaff's technical committee appeared to get it right with White, this remains the status quo. A committee, which consisted mostly of administrators, many whom had their own political agenda, appointed Peter de Villiers in 2008. One would have thought that former players and coaches would have been more qualified to assess the potential of the candidates.

Says Mallett: "I can talk about my experience when England approached me for the national coaching job, and it doesn't compare to any experiences I've heard about when Bok coaches are appointed. I wasn't interviewed by the Rugby Football Union (RFU), but by a rugby committee. The committee was headed by the high-performance director, Rob Andrew, and comprised of the former flanker, Richard Hill, Ian McGeechan [former British & Irish Lions coach] and Connor O'Shea. It was really interesting and we had a proper rugby discussion.

"The RFU then asked the committee for their recommendation. I thought it was a very fair way of doing it. In South Africa, fairness and thoroughness have been lacking, and the elected officials and board members who make the decisions aren't really qualified to make coaching appointments."

South Africa has a lot of coaching expertise and experience to draw on when coaching appointments are made, but Mallett says only one union has ever approached him to help identify or select a suitable candidate.

"When I was still Springbok coach, the Bulls approached me and told me they had a list of candidates they were looking at but didn't know what they should be looking for, and would I help them out. I really respected them for their honesty. I was one of the people who would have helped them make the decision to appoint Heyneke Meyer as [the Bulls] coach.

"But at first they wanted to appoint him for only one year. I said no, they needed to give him time to get things right. South Africa has too much of a short-term view about their coaches, and I think generally there is a lack of calmness about everything. It's because for most of the past 20 years the people running the game haven't understood what they are looking for in a coach and, as a result, when a crisis hits, like it did in 2006, they don't know how to react to it."

That lack of clarity has had a direct impact on Springbok performances, and it has probably destroyed not just a few coaching careers, but also a few playing careers. Mark Andrews, who apart from Joost van der Westhuizen played under more Bok coaches than any other wearer of the green and gold, reckons the turnover of national coaches during his playing career had a massive impact on results.

"When people ask me about my greatest achievement, I don't tell them it was winning the World Cup; I tell them it was being able to adjust my game to suit six different national coaches," Andrews says. "I played my first Test in 1994 and my last in 2001. That's a different coach more frequently than every 18 months, and Nick Mallett was the only one who lasted for longer than that. Every coach had a different idea on how I should play."

This may explain why South African rugby, despite the two World Cup triumphs, has so often given the impression that it's lagging behind the top teams in the world.

It might also have helped South African rugby if it had a better perspective of its capabilities when the curtain was lifted in 1992 and the Springboks were allowed back onto the international stage.

Instead, it lived in dreamland ...

2

"Welcome to your worst nightmare!"

There was never any danger of the New Zealand All Blacks underestimating the challenge posed by the Springboks as they arrived in Johannesburg for the first post-isolation tour of this country. The South African public told them exactly what to expect.

"Welcome to your worst nightmare!" screamed several banners brandished by locals who greeted Sean Fitzpatrick and his team as they walked through the arrivals hall at Johannesburg airport on a Sunday evening in August 1992.

It wasn't just an isolated pocket of arrogance. In his book *The Winning Way*, Wallaby World Cup–winning coach Bob Dwyer described his irritation at the aggressive way South African fans insisted on informing him that the Springboks, and not *his* team, were the true world champions.

Perhaps one shouldn't describe the South Africans' attitude as arrogance, for it is true that there are none so blind as those who cannot see. Being denied international competition for so long had rendered South African sports fans incapable of assessing how good, or bad, their teams were.

The mood on the eve of the All Black visit was driven by three factors: the naivety that had resulted from many seasons of isolation from international rugby; a domestic competition, the Currie Cup, which had been trumpeted as the toughest rugby competition in the world; and a desperate desire to see a country struggling with its identity and undergoing massive changes assert itself in a sport at which it had historically excelled.

The national cricket team had made a good fist of it in an epoch-making comeback year, which had started with a tour to India under the captaincy of Clive Rice, and it had then captured the public imagination early in 1992 by reaching the semi-finals of the Cricket World Cup, with Kepler Wessels as captain. Even though they exited against England in controversial circumstances in a rain-reduced game, the tournament had inspired those South Africans who were about to vote in a referendum on whether or not to accept President F.W. de Klerk's political reforms.

Transfixed as South Africans were by the World Cup in this time of political uncertainty, it became clear then that sport was going to play a big role in determining the nation's self-esteem in future. After all, the country had been the pariah of the world for decades because of race-driven government policies and ideologies. After years of being criticised, banned, expelled and isolated by the rest of the world, it would have been understandable if an inferiority complex had started permeating the South African population.

Not that there was any noticeable feeling of inferiority in the rugby community. A year before their return to international rugby, the Springboks had played a festival game against the Junior Springboks at Durban's Kings Park Stadium. It was designed to give South Africa's top players the opportunity to play together and to get a feel for the green-and-gold jersey ahead of a possible return to international sport. The first-choice team won comprehensively enough to spark at least some optimism.

"It's this, this is what it's all about," said Springbok selector Mickey Gerber, pointing to the emblem on his blazer pocket when I approached him for his thoughts after the game. "Believe me, we can take on New Zealand at 1 a.m., Australia at 3 a.m. and England at 5 a.m., and we will beat them all on the same day," he continued.

His sentiments were echoed those months later, when the All Blacks were preparing for their opening tour match against Natal at the same stadium. Led by the hulking flanker Wahl Bartmann, Natal were top of the Currie Cup table and en route to their second Currie Cup title. Michael du Plessis, who had led the Boks against the Junior Boks in 1991 but had subsequently retired, wasn't shy to tell me that the confidence fans had exhibited at the airport a few nights earlier was thoroughly justified.

"I think Natal will win by around 20 points," said Du Plessis by telephone from his dental surgery in Port Elizabeth.

Noting the incredulity in the tone of the interviewer, Du Plessis extrapolated. "I just think South African rugby has moved on during isolation and forged ahead of the rest of the world."

Phew! Talk about giving the All Blacks motivation. And talk about piling the pressure on South Africa's first post-isolation Springbok coach, John Williams. A former Bok lock, Williams had coached Northern Transvaal to some significant successes in the latter part of the 1980s, but when the All Blacks arrived, he hadn't coached since 1989.

Eugene van Wyk had coached Northerns in the interim, but the movers and shakers on the South African rugby-coaching firmament at the time were Natal's wily, experienced and innovative Ian McIntosh, who had engineered that province's historic first-ever Currie Cup title in 1990, and Transvaal's dynamic young Harry Viljoen. In 1992, those were the two teams that played in the final, and they got there by employing a style that was far more modern than the 10-man rugby Northern Transvaal espoused.

But both McIntosh and Viljoen had one glaring deficiency in their respective CVs: neither of them had played for the Springboks and was in possession of the distinctive green-and-gold ceremonial blazer. At the time, with the ageing Dr Danie Craven still calling the shots in South African rugby's administrative leadership, being a Springbok was a prerequisite to becoming the national coach.[*]

So it came down to a choice between Williams and Western Province's Dawie Snyman. The latter lost out because his provincial team's influence had waned considerably since they had last touched silverware, when they'd shared the Currie Cup with Williams's team in 1989.

If it seems bizarre that South African rugby turned to a coach who had not actually coached in three years to guide the Springboks out of isolation, it was only one of several decisions Craven and his fellow administrators took that smacked of arrogance. The newly formed South African Rugby Football Union was an organisation that was out of touch with reality.

For a start, there was the schedule that they accepted. The Springboks had not played official Test rugby since a South American team and an England side, led by John Scott, had toured South Africa in 1984. There had been an unofficial series against the New Zealand Cavaliers in 1986, and then a mini-series against a weak World XV in 1989 to celebrate the old South African Rugby Board's centenary.

---

[*] The South African Rugby Football Union (SARFU) was formed on 23 March 1992, when the unification of the former whites-only South African Rugby Board (SARB) and the non-racial South African Rugby Union (SARU) was signed at the Kimberley Sun. Craven and Ebrahim Patel were joint presidents, but Craven was vested with the executive power.

The Boks had impressed against a Cavaliers team that included all but two of the players selected for the aborted All Black tour scheduled for the year before, and perhaps it was the memory of how special players such as Carel and Michael du Plessis, Johan Heunis, Danie Gerber, Naas Botha and Uli Schmidt had performed that inspired such confidence six years later. But the 1989 World XV, although beaten in the big match at Newlands, had exposed shortcomings in the South African game. By 1992 both Du Plessis brothers had retired, and the legendary duo of Gerber and Botha were in their mid-30s and coming to the end of their illustrious careers.

While the old traditional rivals, New Zealand, were slated to play the comeback game at Ellis Park, world champions Australia were to tour at the same time and would play the Boks in Cape Town a week after the Johannesburg match. A plan to play Italy and Romania before the tour had fallen through, and thus the Boks were denied the gentle warm-up they needed to prepare for the world's two top teams.

So to Williams fell the unenviable task of coaching the Springboks in their comeback Tests against the two best teams in the world, and that against the background of public expectation on the one side (whites), and the trepidation and very reserved support of a majority population, which, during the apartheid years, had seen the Springbok emblem as a symbol of oppression, on the other.

Not that everyone in South Africa was that gung-ho about the Springboks' chances. A few wise men who had travelled overseas and closely studied the international rugby environment had their doubts. Ian McIntosh had gone to Australia in early 1992 in an attempt to broaden his own coaching education, and after his return I interviewed him for the *Natal Mercury*. He sounded a warning that South African rugby might well be in a time warp similar to the one that had tripped up Rice's cricket team in India.

Piet Strydom, the selection convener for Natal, also noted his concern. He had travelled to Italy as an official with a South African Students team – captained by talented loose forward Andrew Aitken – which participated in the Students World Cup.

"The All Blacks are going to murder us in the rucks," he predicted.

According to Strydom, the ball was coming back from the rucks much quicker than the South African players were used to.

Although influenced by the likes of Michael du Plessis, as a young rugby writer living in Durban, I also had my doubts. Or at least an article that appeared under my name in the programme to the Natal/All Black game suggested I did.

"Nowhere in South Africa has the ball retention been up to the standard we have seen in the NZ/Australia Bledisloe Cup Test," was my contribution to the cautionary lobby. Former Transvaal, Ireland and British Lions scrum-half John Robbie was, however, perhaps the person who best summed up what those first post-isolation Test matches were going to reveal. In his column in the *Rugby World and Post* magazine ahead of the tour, Robbie wrote: "The Boks are either the true world champions or a collection of dinosaurs hopelessly out of touch with the modern game and in for a rude awakening."

Ah, those were to prove prophetic words . . .

But on the eve of the All Black match against Natal, the Durban media displayed a remarkable air of optimism. It was partly fuelled by the confidence of Michael du Plessis, but also by rather inconsequential things, such as the fact that All Black lock Murray Pierce had been playing club rugby in Durban for two years and had hardly had a look-in for the provincial team behind the much bigger trio of Rudi Visagie, André Botha and Steve Atherton.

That, though, might actually just have indicated how much the game had changed overseas; players had become far more mobile than the Rudi Visagies of this world. Certainly the game against Natal served as a wake-up call to anyone who expected the All Blacks to be burnt alive. If anyone was facing a nightmare it was the Boks, and this quickly became apparent as Va'aiga Tuigamala, the giant All Black wing, contemptuously ran over Tony Watson, supposedly one of Natal's better players, as if he wasn't even there.

The scores were close for a bit, but the All Blacks were always in control, and they eventually ran out as victors by the same 20-point margin some had predicted would be the deficit they would face at the final whistle. What was even more disturbing was the way in which Wahl Bartmann, the influential Natal captain and, by all expectations, a big factor for the Springboks in the Test, went missing in action as the hosts were shown to be too ponderous in the battle for the loose ball.

The All Black dirt-trackers also didn't have too much trouble winning their next fixture, against Free State in Bloemfontein, a match that will be remembered for Brendan Venter, anticipated to be an important cog in the Springbok backline, breaking his leg. And so onward to the match against the Junior Springboks at Loftus Versfeld, a clash that everyone hoped would give the All Blacks a proper taste and feel for the strength and depth available to South African rugby.

In his book *Endless Winter*, acclaimed British rugby writer Stephen Jones wrote that the international media had very high expectations as they waited to catch sight of the Junior Springboks at a Pretoria training session.

"We waited on the touchlines for training to start. Now, at last, we would see some Springboks, could prepare the superlatives. We heard so much about these giants, how they would come back into their own with an irresistible surge … Now, at last, we would see these gleaming specimens in the flesh."

But Jones went on to write that the session was one of the most "desultory" he had ever seen. "Kobus Wiese and Drikus Hattingh, next to, say, Wade Doolley or Martin Bayfield, were short."

He never did find the giants he was hoping for, did Jones. Instead, props up and down the country were "porkers in the old style of the years before the conditioning penny dropped", and Springbok lock Adolf Malan was "a trier, but way too spindly".

Again, like they had against Natal the week before, the All Blacks gave the impression that they didn't need to dig too deep to deal with the Junior Springboks, who were captained by Tiaan Strauss, and the challenge they posed.

The All Blacks won 25-10, the game proving to Jones that the South African playing style had been left behind. Writing in the London *Sunday Times*, he described the South African game as one dominated by kicking and in which forwards and backs simply did not combine. The tour was proving that "isolation hammers your game".

After the match, Bok coach John Williams made the first controversial pronouncement of his tenure. The overseas media had criticised the blatant lifting of the home team's line-out forward, Drikus Hattingh, and Williams was moved to defend his team's tactics.

"We don't call it lifting," he said. "We prefer to call it supporting. To us, it is a way of securing clean possession, which must be good for the game."

Indeed, Williams was simply expressing the views of South African rugby experts at the time. The problem was that South Africa was just one nation with its own interpretation, one with which the rest of the world didn't agree.

While it was true that "support" for the jumper was allowed *after* he had jumped on his own steam, the overseas referees did not allow the forwards to be lifted *to* the ball, which was what was happening in South Africa.

South African Albert Adams refereed the Junior Springbok game, and he allowed lifting, but the Test match was going to be officiated by a neutral international referee, who would bring a different interpretation to the law.

Jones wrote that Williams's defence of Adams "wasn't all lies and deception, it was just the first indication that South African rugby in isolation just hadn't kept up".

South African rugby hadn't kept up on other levels, too. In the pre-isolation era, at the time John Williams would have been a player and throughout Danie Craven's tenure as president of the South African Rugby Board, national trials were a massive part of the build-up to any major Test series or tour. There is a long list of players one can consult to prove that trials did have their place in years gone by. Obviously one had to scout for talent in the country areas, and selectors couldn't be everywhere at once. But that was before the advent of television coverage.

By 1992, players considered national trials antiquated. After all, their workload in a season was far heavier than that of a few decades earlier. In calling national trials, the Bok management – Williams and selection convener Daan Swiegers included – was immediately excoriated by the players.

Then, of course, there was another problem, but it was not new to the post-isolation era. This problem was provincialism, and it was exacerbated by the many years in which the Currie Cup had been the primary theatre of conflict for South African players. There had been few Bok teams selected in the preceding years where players from different provinces could bond; instead, players from the various provinces had grown used to playing against each other.

Both Williams and Swiegers were from Pretoria, and they were closely observed for any sign that they may favour the Northern Transvaal players. But there could not have been too many displeased observers from outside Pretoria when, on a calm, early spring evening on the Highveld after the Junior Springbok game, Swiegers announced the first Springbok team of the post-isolation era.

There were just four Northern Transvaal players in the side, although some of the players from other provinces, such as Natal's Robert du Preez and Transvaal's Theo van Rensburg and Heinrich Rodgers, had started off their careers playing for the Blue Bulls under Williams. Du Preez was one of only three Natal players selected for the Boks, and as that province was at the top of the Currie Cup log at the time, there were some murmurs of dissent from the Durban rugby scribes.

What raised *my* hackles, however, was the selection of Northern Transvaal second-string hooker Andries Truscott as understudy to Uli Schmidt, when Natal's first-choice hooker, John Allan, boasted international experience with Scotland. So I phoned the genial Swiegers at his home on the Sunday afternoon following the Saturday-night announcement.

Parts of our conversation were run in the *Natal Mercury*, such as when Swiegers kept on asking, "John who?" before finally saying, "Oh, you mean the *hooker*." I was young back then, and young reporters do stupid things. I doubt I would run a similar conversation in a newspaper if I had my time again. But this anecdotal aside does underline how difficult it is for the Springbok coach and his assistants to make everyone happy.

The Springbok team to play New Zealand read as follows: Theo van Rensburg, James Small, Danie Gerber, Pieter Muller, Pieter Hendriks, Naas Botha, Robert du Preez, Jannie Breedt, Ian Macdonald, Wahl Bartmann, Adolf Malan, Adri Geldenhuys, Lood Muller, Uli Schmidt, Heinrich Rodgers.

Gerber and Botha were the most experienced international players and were the sole survivors of the eventful 1981 tour of New Zealand. But Gerber was now 35 and no longer the player he had been, and was only in the team because of Brendan Venter's broken leg. Eight of the players had not played Test rugby before – not even the soft Tests of the latter part of the post-isolation era.

It would, to put it mildly, be one heck of a thing to play the All Blacks and Australia on consecutive weekends ...

3

"Hello, am I the coach?"

John Williams did not start 1992 thinking that nine months into the year he would be taking charge of the first Springbok team to play a Test match in the post-isolation era.

A professor in the discipline of sports sociology, Williams had left top-level coaching after taking Northern Transvaal to three successive Currie Cup titles, the last one shared with Western Province in 1989. Williams left Pretoria to take up the position of Dean of Students at Potchefstroom University.

It was not the first time that Williams's academic career had forced him to make rugby a secondary interest in his life. In 1976, when his cheekbone and nose were broken playing for the Springboks in the second Test against the All Blacks, in Bloemfontein, Williams decided to call time on a playing career in which he had won 13 international caps and played 64 games for Northern Transvaal.

In those days you accumulated caps a lot slower than in the modern era, as matches were less frequent then, and Williams was already 32 at the time. During his playing career he had coached at school level while also teaching, but he took a break from rugby for the first few years after he retired from the game, as he was working on his PhD. In his own words, the academic world didn't care much for his rugby history.

However, while Williams was lecturing at Waterloo University in Canada towards the end of 1977, Roger Downer, a Zoology head of department, asked him to help coach the three university teams. That was the start of a coaching career that saw Williams guide Pretoria University to three successive Carlton League titles in the first part of the 1980s before he took over at Northern Transvaal.

"When I got the offer to take up a new position at Potch in 1989, I couldn't turn it down; it was my dream job. I served as vice-president of Western Transvaal and president of Potchefstroom University Rugby Club, but I did not actually coach in those years," Williams explained when I caught up with him on his farm near the Limpopo/Botswana border, 60 kilometres from Alldays, where he has lived for the past 14 years.

A hulking giant of a man, as you would expect from a former lock, Williams did retain enough interest in the game to travel to the 1991 World Cup in order to study playing trends.

However, although he would have had long-term ambitions to be the Bok coach if South Africa was readmitted, he was not thinking of it at the time and certainly did not actively seek out the job.

Indeed, the first Springbok team to play a Test match in the post-isolation era was coached by a man who found out from third parties that he had been appointed, and who had to make several phone calls over a period of time to confirm that he actually had the job.

"I started to get phone calls from people in around April 1992 saying that they believed I had been appointed as the Springbok coach," recalled Williams. "I told them that it couldn't be true. Surely there would have been a letter of appointment? At the very least I would have received a phone call from someone at SARFU. But I had nothing of the sort, so I assumed it was all just rumour."

But as 1992 proceeded, the "rumour" persisted. And people in the know kept on phoning him to tell him that he had been appointed as the Springbok coach.

"Eventually I decided that something must be wrong. So I went to Johan Claassen, whom I knew and who had coached me when I was a player. He was on the SARFU executive. I asked him if it was true that I was the Springbok coach. Johan said that as far as he knew, I had been appointed at an earlier executive meeting.

"This was already May, and the Springboks were due to play at the end of August. If we were going to play two tough Test matches so soon, I needed to get cracking with preparations. And yet I still hadn't been officially informed. So I phoned the SARFU general manager Arrie Oberholzer, who also confirmed [that] I had been appointed.

"'Arrie,' I said, 'there are a lot of things that need to be done.' I told him I had had no official notification, no terms of reference. I asked him if I could please be sent something [that would] officially notify me [that] I had the job so [that] I could get cracking with the planning. I had an important job at Potchefstroom University and needed to schedule around that.

"So about a week later I got a letter from Doc Craven. It read as follows: 'You've been appointed as Springbok rugby coach for 1992.' That's all it said."

With his appointment letter now filed away, Williams applied himself to the task of planning for the imminent arrival of the two top teams in world rugby. There was little time, and he needed everything to be plain sailing if the Boks were to be ready by the time they played the All Blacks.

What followed, though, was anything but plain sailing. In fact, events bordered on the insane, with the confusion and disorganisation that had started even before Williams was appointed continuing into the early days of his coaching reign.

"When I asked Arrie if I could fly down from Pretoria to Cape Town to speak to him and start the planning, he said, 'Just carry on with it yourself.' I asked him about the dates for the trial matches. Arrie said, 'You'll be informed in due course. Daan Swiegers will let you know, as he is the convener of selectors.'"

Williams's attempts to get help from Arrie Oberholzer in those early days were akin to smashing into a brick wall over and over again. It wasn't so much the paid employee, Oberholzer, who was the stumbling block, but the SARFU joint president, the ageing patriarch Craven, and an executive dominated by people who, for years, had cared only for the provincial unions over which they presided.

Recalls Williams: "Way back in the day there used to be a system enforced by the International Rugby Board (IRB) prohibiting international teams from beginning their preparations earlier than a Wednesday before a Saturday match. I was good friends with Australian coach Bob Dwyer, and he told me it was nonsense, that it was ridiculous to expect a Test team to be prepared in three days.

"I told Arrie this, and he referred me to fellow SARFU employee Steven Roos. I told Steven that it was impossible to prepare a team for a Test match in three days, but Steven said I wouldn't get my wish, as Transvaal president Louis Luyt had insisted that his provincial team had a Currie Cup to prepare for. So we played against the All Blacks, after nearly 10 years without official Test rugby, with what was effectively three days' preparation."

If the first post-isolation Springbok coach had to put up with that, it is easy to have sympathy for him now. But at the time, Williams was the man who carried the can for every failure. The media was oblivious to the rugby administrators' weird machinations and the amateurish behaviour that had surrounded Williams's appointment and hampered the execution of his duties. What we saw at the time was a man who seemed very much a product of the Northern Transvaal culture – hard, uncompromising and a little dour.

He also didn't have much to say to people he didn't trust or know well, and rugby reporters suspected that he favoured Quintus van Rooyen, the late rugby scribe who was long regarded as the oracle of Northern Transvaal rugby. A colleague of mine recalls trying to interview Williams as he walked through the arrivals hall of D.F. Malan Airport (now Cape Town International Airport) in the build-up to the Australian Test and, in response to questions about the game, all the big man would say, over and over again, was, "We're going to look at it."

In the week leading up to the Ellis Park Test, the All Black midweek team beat a Central Unions team 39-6 after leading 22-0 at half-time, and the Wallabies arrived to start their tour. On their arrival, the Australians weren't greeted with the same level of arrogance reserved for the All Blacks a week earlier, but an advertising campaign that depicted a Wallaby skin drying in the sun with David Campese's No. 14 on the back made up for that.

The world champions started their tour with a regulation 46-13 win over Western Transvaal, then beat a Northern Transvaal team without Naas Botha and their other Boks 24-17 at Loftus the night before the Ellis Park Test match.

South Africa's comeback Test will forever be remembered more for the events around the game than for what actually happened on the field. Because rugby had been perceived as a morale-booster for white people during the years of apartheid, far greater political sensitivity surrounded the Springbok return to the international sporting arena than had been the case with the Proteas, the national cricket side, or, for that matter, the South African swimmers and athletes to the Olympic Games, which was being staged at the same time as the rugby internationals.

That sensitivity was to become an important factor in the considerations and actions of future Bok coaches, and may even have derailed one or two Springbok campaigns. But back in 1992, Williams was relatively shielded from what was taking place off the field. The first post-isolation Bok team, for instance, was all white, and no one batted an eyelid. This may not seem significant, but Errol Tobias had become the first black Springbok as long ago as 1981, and Avril Williams had joined him in the 1984 team that played John Scott's England.

Says John Williams: "We had selectors who didn't know anything about rugby who had been put there for the purposes of the new South Africa, and that was obviously a bit frustrating when you were trying to select for Test matches against New Zealand and Australia in consecutive weeks. But there was no pressure placed on me, as there were no black players coming through at the time."

For the Test to go ahead at Ellis Park, the ANC had laid down certain conditions, to which SARFU had agreed. These were that the old South African flag, which was officially still the national flag, would not be flown, that the national anthem, "Die Stem", would not be sung, that a minute's silence would be held at all Test venues for victims of political violence in the country, and that a message would appear in the match programme that expressed SARFU's support for peace and democracy in South Africa.

When the big day arrived, a few South African flags were waved around, but there was no noticeable demonstration or protest around the ground or in the Doornfontein precinct of Johannesburg, where Ellis Park is situated. But then came the clanger: after having played the New Zealand anthem, "God defend New Zealand", the band – the official band, that is – struck up the chords of the "white" South African anthem, "Die Stem".

Transvaal president Louis Luyt, along with Danie Craven, had been part of the delegation that had visited the ANC when it was still considered to be taboo. But in explaining his decision to play "Die Stem" in his autobiography, *Walking Proud*, Luyt displayed a political naivety and complete lack of sensitivity to the realities of why South Africa was being allowed back into international competition.

"For weeks leading up to the Test, a debate raged in the press and over radio as to whether it would be appropriate to play 'Die Stem' at Ellis Park before the game. I disagreed with newspaper pundits who strongly opposed the playing of our national anthem on this occasion while raising no objection to 'Nkosi Sikelel' iAfrika' being played at soccer matches.

"After all, 'Die Stem' was still our official anthem. And even without the overwhelming support of the rugby public, I would still have pressed ahead. This was, in my view, an issue of principle. I was not about to deny the existence of a national anthem merely to please the ANC or any of the wimps who wished to roll over and play dead."

Of course, as Dan Retief noted in his book on South Africa's quest for World Cup success, *The Springboks and the Holy Grail*, when Luyt spoke of "principle", he conveniently neglected to mention the lack of principle he'd displayed in not sticking to the agreement that the anthem would not be played.

Understandably, the ANC was furious. Sports minister Steve Tshwete thundered that "Verwoerd will not be allowed to rule this nation from his grave." Australian rugby head Joe French declared that if the ANC wanted his team to fly home and not play the match against the Springboks at Newlands the following Saturday, then that is what they would do.

In the end, thanks to the efforts of Tshwete, the Australian part of the tour was saved.

But back to Ellis Park and the Springboks' first post-isolation clash against the mighty All Blacks ... The Kiwis dominated the first three-quarters of the match, leading 27-10 as the game headed into the last quarter. However, perhaps because they were unfamiliar with the effects of altitude, and also because they perhaps felt the game was already won and it had been a long competitive year for most of their players, the New Zealanders released the pressure in the final 20 minutes and the Boks ran in three great tries, contributed by centres Danie Gerber and Pieter Muller.

The next day, in between all the space devoted to the political backlash over the playing of "Die Stem", the newspapers lamented James Small's knock-on when he had the line at his mercy during the second-half renaissance. Had it not been for that, the Boks would have won – or so they said. They seemed to ignore the fact that the Boks' third try, the second to Gerber, was only scored deep in injury time.

"I won't say we felt the coaching was disorganised, but it was a very different style from what a lot of us, who didn't play for Northern Transvaal, were used to," recalls Muller. "Naas and Danie were the older guys in the team, and as a youngster you didn't have a chance to put a marker down. It was all very quick, we didn't have much time to prepare, so I suppose that might explain why there wasn't much that was new in our approach, and [the game plan] seemed very old-fashioned and basic.

"But it was just so exciting to be playing in what, for most of us, was our first Test match, so we were probably oblivious to the other factors surrounding the management. We noticed that more on the end-of-year tour. At Ellis Park, we played on adrenaline."

Muller said that the squad had been fairly oblivious to the shenanigans surrounding the playing of the anthem. "We were told on the way to the stadium that there would be no anthem. But then, when we got to the field, we were told it would be played after all."

The day after the Ellis Park match, the ANC issued a press release in which they stated that the crowd at Newlands held the future of South Africa in its hands. A repeat of Ellis Park would not be tolerated.

"They [the Newlands crowd] can make rugby a reconciler of people or they can use it as a ritual that celebrates conquest and domination of black people," the statement read.

The crowd was informed that there would be no official flags or anthems, and a minute's silence would be observed for victims of the violence. If these appeals were not adhered to, the ANC would oppose future tours to and from South Africa and also the hosting of the 1995 World Cup.

So Australia proceeded with their tour, and beat Eastern Province 34-8 at Boet Erasmus. Incidentally, Christie Noble played that day and was the only black player the Australians and New Zealanders would encounter on their respective tours.

For the Newlands Test, the Boks retained the same team that played at Ellis Park, but the build-up to this game reflected a completely different mood to the one that had prevailed in Johannesburg. No anthem was played, and the minute's silence was properly observed. Unfortunately for the Boks, however, the game itself was also completely different from the one in Johannesburg.

At Ellis Park the Boks had given the impression that they were competitive, but at Newlands they were properly caned in a game that the Aussies won 26-3. Admittedly most of the points were scored towards the end, but the Boks were outplayed at the line-outs where, for the second week running, it became apparent that the South African refereeing approach to lifting in the years of isolation had done the players no favours.

Wahl Bartmann, too, was clearly playing the old tackle laws, and the Springboks appeared extremely naive, both in their approach to the breakdowns and in the general way they played the game.

There was an inevitable media backlash, although *Sunday Times* sports editor Edward Griffiths, perhaps acknowledging the folly of thinking that the Boks could return to international rugby by playing the All Blacks and Wallabies on consecutive weekends, ended his report on the game with the words: "We lost, so what?"

Griffiths' detractors pointed out that those words just proved that he wasn't a born-and-bred South African (he was actually Zimbabwean and British-educated), as most white South Africans considered the two defeats – even after such a long absence from international competition – to be unacceptable. The Springboks were the flag-bearers of a racial identity many felt was in danger of extinction, and as a result there was only one result that was acceptable, and that was victory.

Alas, such an expectation was unrealistic. After the Newlands match, Ian McIntosh, spotting former Bok coach Ian Kirkpatrick near him in the stands, strode over, his wild eyes reflecting the hurt that had been inflicted by what he had just seen.

"Master, have we got problems," McIntosh said to Kirkpatrick.

In his book, *Mac: The Face of Rugby*, McIntosh said that the match had realised his worst fears: the years of isolation had left South African rugby impoverished, both technically and tactically.

"There was massive arrogance in the decision to take on the two power-houses, New Zealand and Australia, in the first games back, before nipping over to play France and England," he wrote.

Obviously the rugby bosses had believed that the South African game was strong enough no matter who the opposition was, but the message was conveyed loud and clear over consecutive Saturdays: South African rugby had stagnated.

Apart from the bit of perspective that flowed from Griffiths' pen, the rest of the rugby media lambasted John Williams and his team. A memorable photograph from the game summed up the general attitude towards the Boks; it showed the backside of Wahl Bartmann poking out from a tear in his shorts as he lumbered to a ruck. The caption read: "Annus horribilus".

But McIntosh felt it was wrong that the players were blamed for the heavy drubbing. He was convinced the country had the talent and just needed some direction. According to him, New Zealand was also playing "old-fashioned" rugby at that time, which was why the chasm at Ellis Park had not been as wide as it was at Newlands. For McIntosh, there was good reason why the Wallabies were the world champions.

The most important fundamental change the Australians had made to their game was to abandon the traditional way of playing to the breakdowns with forwards and backs in clearly defined and familiar roles.

Says McIntosh: "That is what the Bok forwards tried to do at Newlands. They tried to play with the ball under a blanket, but the Boks, when running wide and deep, only succeeded in taking players like Wahl Bartmann out of the game."

So, not only did the Springboks return to international rugby in 1992 after a long enforced break and against a background of political uncertainty and unrealistic expectations, they also returned at a time when the game was undergoing some fundamental changes. And at the helm was a man who had not coached for three years, the very period when these changes to the game had started happening.

For his part, though, McIntosh believes that Williams, had he stayed on, would have got it right in the end.

"John was a clever and astute coach, and I have absolutely no doubt that had he been given the opportunity, he would have figured it out for himself," says McIntosh. "Under pressure, which [John] was throughout, because he was landed with a ridiculous schedule, he had to stay with what was familiar to him and what had been successful for him at Northern Transvaal. [But] he would have adapted and it would not have been long before the Springboks made up lost ground."

And maybe McIntosh was right, as Williams, although committed to his job at Potchefstroom University, had not been completely divorced from rugby in the three years since he had last coached Northern Transvaal. On the contrary, he had anticipated the wake-up call the South African game would receive at readmission, and he might have been better prepared if SARFU had supported him more.

"I realised we needed to get up to date with rugby as it was being played internationally, and that the Currie Cup couldn't be equated to international rugby. That was why I went to the World Cup in 1991, along with a few other coaches. Derek Morgan, who would later become president of the RFU, was a good friend of ours, and he gave us the opportunity to study the preparations of teams such as England.

"I honestly don't think [South Africa] lacked coaches in those days, and we have always had the talent. It just seemed to me that SARFU's whole focus was on issues other than rugby. With all the talking to the ANC and getting politically acceptable rugby structures in place, they neglected the rugby aspect. What we really lacked was top world-class administration."

Three days was certainly not enough time to prepare for the first Test, and New Zealand and Australia were a tough baptism for the Boks after so many years of isolation and with so few of the more experienced international players of the previous era still around to lead them. The Rolling Stones sing about time being on our side, but it certainly wasn't on Williams's side. Raising the Boks' game to international standards was no easy task, and it wasn't going to happen overnight.

Says Williams: "One of the things we needed to do was to [inspire player loyalty] to the Springbok [emblem] again, as [they] had for so long been caught up just in their provincial identities. And we needed experience. The only way to find out if players can play international rugby is to see them play [at that level].

"We needed to find out who would stay on the ship and who would end up swimming. Like Ian McIntosh at Natal, I had experience of [developing] teams and building success by putting systems in place. I had done it with both Tukkies and Northern Transvaal. But it didn't happen overnight. [Doing the same with the Springboks] was going to take two or three years, as we needed to gain international experience."

After the Test against Australia in 1992, Williams was certainly honest in his assessment of where South African rugby stood at that juncture.

"We no longer play rugby like the rest of the world. We play a different game," he said.

If international experience was what Williams felt the Springboks were most lacking, skipper Naas Botha's threat to retire would have increased the worry frowns creasing the coach's brow just as it was time for him to turn his attention to the first overseas tour the Boks would undertake since 1981.

4

The Mickey Mouse tour

Naas Botha didn't do as he'd threatened and retire. Instead, he stayed on for what was to be one final fling, captaining the first Springbok squad to tour overseas since their 1981 counterparts had endured an eventful and demonstration-plagued trip to New Zealand.

South Africa was by now fully readmitted to international sport, but rugby people were nonetheless uneasy at the prospect of touring, particularly in England. The Boks had last been there in 1969/70 for what will forever be remembered as the Demo Tour, and with sections of the British press questioning the sincerity of reforms in rugby, the prospect of demonstrations on the England leg of the trip could not be ruled out.

It was clear that, for South Africa, rugby was far more of a political hot potato than any other sport.

The prospect of having to deal with political agendas cost the Boks their experienced hooker Uli Schmidt. Along with another survivor from the unofficial 1986 series against the New Zealand Cavaliers, No. 8 Jannie Breedt, Schmidt decided to call time on his international career.

"I am sick and tired of the politics in and around rugby," he was quoted as saying in an interview with Rodney Hartmann of the Argus Group.

Schmidt and Breedt's non-availability added to the challenge coach John Williams now faced, as they were two of the few experienced players in the squad who had played against New Zealand and Australia.

"It will be a learning process and a new era," Williams said of a tour that was to last seven weeks, including five weeks in France, where they would play games against regional teams in addition to two Test matches, as well as a fortnight in the UK before the tour would culminate against England at Twickenham.

But if Williams thought the people at SARFU who had appointed him were ready to buy into anything new, he was mistaken.

"I should have been prepared for anything, as the standard of administration when we were hosting New Zealand and Australia wasn't high," says Williams.

The coach felt he had learnt from the first two Tests, and was determined to find a way to quickly gain the experience that was lacking. He didn't see much point in taking older players who wouldn't make the Test team on tour – apart from the primary goal of winning the three Test matches, for him the trip presented a chance to bring young players through in the club and provincial games.

"When I met with the selection committee to choose the 30-man squad, I asked if we could go for a mix of experience and youth. I argued that maybe we would lose some games, but at least we would build up our depth of experience. I asked them if I could give them 30 names. I suggested that where we agreed on the player we would mark [his name] and move on, and we would discuss the others.

"But they weren't interested. And they [also weren't] interested when I suggested that, as the coach, I should have the deciding vote when there was a 4/4 split in votes. I was the coach, but I wasn't allowed [to have] the team I wanted. That wasn't the way I had worked at Northern Transvaal, where I had been the first coach to also be the convener of selectors."

The Free State halfbacks Jannie de Beer and Hentie Martens were two of the youth brigade that Williams wanted to blood as stars of the future, but he never got them close to being selected. Worse – much worse, in fact – was about to follow for Williams when he asked Arrie Oberholzer if they could discuss the composition of the management team he intended assembling.

"Eugene van Wyk, who had been coaching Northern Transvaal, had been a good assistant to me in the matches against New Zealand and Australia, and although we had minimal time to prepare the team, we understood each other and were making a bit of progress," recalls Williams. "But when I told Arrie Oberholzer of my intentions, he told me I wasn't appointing the team. He made it clear that it would be pointless for me to ask Doc Craven if I could take Eugene as my assistant, as Eugene wasn't a Springbok."

So Williams ended up with Ian Kirkpatrick as his assistant. Kirkpatrick had coached the Springboks in Williams's last series as a player against the 1976 All Blacks, but his days at the top level were long gone.

"Kirky was a really nice guy. He had been my coach in the 1974 series against the Lions after Johan Claassen got sick, and he also coached me against the All Blacks. But now, all of a sudden, the guy who had coached *me* was *my* assistant coach. I had never coached with him before. I was starting again from scratch."

The main problem confronting Williams was still the culture of the South African rugby administration. Craven, president of the old SARB since 1956, was still the chief to whom everyone in rugby bowed down. A great man and a gifted thinker of the game, Craven will always be remembered as a legend in South African rugby, but by 1992 he was a doddery geriatric.

The Boks held a training camp in Cape Town before the tour, and management favoured Eugenie Short, a biokineticist, to fill the role of fitness trainer. But Craven quickly put down his ageing foot and made it clear that he did not want a woman near the Bok camp.

So Williams and the team doctor Louis Wessels travelled to Stellenbosch to meet with Craven in the hope that they might change his mind. Although sharing the presidential duties of SARFU with Ebrahim Patel, Craven was still calling all the shots. Williams wanted to keep abreast with modern trends by being scientific, and he wanted to press home to Craven how important it was to have a biokineticist on board.

After appearing to listen to Williams, Craven pointed at Wessels and asked him why, if he was a doctor, *he* couldn't handle the fitness on tour.

"Louis was very frank and direct with him. He told Craven [that] he was a medical doctor and had no specialist training in fitness, and that he would be travelling on tour to do what he was trained to do and no more than that."

In Craven's era, his alma mater, Stellenbosch University, was the first port of call when expertise was needed and, sure enough, that was what happened. The man – yes, of course he was a man – appointed to look after the Boks' fitness was Bokkie Blaauw, who had extensive links with Maties but did not boast any experience in charting fitness programmes for first-class rugby players.

"Who is he?" I asked Arrie Oberholzer when I popped into SARFU's old headquarters at Mill House near Newlands during the Bok training camp.

"I can assure you [that] he is a man with impeccable credentials," replied Oberholzer.

But when I asked him what those impeccable credentials were, all he could do was raise what looked like a confused eyebrow and say nothing. The message was clear – his credentials were that Doc thought he should be with the Boks.

After Blaauw's appointment, I phoned Richard Turnbull, the prominent biokeniticist who had helped Natal prepare for their successful 1992 Currie Cup campaign. In his opinion, Blaauw wasn't the man for the job. And well known Cape Town–based sports scientist, Professor Tim Noakes, shared his opinion.

So the coach was already on the back foot, and touring was going to pose new challenges for a group that consisted mostly of people who had never before left the shores of South Africa to play rugby, and who had been assembled by a hopelessly out-of-touch administration.

From beginning to end, the tour – which I covered for the South African Morning Group – was a logistical disaster. Imagine the industrial areas of the major South African cities, particularly those around the airports, and you will have an idea of the parts of France where the Springboks stayed on tour.

At least in Paris and Marseille, the hotels were central – indeed, the 1992 Boks stayed at the same Paris hotel Jake White's team would occupy for most of the 2007 World Cup – but at the other venues, they mostly stayed on the outskirts.

This might not sound like a problem to people who have never been on an international sports tour, but players need their down time. And staying cooped up in a small hotel in an industrial area far from the distractions of the town centre is a recipe for boredom, and cabin fever soon sets in. Television reporter David van der Sandt became extremely popular with the players, as he had the use of a hired minibus which he ferried the guys around in, and, most importantly, with which he picked up fast food such as KFC and McDonald's.

The French food was a big bugbear for the players, and by the time we reached Marseille, some of them were quite vocal about it. "If I see another prawn, I'm going to puke," a Natal Springbok assured me.

The media gave the players and management a lot of flak for being so unprepared for the trip, but it wasn't really the fault of anyone on tour. The main problem was simply the newness of it all, and SARFU should really have ensured that the logistics were better planned.

"What irritated me," recalls Williams, "was the fact that I foresaw those problems. When I was in that meeting with Doc, I asked him if we could send someone over to check out the hotels and make sure that the playing field was level for us. I had spent some time in France and had toured there

with the Springboks as a player in 1974. The French love organising a training field on one side of Paris while your hotel is on the other, and you spend
half the day travelling through traffic.

"I wanted someone to go over and make sure [that] we would be put up in
comfortable hotels. But Doc said there was no need for it. We ended up not
only staying in hotels that were unsuitable, but also training on fields that
were bumpy and didn't even have rugby posts. Once I had to demand a new
hotel because the bedspreads had holes in them."

Such poor organisation did not endear the management to the players.
Pieter Muller remembers that tour as an event that had happened in a different time and space to his later career.

"From the start it appeared as if there had just been no planning. We were
on buses and modern players find it hard to believe we travelled like that so
relatively recently," says Muller. "We would have a function in the evening,
the next day we would be up early and on the bus to the next venue, and then
there would be a function the night before the game, and we were constantly
on the bus. It was a complete culture shock for most of us, and we struggled
to adjust to the late-night eating and the three functions we had to attend in
every town we visited.

"I enjoyed it as an opportunity to pick up souvenirs and memorable experiences, but as a top-level rugby tour group, we were hopelessly underprepared.
I ended my career in 1999 and, even looking back then, it seemed [as if] that
tour was from the Dark Ages."

If the appointment of the fitness advisor was shoddily done and the
logistical preparation was non-existent, there were other aspects of the
administrators' old-school approach that were even more debilitating to the
Springboks' chances of success.

As the first national rugby team from South Africa to tour overseas since
1981, it was naive to expect it to be "just" a rugby trip. The overseas media,
particularly the British press, were going to be looking for political angles.
More than that, South African rugby's propensity for attracting controversy
made it imperative that an eloquent manager, who could respond appropri-
ately to whatever questions were asked, travelled with the squad.

The local media had a man they thought would be ideal for the job.
Chick Henderson had managed the South African Barbarians team that had
toured the United Kingdom in 1979, and by all accounts he had done an
outstanding job. Henderson eventually did join up with the tour a few weeks

into the French leg ... but as a radio commentator. Henderson wasn't a Springbok, and that is probably what counted against him.

The rugby administration opted instead for Abe Malan, a former Springbok of some renown but who, as a farmer by profession, was ill-equipped to deal with the obstacles and challenges that would present themselves during the seven weeks on tour.

"I got on really well with Abe," says Williams, "and I have huge respect for him as a rugby man. But unfortunately he just wasn't a professional rugby team manager. Not at that time."

Half the time affable, the other half scowling, my abiding memory of Malan is of a man always seeming to be rushed off his feet. Diplomacy certainly wasn't his strong suit, and at one point he told the reporters that they should not be seen in the corridors of the hotels they were sharing with the players. It was also Malan, along with Naas Botha, who orchestrated the walk-out at a reception in Lille late in the trip, resulting in an international incident. And he was almost gloating when he got back to the hotel afterwards and informed the press about what had transpired.

"This is what I've done, and if there is going to be an international incident, then so be it," he said.

One would have thought that on a tour of such importance a press liaison officer would have been appointed to guide and instruct the management on how to go about the important business of selling the Boks to the overseas media. But there wasn't one.

Says Williams: "I saw the role of a media liaison officer as hugely important. We knew we needed to make a good impression, and I told Doc Craven that the pressure would be on us. The 1981 Boks told me how many problems they'd had because they didn't have anyone doing any form of liaison work for them. But Craven refused my request on the grounds that it had never been done before."

A media liaison officer of sorts *had* actually been appointed, albeit briefly: Johan Claassen, another legendary former Springbok. Ironically – and significantly – he had been criticised for his poor management and public-relations skills when he'd managed the 1981 Springboks ... by none other than the tour captain, Wynand Claassen. Apart from being completely unqualified for the job, he never fulfilled that function for the post-isolation Springboks. Instead, he toured as a representative of SARFU, and it was never clear quite what his role was supposed to be.

The old-timers among the media contingent – there were such people in those days – said that Claassen had mellowed, and certainly to the Morning Group man on tour he appeared to be the perfect gentleman. But then the ANC threatened to withdraw their support for the trip while the Boks were already on tour, and the media were keen to record SARFU's reaction to the threat. Two days into the crisis, Claassen had still not received any directive from SARFU.

There is, though, something important to be said in his defence – he was the one member of the Springbok tour group who did not leave when the rest walked out of the Lille function. He later told the media that the walkout was a disgrace and a "misplaced show of strength".

For Williams, this was *the* moment on the tour when a press liaison officer of some kind would have been very useful.

"After an hour, the French team hadn't pitched at the function. Players kept on coming to me and asking me what we should do, but it wasn't my role to deal with that sort of thing. I left it up to Abe, as he was the manager of the team, but he wasn't really a liaison person who could speak to the French. So we got on the bus and drove off, but just as we did so, the French team arrived."

Assistant manager Jackie Abrahams, for many years the president of Boland and a high-ranking SARFU representative, was the only black face in the management and also the man who was frequently caught in the middle whenever the proverbial *bokdrolletjies* hit the fan.

Williams may have struggled to gain concessions from SARFU before the tour, but once the trip through France had started, and with the national selection committee members left behind in South Africa, only Williams was responsible for playing players out of position – something that happened a lot.

"Well, that was because I ended up with a tour squad that I didn't agree with," he recalls on his farm 21 years later.

The players regarded Williams as a hard man who did not accept failure. He was also a strong disciplinarian, which did not appeal to those players used to a different approach from modern coaches such as Ian McIntosh and Harry Viljoen. By then, the days when Afrikaans players referred to coaches as *oom* (uncle) were receding into history.

This was something that the captain, Naas Botha, found problematic, and it soon became clear during the seven-week tour that Naas, too, was part of the problem. Like Williams, Botha couldn't tolerate the new era of rugby players that had emerged from the more democratic player-management-driven systems at Natal and Transvaal, and he considered young players who gave their views at team meetings "cheeky".

"John as a coach was very old school and autocratic," recalls Pieter Muller. "Naas controlled most of the backline coaching, even though Ian Kirkpatrick was supposed to be the backline coach. A lot revolved around John and Naas, and most of it was very basic stuff. There were some moves, but a lot of the game seemed to revolve around just giving the ball to Naas."

Two decades later, Williams makes no apologies for the role that discipline played in his rugby philosophy.

"Discipline is a very important thing. If you look at the years I coached Northerns, you will note that I took over at a time when they had really slumped and their record was poor. We were in a situation where we had to build that team up and bring the pride back. I had been coached by Buurman van Zyl, and he was a disciplinarian, and Johan Claassen too.

"What they taught me remains important to me. Sometimes you can cover it with nice things, but it basically remains the same. In 1987 we had to enforce a lot of discipline in our coaching, as we had young players. It paid off, and against all the odds we won the Currie Cup at the end of that year when we beat a Transvaal team with Carel and Michael du Plessis in the final.

"As the year progressed, guys like Adolf Malan, Johan Heunis, Naas himself and Heinrich Rodgers became such a strong group of leaders that I could lay off a bit. I always remember something that Vince Lombardi, the legendary American football (NFL) coach, said when he was coaching the Green Bay Packers. He said that you never choose talent before character, because the team will pay dearly for it every time."

For me, an enduring memory of Williams on that tour was watching him order spectators and pressmen away from the field, and then getting quite irate when nobody would budge. The problem was that he was speaking in Afrikaans, and most of the people he was addressing were French or English-speaking.

For all the rugby-related problems and the lack of preparedness of the players and management – and one has to remember that this was a completely new challenge for all concerned – the lack of any public-relations expertise was the most serious. The tour might not have been conducted in the same atmosphere as the demo tours, but South Africa's former status as the pariah of the world nevertheless attracted attention from those sectors of the media that weren't interested in sport.

Politics reared its ugly head for the first time soon after the Springbok squad arrived in Bordeaux, where they played their first match, against the French Espoirs (French Youth). The French sports minister, Frederique Bredin, criticised the Boks for their lack of black players, and even made the laughable suggestion that one should be flown over. The reaction of the Bok management – which was no reaction at all – left none of us media people in any doubt that they would not be able to deal with any serious problems that arose on the tour.

Sunday Times sports editor Edward Griffiths had actually discussed the potential shortfall in public-relations expertise, as well as the inadequacy of the management team, in his "One Small Voice" column. Observing that the tour group's itinerary included a visit to Euro Disney, Griffiths called the trip "The Mickey Mouse Tour", a label that stuck for the duration of the trip.

Nick Mallett, playing and coaching in France at the time, anticipated the prospective problems the South African group would face, and offered his help when he visited the squad in the early days of the tour. Mallett says he was told in no uncertain terms where to get off, with Abe Malan informing him that not only did he "look and behave like a Frenchman, you smell like a Frenchman too"!

But the biggest problem was newness to touring. In Stephen Jones's book *The Endless Winter*, he quoted Naas Botha on the challenges the Boks faced on their first major tour since 1981:

[Firstly] there is the tour itself. In South Africa we leave for a match on a Friday night and we are back home by Sunday. Suddenly, these guys are away for seven to eight weeks, which for some is a shattering experience ...

Another factor is the tribal structure of South African rugby. For many decades we had been divided into provincial entities. There are guys who left Northern Transvaal because they hated me and who are now touring with me. For years, players in Natal, Transvaal and Western Province regarded me as their foremost enemy. It is very difficult to change their mentality overnight and to make them think now, I like Naas Botha.

Williams, looking back, has a lot of sympathy for Botha. "There was a lot of pressure on Naas on that tour, both as a captain and to be the match winner," says Williams. "As the experienced player, it was his job to [make] the team [win]. It was the end of his career, but I still thought he played well on that tour. I was aware that he wasn't popular with all the players, and there were a lot of different camps. Naas had beaten most of those players when playing for Northerns, and some liked him and some didn't."

The Natal players were always together, all five of them – Hugh Reece-Edwards, Pieter Muller, Robert du Preez, Steve Atherton and Wahl Bartmann. And once they had got into the meat of the tour, they never made it a secret that they were unhappy. They had reason to be, too – they had won the Currie Cup, and yet they were drastically outnumbered by players from Northern Transvaal and Transvaal.

"Hey, aren't you the guys who won the Currie Cup?" I chided them as they sat together at a training field towards the end of the French leg of the tour. They immediately started reciting their list of complaints.

But it wasn't only the Natal players who had drawn the short straw. The team announcement for the first Test against France, in Lyon, was itself bizarre. The touring media were invited into the room where the team would be announced to the players. In other words, we were going to hear the team at the same time as the players, and then, unbelievably, we were to ask them questions. When it was announced that Reece-Edwards had been included at fullback ahead of Theo van Rensburg, Deon Viljoen of the Argus Group decided he had a job to do, and he did it. He asked the management how Reece-Edwards had got the nod ahead of Van Rensburg. The two players shifted uncomfortably in their chairs as the explanations were given, and most of us didn't know where to look.

The relationship between the players and the media has seldom been as tetchy as it was on that inaugural post-isolation tour. Botha had major words with Deon Viljoen over an article that had run in the *Daily News* in which Deon had praised Hennie le Roux and compared him to Botha. Later on the trip, players told us that they had been instructed not to speak to us, and that Viljoen was considered persona non grata.

Although I didn't know him then, I found Botha fairly approachable, and I even had a few rugby discussions with him and some of my colleagues where we exchanged opinions, though the atmosphere got a little strained at times.

For instance, after the Boks lost to a French Universities team in Beziers,

Botha, who did not play that day, awaited the team at the hotel. "How come you always write these guys off?" he inquired in Afrikaans of a Sunday newspaper scribe as the team trooped into the foyer.

"Because they play like a bunch of..." responded the reporter, and we will leave the sentence unfinished.

The tour itself started with the match against the French Espoirs, and Craven was invited onto the field to perform a ceremonial kick-off. It was to be his last public appearance, as he would pass away three months later in Stellenbosch.

For the Boks, it wasn't a happy resumption of contact with the French, and they lost 17-25. The superiority of the French team was disturbing, and few would have quibbled with Stephen Jones's contention that "the Springboks had no line-out and no back-row balance either".

The issue of balance in the team was to be a constant problem, as was Williams's eagerness to play players out of position, such as prop Willie Hills as a hooker. Deon Viljoen referred to the South Africans in the *Argus* as the "retro-Boks", a name that would also start to stick. The retro-Boks were on a Mickey Mouse tour ...

Going into the second tour match, in Pau against an Aquitaine XV, the media sensed that the tour was already verging on disaster, but thanks to a barnstorming performance from stand-in skipper Wahl Bartmann, the tourists won 29-22. That was followed by a close win over a Midi-Pyrénées XV (18-15), where the Boks started well but then faded badly in the second half.

This was one occasion where the newness to touring was exposed in the media reports too. I lambasted the decision to give the Bok squad "an extensive workout just one day after playing a hard game in midweek", which accounted for their exhaustion in the second half, and claimed that "only poor finishing from the hosts prevented them from winning".

But unbeknown to me, Williams's intention had been to drive the players extra hard that week so that they could slack off a bit in the days leading up to the first Test. Many of the players had obviously been surprised by the hard practice, but the Bok mission was to win the Tests, and on later tours some Bok coaches would be criticised for focusing too much on the provincial and club games at the expense of building towards the big matches.

The Boks won their next match, in Marseille, more comfortably, but there was a massive fight during the game. It seemed to galvanise the Boks, as for once they seemed to be united, and when they later beat the French 20-15 at Lyon's Stade de Gerland in the first Test, they were able to thumb their noses at those who had criticised their team selection. Botha was at his best, orchestrating matters both as a tactician and a goal-kicker, and James Small and Danie Gerber scored the tries.

Williams supporters like Quintus van Rooyen lauded the selection of Willie Hills at hooker (he had been selected to tour as a prop), but in reality the French had paid dearly for their decision to try to run at the Boks on a soft and wet field, even though it wasn't raining. The result meant that the Boks retained their proud record of never having lost a Test match on French soil.

But that record would be consigned to the history books in the next Test, in Paris. The game was played at the old Parc des Princes, and after holding their own in the first half, the South Africans fell away to lose 15-29, a score that flattered them.

At the post-match press conference, I asked the French management what chance the Boks had of winning the last Test match of the tour, at Twickenham, and the hacks who had flown over from England to watch the game against France, including the recently retired international lock Paul Ackford, laughed uproariously. It had been another game in which the Springboks had shown how far behind South African rugby really was.

The Boks lost their two remaining games in France, to French Universities in Tours and then to the French Barbarians in Lille, before we all travelled across the English Channel by ferry – these were the pre-Eurostar days. The Boks were looking forward to England because of the promise of more familiar food and a language they could understand.

And it did go better than the French part of the tour, with the Boks hammering a Midlands team 32-9 at Leicester's Welford Road and then winning a great game, the most exciting of the tour by far, against the England A side at Bristol's Memorial Ground.

After a 19-3 win over North Division at Elland Road in Leeds, it was time for the Test against England, and the coach again surprised, this time by selecting F.C. Smit, who was not part of the original tour group, on the flank.

The Boks led 16-8 at half-time on a dank, wet day at Twickenham, but then got undone by the England kicking game as the hosts took control to eventually win 33-16, scoring 25 unanswered points in the second half.

The loss was seen as an abject end to a miserable first year back in the international fold.

Flying home from London on that Sunday night, the passengers on the SAA 747 were an interesting mix of South African celebrities, sportsmen and even politicians who had flown out to watch the Twickenham game. I remember seeing radio personality John Berks on board, as well as politician-cum-rugby manager Abe Williams, and former Bok captain Wynand Claassen.

The conversations were animated and lasted long into the night as the aircraft flew across African airspace en route to Johannesburg. The consensus was that the Boks had failed, and that Williams had failed.

Once back home, the post-mortems and recriminations continued. Hugh Reece-Edwards and Wahl Bartmann made a speech on the Natal South Coast that they thought would go unreported, but it somehow made its way onto the front page of the *Citizen* newspaper. The gist of it was that the Broederbond was still running South African rugby.

So was Williams given one of those high-profile dressings down and public sackings that some of his successors would suffer? As it turns out, he got anything but – he was simply shown the door by just not being appointed again.

"I knew that I wasn't the Springbok coach any more when I heard from Quintus van Rooyen that someone else had been appointed," says Williams. "I didn't think winning one and losing two Tests on tour was a good performance. But I thought some players were coming through, and had we had some of the players we'd left behind, I think it could have [made] a very big difference.

"When I got back, I took some time out to write a report. In it I said [that] the coach needs much more authority in the selection of the team, and that when it came to match preparation, we were caught in a very old dispensation. I warned that we would not be able to be successful if we continued [in the same manner]. I also said that the coach would need his own support team.

"A board meeting was going to be held in Cape Town, so I called SARFU and asked where I should send the report. I was told that if it was necessary they would contact me, but they didn't need a report. Maybe they thought I was trying to save my job. But I wasn't, I was just trying to be helpful so that the mistakes [would not be] repeated."

As it turned out, some of them weren't, but many of them were, several times over, in the next two decades ...

5

Wild eyes wide open

"So are you guys still going to want to talk to me when I've been axed?"

Those were Ian McIntosh's words when I phoned him after learning that he would be taking over as Springbok coach following Gerrie Sonnekus's dramatic exit. The former Bok and Free State No. 8 had doubled his role of provincial coach with that of union marketing manager and had become embroiled in a scandal over the misappropriation of funds. Club 300, which was set up to raise funds for the Free State Rugby Union centenary celebrations, was a Sonnekus project, and it was the subject of an investigation when it was alleged that it was operating for profit.

The furore, which bubbled under for some time in Bloemfontein, led to the resignations of other high-ranking Free State Rugby personalities, including president Steve Strydom. With Sonnekus under such a cloud and having to fight to clear his name, he had little option but to resign the Bok coaching role soon after his appointment, and it offered a gap to McIntosh. Often singled out in the crowd by television cameras for what commentators called his "wild" eyes, those eyes were nevertheless wide open. McIntosh knew what he was getting himself into, and when I interviewed him in his Durban North flat in March 2013, almost exactly two decades after his appointment, he said that he had always known he was inheriting a poisoned chalice.

"I knew that I was breaking the mould for Springbok coaches, and I knew that there would be people who wouldn't accept me. I anticipated the opposition I got," he said.

By "breaking the mould", McIntosh was referring to the traditional policy of only appointing former Springboks to the national coaching position. McIntosh should have been the obvious choice to succeed John Williams. Natal had won two out of the three most recent Currie Cup titles under his mentorship, and his playing style, which had come to be known as "direct rugby", while not universally popular, was certainly innovative. However, even though Dr Craven had died earlier in the year, the Springbok credentials were still a prerequisite for the job of national coach.

"I don't think that was the only reason I was regarded with suspicion," recalls McIntosh 20 years later. "There was also the not-so-insignificant point that I was Rhodesian. There was very little respect for Rhodesian rugby, and no one let me forget that. Never mind the fact that both my parents were South African; my mother was born in Matatiele and my father in Newcastle."

Although not a favourite of the traditional and conservative elements within the rugby politic, McIntosh was the popular choice within at least some significant sections of the South African population. As he recalls: "The *Sunday Times* ran an opinion poll the week that they were making the initial appointment. I got about 80 per cent of the vote, and the next best was Dougie Dyers. Sonnekus only got about 5 per cent."

But history reflects that Sonnekus was SARFU's first choice, with McIntosh winning the consolation prize: coaching the Junior Springboks.

"My initial reaction was to tell SARFU where to stick it," McIntosh says. "But then Nick Labuschagne, who was on the SARFU executive, phoned me and advised me not to turn down the job. He obviously had wind of what was happening with Gerrie.

"I am convinced that if I had not taken the SA A job, I would not have been appointed [Springbok coach]. I think [the fact] that [I was] the South African A coach forced their hand."

Former Springbok centre Pieter Muller said that the Natal coach was never completely accepted by his new bosses, a perception with which most of his teammates agreed.

"When Mac took the job, it was a bit of a double-edged sword; you got the feeling that SARFU had picked him because there was no one else," recalls Muller. "He was like a lamb to the slaughter. There was definitely a feeling that the administrators didn't want him as the coach."

The many pitfalls and obstacles McIntosh would encounter during his Springbok reign were anticipated in an article I wrote for the *Natal Mercury* on the day SARFU announced his appointment:

> While he presents himself as the obvious choice, it would be a fool who
> would anticipate overnight success. Williams's main failing was not that his

team lost, but that it failed to establish any pattern. To do that, McIntosh needs time ... Other guarantees he must seek are a place on the Springbok selection panel and, most importantly, that he gets enough time to prepare his team for the Tests [against France].

And even if those guarantees are given, can McIntosh really be sure that he will have the free hand he needs, or will the SARFU hierarchy poke their noses in and interfere with the running of the team, as was the case before the death of Dr Danie Craven? A coach lives and dies on the success of his team, as the Williams case proved, and as such he must be given the power to make his own decisions, and surround himself with his own management team ...

McIntosh didn't take my advice and insist on his own management team, but then he probably wouldn't have got his way anyway. Those times were different to the modern age, when the coach gets to call all the shots.

"I had no say in the coaching team whatsoever," McIntosh says. "I didn't mind because I had coached [that way] all my life. It was the way then and it really didn't faze me, but looking back, it was wrong."

McIntosh was appointed to the selection panel, but he was just one of the selectors and had no overriding say. In retrospect, he can see that apart from coming into the job at a trying time for South African rugby and at a stage when the sport was undergoing dramatic changes in the way it was played, he was also in a transition period regarding how coaches were contracted.

"Back in the 1950s and 1960s, you often didn't have a coach, with the captain taking complete charge of the tactics. It was only from the late 1960s and into the 1970s that coaches started to have an impact, but even then you still had a manager who ran everything," he explains. "When I was appointed as Springbok coach, I was selected just like a player. I did not apply for the job. The manager still called all the shots. And I was really just given my team. Only after me, when Kitch Christie became coach, did the Springbok coach become number one. Kitch got everything he asked for, and he was the sole selector. It was just unfortunate for me that I fell bang in the middle of the different eras of coaches."

But the brickbats and the pitfalls were still all in the future for McIntosh when I interviewed the beaming new national coach at Kings Park in the late summer of 1993. Although reluctant to criticise Williams, who would now serve as one of the national selectors, McIntosh made it quite clear that he was going to get the Boks to play his "direct" style of rugby.

"I believe we have lots of talent in this country – all we have to do is harness it correctly and play the right game," he said. "The whole philosophy of direct rugby is about playing in front of the forwards. The way the game is played now, no side can afford not to play it in front of the pack – at least not if they expect to win."

McIntosh was also delighted with the appointment of Jannie Engelbrecht as the Springbok manager, and thought it was the best time to be involved as Springbok coach.

As he recalled in his autobiography *Mac: The Face of Rugby*: "I was convinced that South African rugby was ready for something new, and the Springboks, after their outdated rugby of 1992, needed a change. If the Springboks could play the style of rugby that I was seeking to play in Natal, I was confident they could win the World Cup. We had the talented players. The resources just had to be harnessed properly. And the Wallabies were showing the world how modern rugby worked. I almost felt I had a mission – to spread the modern style of rugby and change the conservative face of the game in South Africa, as Bob Dwyer and Rod McQueen had done in Australia."

The difficult part was getting that message across to people who wanted things done as they had been in the past. McIntosh didn't have much of a honeymoon period before the Afrikaans press started targeting him.

"They turned on me straight away, but I had become used to it," said McIntosh. "Up until [Natal] won that first Currie Cup in 1990, they were all praising what we were doing, backing my direct rugby style, but it always came across as a slightly patronising attitude. Once we had won the Currie Cup, however, it all changed. It was as if the press just suddenly turned on us, accusing us of playing a bad and illegal style of rugby.

"I [did make] a lot of mistakes, so some of the criticism was justified, and as you go along you learn to build bridges and not burn them. For instance, I knew that during the John Williams era, Quintus van Rooyen had been in on team selection meetings. So I made what was perhaps a stupid joke by telling him that now he would have to get in the queue like everyone else. I also had a major fight with Louis Luyt when he was Transvaal president and I was coaching Natal. I showed him no respect, and that might have come back to bite me too."

In those early days, following Craven's death, Ebrahim Patel was the president of SARFU, and McIntosh was impressed with him after their first meetings.

In his two years as Bok coach, McIntosh worked with eight selectors, but the group he worked with in 1993 gave him fewer headaches than the one that was to be ushered in when Louis Luyt became president of SARFU in early 1994. The 1993 selectors were Jackie Abrahams, Bill Jardine, Hennie Erasmus, Daan Swiegers, John Williams and Vuyisile Zwelibanzi.

McIntosh managed to get permission from the SARFU executive to host squad sessions in Johannesburg, designed to spread his "direct-rugby" approach to players who weren't acquainted with it. I flew up from Durban to watch some of those sessions, and detected a noticeable energy and vibrancy as the players practised, which was a far cry from the training sessions the Boks had endured before they'd departed for France and England the year before.

McIntosh had his first taste of coaching a national side when he mentored the SA A side in their match against France in East London. On a blustery day at the Basil Kenyon Stadium, the A side (which was also referred to as the SA B side and the Junior Springboks, depending on which newspaper you read) scored an emphatic 35-22 win over the opposition. The final score flattered the outplayed French side, which included most of their Test players.

I started my match report for the Morning Group of newspapers thus: "Now you can write it down in indelible ink – South African rugby is back and ready to roar in the coming months."

The prophecy proved incorrect, but McIntosh reckons it might have been different had he paid more heed to what he saw that day.

"It was a virtual Test team we beat and we were outstanding, with players like Henry Honiball, Joost van der Westhuizen, Hugh Reece-Edwards and Ruben Kruger all brilliant in executing my game plan," says McIntosh. "In retrospect, I should have taken more note of how that team played, because at Test level I battled to get my game plan through to the Springboks."

McIntosh wanted to make Wahl Bartmann, his Natal skipper, the Bok captain, but an untimely injury ruled him out of the series against France, and McIntosh had to choose between Transvaal captain François Pienaar and his Western Province counterpart Tiaan Strauss instead, with Pienaar winning the day on the advice of Harry Viljoen, who had replaced McIntosh as Natal coach.

"It's funny to think how differently South African rugby history might have turned out had Wahl been fit to play in that series," McIntosh says today.

Indeed, with Bartmann as his captain, McIntosh might have had more success in conveying his game plan to the players.

"A lot of Transvaal guys got selected into the team, and they needed to be convinced about Mac's way," recalls Pieter Muller. "We were all very cocky from a provincial point of view in those early days, and we all thought we knew best. Even Mac was a bit guilty of that at times. There were occasions when I thought he could have listened more to other views, too. But in 1993, Hennie le Roux and those guys couldn't really understand what Mac was trying to do."

McIntosh's approach was very different from anything those players knew, and one could perhaps understand why they found it hard to adapt to the new playing style.

McIntosh had "invented" the direct style of play after he had a brainwave following a Currie Cup match against Eastern Province in Port Elizabeth in 1987. Natal had lost that match 15-29 and never looked like scoring a try. Aware that the old trick of bringing the fullback into the line to create the overlap just wasn't working any more, as the cover defence had him in their sights, McIntosh started to think about attacking closer to the pack and getting across the gain line sooner. It would mean that if the move broke down, the loose forwards would be there to retain possession and carry the ball forward. McIntosh discussed the tactic with Natal flyhalf Henry Coxwell, and asked him, "What if you start moving early, before the ball is out, and take it flat?"

Coxwell became the pioneer of the approach, as he was physical and strong, and in the next six games Natal scored 13 tries after having hardly scored any in the first round. The province then won the Currie Cup in its centenary year with Joel Stransky at flyhalf, playing the direct way. It's therefore not unreasonable to ask why McIntosh had not deployed the naturally gifted Maritzburg College old boy in his first Test series.

"I couldn't get Joel to first base with the other [Springbok] selectors," McIntosh explains, "and I never got any support from the assistant coach, Gysie Pienaar. I think one of my faults as Bok coach was that [perhaps] I wasn't as firm as I should have been in selection meetings. I have tended to be a person who goes with the consensus, and if I wanted to get my way across, I should have been more forceful."

The critics – and some of the players who did not understand his game plan – often accused McIntosh of stifling flair and promoting crash-ball rugby.

"What people never understood was that direct rugby was just a starting point to break up opposing defences, to create the 15-against-seven situation. When Natal perfected it, they scored a record number of tries. And of course, ironically, it is the way modern rugby is played today. Critical to the style was the decision-making of the halfbacks. If you had the wrong halfbacks, you were in trouble."

So there was no Stransky when the Boks lined up for McIntosh's first Test in charge, against France at Kings Park in 1993. Uli Schmidt, the hero of Transvaal's triumph in the Super 10 final against Auckland, had come out of retirement, so there was at least some experience to offset the retirement of Naas Botha. McIntosh also called up Natal's meaty lock, Rudi "Vleis" Visagie, who had last played for the Boks in 1984, a decade earlier.

Meanwhile the French, apart from their defeat to the South African second-stringers, were duping the country into a false sense of complacency with some underwhelming performances in their tour fixtures. Apart from the East London game, they were smashed 38-19 by Northern Transvaal at Loftus, and only managed to snatch a draw against the Cheetahs in the last minutes.

The Springbok team that lined up for the Durban Test read as follows: Theo van Rensburg, James Small, Pieter Muller, Heinrich Fuls, Jacques Olivier, Hennie le Roux, Robert du Preez, Tiaan Strauss, Ian Macdonald, François Pienaar (captain), Rudi Visagie, Kobus Wiese, Keith Andrews, Uli Schmidt, Willie Hills.

The South African media does tend to be parochial, as was reflected by the *Sunday Tribune* headline on the day of the team announcement: "Natal get four as Pienaar takes charge of the Boks".

McIntosh wishes now that it had been more than four, for Joel Stransky or Henry Honiball would have been more willing to play his game than Hennie le Roux, and it's not only these years later that he recognises this as a reason for his team's flat performance in a game they were lucky to draw (20-all).

Late that night, in the floodlit Kings Park outer-field precinct, as the braai fires were burning down to their last embers, I was chatting to some acquaintances when a glum-looking McIntosh joined us. One of our group was Warren van Zyl, now a well-known KwaZulu-Natal chiropractor, but then a student who knew McIntosh, as he had attended Beachwood High with Mac's son, Craig.

As Van Zyl reminded me recently, that night McIntosh made no secret of the reasons why his team hadn't played well: the players had simply not played it his way. Looking back now, McIntosh reckons his captain might also have been part of the problem.

"When I wanted to bring in the auxiliary runner, which we had always done on the inside of the flyhalf at Natal, [Pienaar] insisted that the runner had to be outside the flyhalf. They wanted the inside centre to take the ball flat and not the flyhalf, and that was how it became a crash-ball," explains McIntosh. "Throughout my time with the Boks, I was criticised for supposedly playing crash-ball rugby, but we never played crash-ball at Natal. But the really sad part for me was that first Test in Durban. While the guys followed my game plan during training, when everything worked smoothly, suddenly that changed in the game itself. Hennie was standing deep and kicking for position in situations where we should have taken the ball up."

But instead of the flyhalf, the two locks, Visagie and Kobus Wiese, were made the fall guys and were omitted for the second Test, which was played in Johannesburg on a Friday night under what Dan Retief described in his *Sunday Times* match report as "an ominous moon".

In the week leading up to the Test, the match was overshadowed by the tragic deaths in a motor accident of two popular Transvaal players, Cameron Oliver and Stef Nel. You couldn't blame the Transvaal players if they lacked focus for that Test. Nico Wegner and Hannes Strydom were the new locks, and McIntosh reckons his game plan was followed more closely that night than it had been in Durban the previous week.

"But then Theo missed that kick," laments McIntosh, referring to Theo van Rensburg's failed penalty attempt in the dying minutes that would have given the Boks victory.

Defeat meant that the pressure McIntosh was already feeling now intensified. It also meant that the Boks had yet to win at home since the end of isolation, and now they faced a three-match away series against Australia. If they couldn't win at home against France, what chance did they have of beating the world champions in their own backyard?

The tour started off with some easy games, which allowed the Boks to relax and gave them the opportunity to work on their game plan. McIntosh later described it as the happiest tour he had ever undertaken, something he ascribed to the support he received from team manager Jannie Engelbrecht and SARFU president Ebrahim Patel.

One man who was impressed with McIntosh in those early days on tour was Pienaar, who writes in *Rainbow Warrior*: "In less than three weeks during the Australian tour, I had developed a profound respect for Ian McIntosh, not least because his coaching was based on a passionate love of the game. He was evidently a student of rugby not because he thought it would make him rich or famous, but because he truly loved the game."

Engelbrecht's opening line to McIntosh went something like this: "Listen, partner, you coach the side and don't worry about anything else. I'll do the management stuff."

It worked on that tour, though it wasn't always plain sailing. Some of the players found Engelbrecht a bit dictatorial, and after he instructed the management at one of the team hotels to stop the video feed to players' rooms, Pienaar asked McIntosh to intervene and tell Engelbrecht to back off.

"Coach, we must get this straight. This is not just Jannie Engelbrecht's tour, it's also our tour," Pienaar told his coach. McIntosh backed the players and suggested they be treated like adults. He had always been big on participatory management at Natal.

Engelbrecht had also suggested a ban on punching at the start of the tour. McIntosh, while not wanting to be soft on discipline, knew that it was a ridiculous expectation.

"You can't have a situation in rugby where the opposition knows they can hit your guys and they won't hit back," he said.

As it happened, Pienaar was badly trampled in the match against the Waratahs and suffered a severe cut under the right eye. South Africa had taken a lot of flak for foul play and did not have a good record, and with this on his mind, Pienaar quickly found a roundabout way in which to criticise referee Barry Leask.

"It's a pity that the referee saw how I was trampled, how the player jumped on my face, and yet he did not penalise him for it. It has happened and we will now let the matter rest," Pienaar was quoted as saying in the media the next day.

Up till that point the tour had gone swimmingly from a results perspective, and by the time they got to Sydney, the points tally for the Boks across the three matches was 239 points to 13. New South Wales, who were welcoming back the Wallabies' World Cup–winning captain Nick Farr-Jones from retirement, would provide the first big test, and McIntosh had some big selection calls to make.

"I started with Joost van der Westhuizen and Hennie le Roux as my halfback combination, and would have started the Test the following week with them at No. 9 and No. 10 respectively, had they come through," says McIntosh. "However, Joost didn't kick well in that match, and once again Hennie failed to execute the game plan."

According to McIntosh, Van der Westhuizen and Le Roux's performances had contributed to the 28-29 defeat to New South Wales in a match that was more one-sided than the score line indicated. In retrospect, though, it may have been a good thing for the Boks that the game plan did not take off, as it enabled them to take the world-champion Wallabies by surprise in the first Test.

In order to see his game plan implemented in the Test, McIntosh went for the "safer" option in the Natal pairing of Robert du Preez and Joel Stransky.

"Boy, did the Transvaal media rip into me for making that decision. But the way I saw it, I had little option. Joost was a brilliant player. You could see he was going to [be a great player one day]. It was just that at that time he still had rough edges that would have made him a risky selection. I was determined to see my direct game properly implemented."

Stransky and Du Preez certainly played their part as the Springboks scored three tries to nil, two of them by James Small and one by Pieter Muller, the latter combining superbly with Heinrich Fuls on the day, as the visitors ran out 19-12 victors in Sydney.

"Joel did brilliantly playing to my game plan and more than vindicated his selection, and it was what we needed in order to start getting the confidence to believe in our ability," McIntosh recalls. "That day and Natal's 1990 Currie Cup triumph at Loftus Versfeld were my happiest and most satisfying moments in rugby."

Back home, the result was greeted with euphoria. "Experts" were claiming that South Africa were now back in the "big league", remembering, of course, that the Wallabies were the incumbent world champions and had been roundly beaten on their home ground.

But the Boks didn't – or couldn't – sustain the momentum. They lost 20-28 in the second Test, after which McIntosh admitted that he had been out-coached by Bob Dwyer, who had wisely selected big flank Ilie Tabua to "look after" the Boks from the blindside. The defining moment of the game, though, was when Ed Morrison brandished a red card at Small, who suffered the ignominy of becoming the first Springbok to be sent off in a Test match.

The incident happened half an hour into the game, when Morrison penalised Robert du Preez for playing a ball that was clearly out of the scrum.

When Du Preez remonstrated with him, Morrison advanced the penalty. In the Boks' opinion, he did so by at least 15 metres as opposed to the usual 10, and at a more favourable angle to the posts. Small clapped his hands and remarked that perhaps the referee should just put the ball *under* the poles.

McIntosh assumed that Small had been sent off for foul language, and with the score 10-all at the break, he followed the referee into the tunnel, where Morrison told him that Small had not, in fact, used foul language after all.

"No player questions my decisions, and that's that," said Morrison.

McIntosh thought Morrison was guilty of double standards, as earlier in the game a Wallaby had been penalised for punching after being spotted by New Zealand linesman Ian Bishop and Morrison hadn't even admonished him.

"Sure," said McIntosh in his book, "James Small should have kept his mouth shut, but it never warranted being sent off. Again it was a situation where a Springbok was singled out for special treatment."

The Boks lost the third Test by the same score (12-19) they had won the first, and there was more controversy around the refereeing. McIntosh had spoken to Morrison before the game, suggesting that the Wallabies constantly left the line-out illegally, and Morrison promised to have a look. Instead, even though the Australians continued to infringe, Morrison awarded a string of penalties against the Boks in the opening quarter.

Then, in the final minutes, the Boks thought they might have been on their way to scoring a try when David Campese obstructed James Small, but instead of blowing up Campese, Morrison blew Small for obstruction.

So the series was lost, but some progress had been made since the tour to France and England the year before, and the Boks had outscored the world champions by seven tries to four on their home turf. McIntosh should have started to feel settled. Australian Rugby Union (ARU) president Joe French may have given the most accurate summary when he lauded the Boks at the post-match reception for the progress they had made "in a very short space of time".

But the next day, when the Boks arrived at Johannesburg International Airport, the newspaper posters the incensed fans brandished would have left Mac in no doubt that French's view wasn't shared by all his countrymen.

"*Dis Mac se skuld!*" they screamed. McIntosh, though educated in the former Rhodesia, knew enough Afrikaans to know what that meant.

Some ex-Springboks also severely condemned McIntosh's tactics, particularly his supposed crash-ball rugby, saying that the Boks were playing "stock-car" and "robotic" rugby. Former captain Wynand Claassen and fellow 1981 tourist Rob Louw led the charge against McIntosh, asking in newspaper articles why there had been no Plan B.

I interviewed McIntosh after the tour, and he blamed the defeats on not winning sufficient possession, which was borne out by the statistics. So I wrote in a newspaper feature that I was looking forward to the book co-written by Claassen and Louw titled *Plan B: How to Win without the Ball.* Claassen wasn't happy with that, and he let me know all about it two years later at a cocktail party in Hong Kong.

But McIntosh did get backing from up high, and a week after the Australian tour he was in Louis Luyt's office at Ellis Park signing a contract that would bind him to the Springboks until the 1995 World Cup.

"There's your contract, and that will cover you, but you know the pressure is on you and you could still get sacked," Luyt said as he signed the agreement.

But the pressure gradually started easing, and there was an interesting development that went unnoticed by most critics in the months after the Australian tour.

"What was that headline all about, master?" McIntosh asked me early one August morning when we bumped into each other in a Durban North gym. "I've just seen a poster while driving here saying: 'Mac is helping Transvaal'."

"It's just an article saying that Transvaal are starting to play your rugby," I replied.

"Ah," said McIntosh. "I was wondering when someone was going to pick that up."

But if some of McIntosh's ideas were being appropriated by another team, there were also areas where he and the Transvaal players were not on the same page. An event two months later could have sounded the death knell to McIntosh's hopes of coaching the Boks until the 1995 World Cup when Transvaal, including several of McIntosh's Boks, beat Natal in a dramatic 1993 Currie Cup final in Durban.

"I knew when that happened that I was in trouble," McIntosh says now. "If there is one thing I have become very certain of through my coaching career it's that you cannot coach another man's successful team."

It was an acrimonious Currie Cup final, following on some tempestuous clashes between Natal and Transvaal during the course of the season. So it wasn't going to be easy for McIntosh to bring the players together as a unit on the end-of-year tour to Argentina.

Selecting the squad proved what a drawback it was to have a large selection panel dictating to the Springbok coach. McIntosh wanted to continue building his team and let the future take care of itself, but the selectors had other ideas – they were looking ahead to the 1995 World Cup.

"In many ways the group we took to Argentina was experimental, and I wasn't entirely happy about that," says McIntosh.

The Battle of Tucumán was a really ugly game remembered for the brawl on the field as well as for the way the tempest threatened to spill over onto the terraces. The Boks won the game 40-12 despite having players sent off, but then they lost to Buenos Aires, where the Boks acknowledged the referee as the Man of the Match – for what he did for their hosts.

The Boks went on to win both Tests, though they won the first one by a much less significant margin than the second. In the opening Test, the Boks were cantering until half-time when the Pumas, not for the last time in the history of their encounters with the Boks, came storming back in the second and were pushing for victory at the final whistle.

Once on tour, McIntosh was given more input as a selector, so it is ironic to reflect now that the man who had been accused of selecting too many Natal players actually dropped three of his former provincial prodigies for the last Test of the year.

"André Joubert, Joel Stransky and John Allan were very disappointing on that tour and I took the decision to leave them out. Boy, did they let me know about it, though," McIntosh reminisces.

Gavin Johnson, Chester Williams and Henry Honiball were brought in. Unfortunately Honiball was injured for most of the following year, but he showed McIntosh what might have been in 1994 with a starring role in the Boks' 52-23 win in the second Test, which provided a rousing finish to an up-and-down year.

Progress might have been made, but it was progress that was not universally acknowledged.

6

"Thanks for the tour, but we're fired"

If Ian McIntosh thought Transvaal winning the Currie Cup might have an impact on his second year in charge of the Springboks, it would have been confirmed if he read the following quote attributed to François Pienaar during the Transvaal Super 10 tour of Australia and New Zealand.

"I know I am going to sound controversial, but Transvaal are better as a team. We have the big-match mentality and we don't change the line-up all the time," Pienaar said after a match in Brisbane.

Pienaar was obviously having a go at the Springbok selectors, and McIntosh might even have agreed with him on that. But the Transvaal captain's words were nonetheless indicative of an attitude that McIntosh felt permeated the 1994 season.

As he recalls: "There was no doubt [that] the Transvaal players were taken with Kitch [Christie], and it was understandable, as they had broken a Currie Cup drought of more than two decades, and [they] had also won the previous year's Super 10.

"When we started preparing for the new international season, it was obvious [that] the Transvaal players wanted to play Kitch's way, with an accent on [obtaining] field position. The big irony, though, was that Transvaal were also using many of my drills and many aspects of my approach. I remember watching Transvaal train before a match against North Harbour and their manager, Wally Walters, came up to me and said, 'Look, we're doing all of your drills.'"

But the rug was taken out from underneath McIntosh's feet in more ways than one at the start of 1994. Headmaster Ebrahim Patel had taken over the presidency of SARFU when Danie Craven died the year before, but he had an uneasy reign, as it was clear that Louis Luyt was gunning for his position. Although the so-called Currie Cup A-section provinces were solidly behind Patel, the B-section unions and Eastern Province backed Luyt in what turned out to be a protracted power struggle.

Patel's decision to retire from rugby administration had been anticipated and did not come as a surprise. With him leaving, the upshot was that Luyt, who had already been a powerful figure the year before, was now all-powerful. And apart from having a national team half made up of Transvaal players, the Transvaal president, and a Kitch Christie supporter, was now McIntosh's boss.

Of equal concern to McIntosh, however, was the newly elected Springbok selection committee, headed by the former Bok captain Hannes Marais, who had been one of the most vociferous critics of his playing style the year before.

"The first thing he said to me was that there were mutterings about my coaching methods – I knew he was talking about the direct style of play – and the influence I was having over selection. He implied that I had been getting my own way [by selecting] too many Natal players.

"I was upset because I certainly hadn't been pushing my team down the throats of the selectors. I challenged [Marais] to come up with a team. He came up with one that had no fewer than seven Natal players in it. I told him that selection was one area where we had to discuss and compromise, but that when it came to my coaching, the issue was a non-negotiable.

"I was worried. I knew rugby was evolving and had changed dramatically over the past five years, and now we had someone who had come in from the distant past, with limited exposure to the modern game, and he was talking about coaching and playing styles."

McIntosh felt as if he was coming up against a brick wall whenever he spoke to the selection panel. The selectors neither listened to him nor paid any heed to the videos he showed of the good tries that had been scored, or the statistics that showed improvement in vital areas of the game. The new selectors also wanted a series of national trials, something McIntosh vehemently opposed. There was disagreement and dissent all round.

McIntosh wanted squad training sessions, but the rest of the selectors would not give him the green light for this. So he eventually travelled to Ballito to meet with Luyt, who gave his permission, much to the chagrin of Marais, who felt McIntosh had gone against protocol.

"They really gave it to me at the next meeting. Hannes had a full go at me, and so did Johan Claassen. Of course they were all [former] Boks, so they used all that brotherhood stuff against me. I decided to lose all sense of diplomacy and I ripped back into them. It was all very unpleasant."

The national coach and selectors had gathered in Bloemfontein to watch the England touring team in action, as South Africa were to play England in a two-Test series. McIntosh wanted 35 players for the initial squad, and Luyt agreed, but when Marais argued for a bigger one, Luyt reluctantly acquiesced and McIntosh ended up with a squad of 50. He was also forced to go along with a decision to delay the Springbok team announcement for the first Test, and the announcement was made only after the Bok B team had played England in Kimberley, which was just four days before the Loftus Versfeld Test match.

Although England had lost a few provincial games on their tour, they were still formidable opponents, and the scant preparation opportunity that McIntosh was allowed was rugby suicide, pure and simple.

The coach's intention was to turn the England forwards around with box kicks and then to play direct rugby from the possession they would win as a result, but the minimal time set aside for training just didn't allow for that level of preparation. The Boks went into the Loftus game hopelessly underprepared, and they were punished by an England team that ran up a big lead early on and was never under any threat.

The final score was England 32, South Africa 15. It was a humiliating day for South African rugby, particularly as it had been the first rugby occasion at which the new national anthem was played before kick-off. The country had completed the transition to democracy with the first election that was open to all population groups at the end of April. For the first time the Boks really were representing *all* of South Africa's people.

A somber mood permeated the marquee erected next to Loftus where the teams gathered for the post-match function. I had a drink with Springbok prop Keith Andrews, who had played in a curtain-raiser that day (a game that would have implications for the Boks in future), and he summed it up thus: "I guess that is the end of Ian McIntosh." Earlier he had told his cousin, Mark Andrews, "This is a good game for us to be missing."

Of course, this time it shouldn't have been "Mac's fault", as he was not to blame for the inadequate preparation, and Andrews knew that. The blame should have been laid fairly and squarely at the door of the administrators, who had prevaricated over what assistance the Boks should be given.

Louis Luyt, the SARFU president, was himself under pressure, though. As he wrote in his autobiography, *Walking Proud*:

> After 17 shocking minutes that left us speechless, the English led 20-0 through two penalties and two converted tries. President Mandela stared straight ahead of him. So did I. There wasn't much to celebrate or talk about. Our team struggled back somewhat, but as the day ended, the score stood at 32-15 to England. President Mandela looked at me.
>
> "Louis," he said, "what are you going to do about this?"

Luyt then went on to explain how it was no longer merely rugby that was on the line, but the whole 1995 Rugby World Cup, as it would be a damp squib if the Boks didn't perform there.

So he called virtually every coach in the country, as many as 19 of them by some counts, to a meeting at Ellis Park on the Monday to hear their views on how the tide could be turned. But surprise, surprise, instead of the coaches being helpful, Luyt found that they were just the opposite, as provincialism reared its ugly head again.

McIntosh thought the whole situation was crazy.

"That meeting was ridiculous. Kitch Christie was the first guy to speak, and he said, 'You have *got* to have Guy Kebble.' But then, later in the year, when we were struggling in New Zealand, he questioned why Guy was on the tour," says McIntosh. "They all rubbished the game we were playing, but we went in with the same tactics when we beat England five days later in Cape Town."

"I think Louis thought the meeting had galvanised us [for the second Test], but what really happened was that, at the training session at the Wanderers, I was very straight with the players. I said that if I was going to get fired, I wanted to get fired for what I was doing, not for the way 'you pricks want to play'. I told them I didn't want to hear another word, not 'even from you, François, or you, Hennie le Roux'. I told them that if they didn't like the way we were playing, they could piss off now."

On the morning of that game, with most of the country expecting a similar result to Loftus, I bumped into Brian van Zyl, the Natal chief executive, at breakfast at the Holiday Inn in Woodstock. Van Zyl was emphatic that the Boks would win, and he put it all down to one word – "gees", meaning spirit.

His prediction proved spot on, and the Bok reputation for back-to-the-wall wins during the post-isolation era was established on what happened on that clear but chilly autumn afternoon at Newlands. The Springboks played like men possessed; they rucked the England pack to pieces and dominated the tactical battle, and the 27-9 win was every bit as emphatic as the defeat had been the week before.

"I was one of the new players selected [for] that game," recalls debutant Mark Andrews, "and I remember how hyped everyone was. Mac had got hold of a *Cape Times* report that asked: 'Is this team a joke?', and he made sure it was pinned to the mirrors in our hotel rooms when we arrived."

What would have happened had the Boks lost is open to conjecture. Rumours had circulated that the defeat could mean the end of the road for McIntosh, and Harry Viljoen even told McIntosh that Kitch Christie had approached him to take over at Transvaal because Christie would be taking the Springboks to New Zealand.

Afterwards, McIntosh said that the win had brought him relief rather than elation. He knew a long, hard road lay ahead, and that the battle lines were being drawn between him and Luyt.

The tour squad for New Zealand was finalised immediately after the game, and Luyt was unhappy with the inclusion of Natal strongman Guy Kebble ahead of Japie Barnard, who had been on the bench that day. Kebble, though, had been injured and was just coming back into rugby. He would also more than likely have been included in the match-day squad for Newlands had he been fit.

But Kebble, who had consistently been one of the strongest props in the Currie Cup, was hardly the main issue. McIntosh was working with seven other selectors, and they were far too impressed for their own good and the nation's good with Northern Transvaal's 41-9 win over a Rest of South Africa XV in the curtain-raiser to the first England Test.

As a consequence, they pushed for the mass inclusion of Northerns players, which accounted for the selection of centres F.A. Meiring and Jannie Claassens, two players who had never come anywhere near a Bok team before, as well as flyhalf Lance Sherrell. McIntosh wanted Joel Stransky and Henry Honiball as his flyhalves, but he was shot down by the rest of the selectors. Hennie le Roux would only have travelled as an inside centre and utility back had McIntosh been given his way.

"Apart from the curtain-raiser to the Loftus game, another thing that skewed everything was that meeting Louis had called at Ellis Park with all those other coaches," says McIntosh. "Several points [were] mentioned there, and one of them was that we needed a recognised goal-kicker. That was what brought Lance Sherrell into the mix. But while Lance was a brilliant place-kicker, I couldn't see how he would make the Test team, as he just wasn't good enough for that level of rugby. I made this point to the other selectors, but they weren't listening."

McIntosh felt in his heart that he had the wrong players from the outset, and he had serious misgivings as the squad boarded a Qantas flight on a Sunday in mid-June, with Ernie Els about to win his first Major golf title. The flight took them to Perth, where they watched some of the golf on TV, and then Sydney, where they stayed overnight before picking up their connecting flight to New Zealand.

McIntosh's frustration with the system was no secret to the players.

As François Pienaar wrote in his autobiography: "At various stages of the tour, he [McIntosh] gave me the impression that he felt frustrated by the outdated system in which the national coach was just one of several selectors, thus creating the situation where he could not be sure of getting the squad he wanted."

The Boks started off the tour in the lakeside resort of Taupo against King Country. The home team didn't put up much opposition, and the Boks may have suffered for not playing against a strong provincial team like Auckland in the build-up to the first Test.

The series opened in Dunedin, and an injury to François Pienaar prompted McIntosh and the management, who became the selectors once the tour started, to move Tiaan Strauss to flank, from where he captained the side. Jannie Engelbrecht had set up a little competition among the journalists to see who would come closest to predicting the team for the first Test, and when I got it right, including Strauss's selection at flank, Engelbrecht rewarded me with a case of his Rust and Vrede wine, which I carted around with me for the rest of the tour.

In the opening match, Hennie le Roux and André Joubert missed several kicks at goal that could have won the game for the Boks. At the same time, ill-discipline let them down at crucial times, and New Zealand punished them by kicking their penalties to run out 22-14 victors.

In the build-up to the series, the Kiwis had suffered a rare series defeat on home soil to France, so in some eyes the Boks started as favourites. This meant that there was massive pressure on them as they headed to the North Island – there would be a lot of island-hopping and long journeys from north to south and back on that trip – for the next leg of the tour.

The Boks scored a narrow win over Taranaki in New Plymouth, but the pressure on the team further intensified when a big fuss was made over the stuffed Springbok head the squad carried with them on tour, which would be awarded to the first non-Test team to beat them. This was part of an age-old tradition, but some players felt the head should have stayed at home.

"The Bok head is hanging over us," wrote James Small in his column in the *Natal on Saturday* newspaper. "What we don't need right now is the added pressure of having the Springbok head hanging over OUR heads."

As it turned out, the Boks thrashed Waikato 38-17 in Hamilton in a match that should have built them a lot of momentum. This was the match that didn't take place in 1981 because of a field invasion, so there was a lot of hype around it. Sadly, there was also a lot of hype over an incident involving Small, who was severely censured for a collision with Waikato's former All Black lock Steve Gordon.

I say "collision", because that was what it looked like to me, and many years later, in a retrospective newspaper feature I did on Small, he still, quite justifiably, protested his innocence: "I played a lot of soccer when I was younger. Check out that incident and see what a soccer challenge looks like."

As we were preparing for our bus journey from Palmerston North to Wellington on the day after the midweek Manawatu clash, Jannie Engelbrecht announced the team for the second Test. There was an audible gasp from the media contingent, me included, when the penny dropped that André Joubert was not going to be starting the game. I caught sight of McIntosh a little while later as he made his way to the bus that was going to take the Boks to the airport, and he stopped for a chat.

"Master, what do you think of us leaving out André Joubert?"

"Mac, I can't believe it. I think you've made a massive mistake."

"I think so too. I think so too," he said, shaking his head.

Years later, McIntosh doesn't hide from the fact that he had been party to the decision and was thus as culpable as anyone else. "My weakness was the way I would go with the majority; I have always been like that. That was my big mistake in Palmerston North. But the situation had been created by the pre-tour squad selection. We did need a kicker, but Lance Sherrell wasn't good enough to make the Test team."

Whether or not Joubert would have made a difference to the Boks if he'd played from the start in Wellington is a moot point, as the All Black win was built around a devastating scrumming performance early in the game. Later the Boks made a bit of a comeback, and Joubert was on the field for the second half, but the All Blacks eventually squeaked home 13-9 in a desperately tense affair.

If nothing else, dropping Joubert to the bench did have an impact on team morale – once we got to Wellington, quite a few of the players told me that they weren't happy with the selectors' decision – and it is probably fair to say that it was a watershed moment in McIntosh's coaching career, as people who had previously supported him now started to doubt him. I was among them.

However, Dan Retief, who had covered tours in the pre-isolation era and was more of a traditionalist, was even more vehemently opposed to McIntosh. After the Wellington Test, which clinched the series for the All Blacks, Retief insisted that McIntosh should be sacked, and he kept repeating his pre-tour assertion that New Zealand was the "graveyard" for Springbok coaches.

Indeed it was, but today Dan would probably be the first to admit that he may have called it differently if he'd known how poorly the Boks would fare in New Zealand in the years that followed.

In the immediate aftermath of the match, the defeat was completely overshadowed by the Johan le Roux ear-biting incident. The Transvaal tighthead was caught on camera taking a munch out of All Black captain Sean Fitzpatrick's ear, and even before the final whistle blew, there was a buzz around the press box.

New Zealand can be a claustrophobic place when something like the Le Roux incident happens and you hail from the offending country. At the start of the tour, after the All Blacks had lost to France, we saw how seriously New Zealand took their rugby. Every radio talk show and current-affairs television programme was dominated by the All Blacks' defeat and speculation over the future of their coach, Laurie Mains.

Walking towards the taxi ranks from the rickety old Athletic Park Stadium on that cold winter's evening, I could hear how the Le Roux incident was being discussed on car radios as spectators sat in the post-match traffic jam.

With New Zealand so far ahead of South Africa time-wise, journalists would work late into the night to meet early-morning deadlines that, at home, normally hit you straight after a match. It was the middle of the night and most of us were in our rooms working on our laptops, or what Stephen Jones calls "facing the loneliness of the empty screen", when we were summoned to the team room for an impromptu press conference.

The first person I saw when I got to the room was McIntosh, sitting slumped in a corner and staring at a television set. The screen was blank except for the snow that appears when there is no picture. McIntosh just sat staring at the TV even when the press conference commenced and Engelbrecht informed us that Le Roux was being sent home.

"We can't deny what happened, we can't defend him … We can either leave it up to the disciplinary hearing or we can take action by punishing him ourselves."

Some of the New Zealand media who had pitched at the late-night briefing were shocked at the swiftness of the Bok management's reaction. So was Louis Luyt. The SARFU president felt his organisation had been upstaged, and a bitter stand-off between Luyt and the management ensued. Luyt had flown home to South Africa, but when the Le Roux incident happened, he was travelling back to New Zealand. In his autobiography, he writes that some of the players were acting "like a bunch of college kids out to have a good time" in New Zealand, and that the night before the Wellington Test (he wasn't there, so someone must have told him) several of the players had been seen living it up with young women at their side.

Also, he wrote that after one game he walked in on McIntosh and James Small "diligently finishing off a bottle of Scotch in the team room". But McIntosh has a reasonable explanation for what Luyt alleged in his book.

The incident Luyt referred to happened in Invercargill, in the far south of New Zealand's South Island, following a mock initiation ceremony that had involved the management, the players and the media, and which had been intended to improve the relationship between the squad and the members of the Fourth Estate. A lot of drinking was done that night and, while there was so much bonhomie in the air, McIntosh took the opportunity to do something he perhaps should have done straight after the Cape Town Test.

McIntosh explains: "I called François, Hennie le Roux and James Small into a meeting to discuss a simmering tension that had been developing since the Newlands Test against England. François had walked off the field and barked at me that he wasn't going to play for the Springboks again as long as James was involved.

"I asked François what was eating him, and he told me that James had told him to 'ef off', like he does with everyone at some stage. I had promised to sort it out, and Invercargill, after that media event, was our first opportunity. I called François, Hennie and James in, and there were a lot of accusations and counter-accusations.

"It didn't really resolve anything, as James took on a victim mentality and asked, 'Why is it always me?' I kept him in my room to try to calm him down after the others had left, and that was when Louis walked in. He never, ever slept, that guy. Why didn't he just ask what we were up to rather than steaming about it? But he just walked out of the room without saying a word."

The fallout from the Le Roux incident, the subsequent dropping of Small after a rumoured altercation with his teammates at a training session in the build-up to the last Test, and Luyt's constant interfering and carping via the media turned the last two weeks of the tour into a media circus where controversy was ever present.

I stayed on in Wellington when the squad and the rest of the media first flew to Dunedin for the tour match against Otago so that I could report on Le Roux's disciplinary hearing, which had been called after the inevitable citing.

If New Zealand felt claustrophobic immediately after the second Test, it became even more so on that Sunday and Monday in Wellington. The foyer of the hotel the Boks had recently vacated was filled with Kiwi journalists eager to get comments from or a photograph of Le Roux. I can't condone the offence, but I did feel sorry for the player, as the media frenzy was completely over the top.

The hearing was held in the New Zealand Rugby Union offices in downtown Wellington on the Monday night. Fitzpatrick scurried into the hearing declining to comment, and shortly thereafter Le Roux was banned from the game for so long that it ended his international career.

And he was not the only one whose career ended that week – that was pretty much what happened to McIntosh, too. The day after the hearing, he watched his team surrender the Springbok head to Otago after a pitiful display in a wet-weather game.

Of course, afterwards the media immediately started writing about the end of the McIntosh era, as if it was already a foregone conclusion. Ironically, it was also the day that McIntosh finally lost patience with Hennie le Roux. It marked a turnaround in the player's mindset, and he started implementing the coach's game plan.

"Hennie came to me after the tour and said that he hoped I would stay on as coach, as he could see now that my way worked if it was properly implemented," said McIntosh.

But the tactical naivety of the team on that miserable Tuesday afternoon in Dunedin was something McIntosh would not survive. When we got to Christchurch for the second-last game against a provincial team, Canterbury, Louis Luyt called a press conference. We were told that everyone was being unfair to the coach, because he was under "terrible, terrible pressure".

McIntosh, Luyt informed us, had a job to do and he definitely couldn't "be sacked now, as that would be inhumane".

My Independent Group colleague Mike McGrath fired off a story that proclaimed McIntosh's job was safe. I didn't agree with him. I had picked up on Luyt's semantics; he was clever with words. I approached him after the press conference and said to him: "The way I understand it, you are not saying he is *not* going to be sacked, you're saying he's not going to be sacked *this instant*."

Luyt stared at me before nodding his head and saying that my interpretation was correct. So he never did lie at that media conference as some later claimed; it was all just clever wordplay.

Behind the scenes several showdowns and stand-offs took place between Luyt and Engelbrecht, all of them well documented in McIntosh's book. Selection protocol was one of the big bones of contention, as was Luyt's accommodation – for much of the tour he was apparently accommodated in rooms that were too small for him, while Engelbrecht enjoyed the spacious elegance of a suite.

Luyt was also unhappy that instances of foul play had gone unpunished on the tour because the Boks wouldn't cite the New Zealanders. And he claimed that after he had heard about the ear-biting incident in Wellington, Kitch Christie, who coached Le Roux at Transvaal, had phoned him. "We should never choose that animal Le Roux ever gain," Christie had allegedly shouted over the phone, calling on Luyt to announce Le Roux's immediate expulsion. But Luyt took a slightly different tack – perhaps because Engelbrecht had got there first.

"The Le Roux incident was not nearly in the same biting league as that of boxer Mike Tyson. And there was also probably provocation from Fitzpatrick," Luyt pronounced.

He tried to contact Engelbrecht en route to New Zealand, but without success, and then asked Johan Claassen to pass a message under Engelbrecht's hotel-room door. Engelbrecht's response was that he wouldn't respond to messages delivered by third parties.

The result was that the last week of the tour was dominated by the bickering between Luyt and the management. It was like watching two bulls circling each other. And in the midst of all that drama, Small was omitted from the team for the third Test, which cast McIntosh in the role of villain, even in his home town of Durban.

The match, played at Eden Park, was typical of the tour itself – the Boks had plenty of opportunities to win the match and even outscored the All Blacks two tries to nil, but had to settle for a draw. It was a pretty hollow end to a tour that had never really lived up to expectations.

But while the on-field part of the tour was over, the action off the field continued. In Auckland, I had a late-night drink with McIntosh in the team hotel, and he told me then what he had just told the team: "Master, I think that is me done. I think that was my last Test match. I've told the players that. I would love to carry on, but I hear I am out."

I hadn't yet written my wrap-up of the tour at the time, but I hurried it out in the early hours of the morning, just in time for me to catch the 5 a.m. flight across the Tasman Sea to Sydney, from where we would all head back to South Africa via Perth. I wrote that McIntosh had told the team that his days were numbered.

But somewhere between leaving Auckland and the *Sunday Tribune* hitting the streets of Durban, a sub-editor somewhere had misinterpreted my words and rewritten them to say that McIntosh had resigned. He had done no such thing, but that didn't stop the article from saying that he had. As a consequence I had to deal with a very angry Rona McIntosh, Mac's wife, when I got back to Durban many hours later, on the Sunday night.

My report was not the only one that was inaccurate, however. Luyt claimed that another one was too. Phil Saayman of *Rapport* had had a beer with Luyt in his hotel room, where he asked him if he would be firing the management at the end of the tour. Saayman then reported that the management would indeed be shown the door, something Luyt would later deny he had said.

Having got wind of Saayman's report, Jannie Engelbrecht got onto the bus that was ferrying the Boks to the airport and famously pronounced: "Gentlemen, I want to thank you all for a most enjoyable tour. Your whole management team has been fired."

During the stopover in sunny Perth, we heard that a press conference might be held on arrival in Johannesburg to set the record straight. The other passengers in the airport transit hall probably wondered why little pockets of officials and journalists were chatting together so animatedly.

When we finally reached Johannesburg and were walking into the arrivals hall, I happened to walk in behind McIntosh and Pienaar. The angry captain swung around and confronted me. He was incensed because I had told McIntosh that he, Pienaar, did not back him, based on something I had heard from another reporter.

"I am tired of this shit," said Pienaar.

I think we all were.

While I was rushing through the airport to catch the connecting flight to Durban, André Joubert caught up with me and asked me if I was going to be writing "pro-McIntosh" stories. I couldn't answer him. I honestly didn't know. A lot of mistakes had been made on tour. It only became clearer much later, when I was away from rugby and enjoying a holiday in the Drakensberg, that McIntosh had been done an injustice.

Engelbrecht would survive to fight another day, thanks to the support he received in the Cape during the unseemly public spat that followed, but no one rallied to McIntosh's defence.

But later, as Mark Andrews recalls, François Pienaar also acknowledged the role McIntosh had played in laying the groundwork for the Boks to win the World Cup the following year.

"I think one of the biggest compliments I ever heard paid to Mac was when François said that we had played smart rugby to win the World Cup, but had stuck to the McIntosh game," said Andrews. "I was young on that [New Zealand] tour, but what I do remember was the strong provincial cliques. I would love to have played under McIntosh for longer, as I found it very easy to understand what he expected and what game plan he wanted us to play. But he also encouraged us to think, and players who were used to a more rigid set-up and more structured way of playing struggled with that.

"François was also a very strong leader, and I got the feeling that he was afraid of losing the support of his fellow Transvaal players in that set-up if he was too supportive of Mac. It was like he was between a rock and a hard place. I got the feeling he did rate Mac, but that Mac was his second choice as coach."

Nick Mallett, however, has no doubt that McIntosh was the best of the early Bok coaches.

"McIntosh was ahead of his time," Mallett told me, "and I do think he was treated badly. The irony is that the game most of the rugby world has played for the last 20 years has been the game that McIntosh was trying to [establish]."

Although McIntosh requested a meeting with the SARFU executive, it never happened. In that sense, his fate, and his dismissal, was similar to that of John Williams – although this time the sacking was public and brutal. Luyt had no compunction about using the media to criticise the way in which McIntosh had handled the tour, and although it was obvious his days were numbered, the affair dragged on for weeks.

McIntosh perhaps fared slightly better than some of the other Bok coaches who had been sacked; he just got on with his life. I was surprised when he popped up on the next tour, to Wales, Scotland and Ireland at the end of the year, as a spectator. Pienaar was right – McIntosh really did love rugby.

"Look, it did hurt, obviously; it hurt a lot," reflects McIntosh, "but I grew up with the code that you get dropped, and playing rugby, you understood that. Whether it was as the flank for the A side when you are [playing] under-13, or from the Springbok side, if you play the game there is a chance you will be dropped. It comes with the territory, and it is the same with coaching. I always asked my players not to go and rubbish the coach and the team when they got dropped. I accepted [SARFU's] prerogative to make a change if they deemed it necessary.

"It would have been nice, though, if Louis Luyt had called me in and at least thanked me for what I had done. I could then have walked away with my head held high and we could all have moved on. But he didn't do that. And I think it was a similar story with many of the Bok coaches who succeeded me. That's really what makes me sad."

The great irony is that the style of rugby that made McIntosh so unpopular back in 1994 is now the modern way of playing, and that, later that same year, at Swansea under Kitch Christie, the Boks finally managed to perfect "Ian McIntosh rugby".

7

An ambulance job

The feud between Louis Luyt and Jannie Engelbrecht was still simmering in the media when the Springbok manager packed his bags in preparation for a fact-finding mission ahead of the year-end tour of the Celtic nations.

"As far as I, and I am sure SARFU, are concerned, the disagreements of the past week are now behind us and we have to start planning ahead as soon as possible," Engelbrecht said.

An uneasy truce had been called, as both Engelbrecht and Luyt had garnered some public and media sympathy during their spat – Engelbrecht through the press in the Cape, which backed him to the hilt, and Luyt by announcing his resignation via the *Sunday Times*, though he changed his mind later that same day.

"Small men will cheer," Edward Griffiths wrote in his "One Small Voice" column, which ran in the same edition in which Dan Retief broke the news of Luyt's resignation.

By referring to Luyt's opponents as "small men", Griffiths was insinuating that Luyt was a big man. Which of course he was, and he had a big appetite, too. Whenever Luyt's name came up in a book, he seemed to be tucking into a plate of spare ribs in the midst of making important decisions.

For instance, in 1996, the SANZAR delegation was waiting to hear from Rupert Murdoch's lieutenant, Sam Chisholm, what his boss thought of the US$555 million on offer to southern hemisphere rugby for a decade of exclusive broadcasting rights. Luyt was tucking into a large helping of ribs when the call came through to say that Murdoch had approved the deal.

"What about the ribs? I'm not finished," Luyt complained to the rest of the delegation as they got up to go to the News Corporation offices to sign the deal.

But when Luyt unexpectedly called Kitch Christie and asked to meet him for lunch, the two sat down to enjoy some prawns rather than ribs. At the time, late in 1992, Christie was on the way out at Northern Transvaal, where he had long served as an assistant, and was coaching the Harlequins second team. Luyt remembers their first conversation thus in his autobiography, *Walking Proud*.

"It's Louis Luyt here."

"Who did you say you were?"

"Louis Luyt. I want to talk to you about the head coaching job at Ellis Park."

"This must be a joke," responded Christie.

"No, I am serious. If you have any doubts, why don't you call me back at Ellis Park so we can talk further."

Christie didn't bother to phone Ellis Park. Instead, he left his office in Midrand and drove straight to Luyt's office at the stadium. In another half an hour they were at a restaurant called LM Prawns, enjoying the restaurant speciality and drinking wine while Luyt thrashed out his plan. Christie listened, accepted the job offer, and by the end of the afternoon, both tanked up on wine, Luyt introduced Christie to the Transvaal team ahead of a training session.

Harry Viljoen had departed the Transvaal job after his team had lost to Natal in that year's Currie Cup final at Ellis Park, and Avril Malan had declined an offer to take over.

Kitch had been undervalued at Northern Transvaal for a long time, and the fact that he was English-speaking had counted against him on several occasions when the top job became available. The word from the Northerns cognoscenti, though, was that Christie was not only "too English", he was also too strong-minded and opinionated. But those characteristics worked in his favour in his first dealings with Luyt. With him, one had to establish the ground rules fast, as he was notorious for interfering in the coaching of the Transvaal team.

Luyt, in fact, had filled in as coach for Transvaal after Viljoen's abrupt departure, as the Lion Cup was played after the Currie Cup that season. Luyt had been in charge of Transvaal for four games when he and Christie met for their prawn lunch.

In his book, Christie recounted the meeting thus: "Luyt took me to lunch and we agreed the ground rules of our association. He would run the union, I would run the team and neither of us would interfere in the other's business. We were eating prawns, and after a while, I asked him when he wanted me to start. I will never forget his reply – it was typical of the man. He said 'tonight' and we drove straight to the Transvaal team hotel, where the players were preparing for a Lion Cup semi-final against Northern Transvaal the following day."

Christie called in former Springbok wing Ray Mordt to work with him as his assistant. Mordt had been part of the Harlequins team that had brought Christie his greatest rugby achievement up till then – victory in the prestigious National Club Easter Tournament in 1983. They beat Maties, coached by Danie Craven, along the way. After the game, Craven called Christie "a bloody amateur".

But Christie was no amateur, for Transvaal quickly started to find success under his guidance. They won the Lion Cup, the province's first title in five years, and followed that by winning the Super 10 the following season, beating a star-studded Auckland outfit that included Zinzan Brooke and Sean Fitzpatrick in the final. From there they won the Lion Cup again, as well as the Currie Cup.

Luyt kept his nose out of Christie's business, which was probably not hard to do with the side almost always winning. Christie wrote about the family atmosphere that reigned among the Transvaal players.

"I took him [Luyt] as I found him, and he was straight and fair with me. We developed a relationship which suited us both. I needed him because I desperately wanted to coach a provincial team, and he needed me because he wanted to win trophies and fill the stadium."

There was some irony in Christie being employed at Ellis Park. His father, William, a Scotsman, had come to southern Africa at the age of 19, initially working in the copper belt of northern Rhodesia. Christie was born in 1940, four days before his father departed for World War II, and it was at Ellis Park that father and son were reunited when the war was over.

Kitch was sent to Scotland to study at Leith Academy in Edinburgh at the behest of his grandparents, and his coaching career started at Harlequins, Pretoria's English club, in 1968. By 1971, the success of his under-20 team was starting to be noticed, and from there, Christie, who friends and colleagues described as "incredibly intense", progressed through the ranks until he became first-team coach. Twenty-three years later, and following his success at Transvaal and the axing of Ian McIntosh, Christie would accept the top job in South African rugby – that of Springbok coach.

"I told him [Doc Luyt] that I would do an ambulance job," Christie recalled later in his biography, *Kitch: Triump of a Decent Man,* referring to the perception that South African rugby needed emergency resuscitation. "I said I would take the Springboks to the 1995 Rugby World Cup but, after that, it would be my preference to regain the coaching position at Transvaal. Doc Luyt said we could handle that issue later, but that was the understanding."

At Transvaal, Christie had placed massive emphasis on discipline and physical fitness, as François Pienaar remembers in *Rainbow Warrior*: "I remember thinking during those early days of training that 'this guy just refuses to lose'. Everything he did gave the impression that he knew exactly what he was trying to achieve and, more than that, that he had no doubt at all that the Transvaal team would achieve it."

It wasn't as if Christie was asking the players to do anything he wouldn't have done himself, if he could. He had been forced to hang tough since 1979, when he was first diagnosed with lymphatic cancer, and like many who struggle with that disease, Christie saw everything sunny-side up and endeavoured to make the most of his time.

It helped that he was in a position to lay down the ground rules with Luyt. He became the first national coach to operate without a selection panel telling him whom he could select.

Christie's emphasis on discipline was one of his big strengths, and it may have influenced the coaching career of one of his prodigies, Rudolf Straeuli, who played under Christie at Northern Transvaal, Transvaal and the Springboks, and who would later himself coach the Boks. Christie felt there had been a lack of discipline during the Boks' tour of New Zealand, and from the outset he was determined to stamp his authority on the team.

"I remember getting the shock of my life when I first started training under Kitch," recalls Mark Andrews. "In one of our first encounters I asked him something and addressed him as Kitch. Boy, did he come down on me like a ton of bricks. He very firmly told me that I was not ever again to address him as Kitch, and that henceforth I should refer to him either as 'coach' or Mr Christie, and nothing else."

Andrews wasn't sure whether the Transvaal players felt the same as him, but he says he never felt settled under Christie.

"We obviously had our successes under him, but I can't say that the time I spent in the Boks when he was coach was my most enjoyable time in rugby," says the former lock forward.

In order to enforce his discipline on the team, Christie felt it necessary to remove those players he considered lax or lazy, and he shocked the nation when the 37-man training squad he named for the early part of his tenure excluded no fewer than 19 of the 36 players who had toured New Zealand under McIntosh.

Christie said that when he accepted the job, he told Luyt that he wanted to pick the team; he did not want to be given a list of names by a panel of seven selectors. Luyt agreed to the request, so Christie gave it some thought and picked what he thought was the best team. Christie said it was actually a "straightforward process". He simply worked out what game plan *he* wanted the team to adopt and then selected the players who would best serve that game plan. According to him, the Springbok team should consist not of the best 15 players in the country, but the best combination to execute the game plan.

As Brendan Venter recalls, however, tactics and game plans were not something discussed with the players, which was one of the areas where Christie differed from McIntosh. "To me, Kitch was not a tactician, and the fact that he went on to win the World Cup may be an indication that sometimes it doesn't matter how strong you are tactically when it comes to whether or not you are a good coach. Kitch succeeded by making people believe in him, and he succeeded at the Boks by surrounding himself with people whom he believed in and who believed in him.

"He picked 13 Transvaal players, and then even called up the Transvaal B hooker when one of the hookers fell out. The plan to win the World Cup was purely and simply that there was a low road and a high road, and that we must take the high road by beating Australia. That was not a tactic.

"He may have communicated tactics to the Transvaal players, particularly François Pienaar, but there weren't meetings where we discussed tactics and strategy. It was all about fitness and discipline, and in that sense he was extremely old school. Whether you agreed with it or not, McIntosh had a plan and he spent a lot of time trying to communicate that plan to you."

Christie utilised some of the Transvaal players to guide him in the selection process. He asked Uli Schmidt, who had followed him to Transvaal in 1993, to name the strongest props in South Africa, which led to the selection of the immensely powerful Pieter "Os" du Randt from the Free State, and the equally immovable Western Province tighthead Tommie Laubscher, a 30-year-old farmer from Velddrif on the West Coast.

The players who had toured in New Zealand and were now omitted from the first training squad included F.A. Meiring, Jannie Claassens, Cabous van der Westhuizen, Lance Sherrell, Guy Kebble, John Allan, Johan le Roux, Wahl Bartmann, Steve Atherton, Adri Geldenhuys, André Joubert and James Small.

The omission of the last two names caused the most controversy. The Natal pair had landed themselves in hot water for being spotted having a drink in Port Elizabeth on a Friday night before a match against Eastern Province not long after the Boks had returned from New Zealand. It was the perfect opportunity for Christie to make a public example of players who did not take note of his message that any kind of indiscipline would not be tolerated.

Joubert and Small contacted Christie quite soon after the squad announcement and, after promising to clean up their act, were immediately brought into the training group.

Christie's move did not go down well everywhere in South Africa, and in Natal, in particular, the new coach was regarded with suspicion.

"There was a lot of fuss about Kitch being tough on discipline and being hard on the players in order to get everything right, but as far as I can ascertain it was always Natal players who were cut from the squad and Natal players he made examples of, and not his Transvaal players," Ian McIntosh recalls.

He makes a good point. In Christie's book, he mentions a couple of occasions during his first tour where he punished players for being late and made examples of them – the names that were mentioned were Western Province's Tiaan Strauss and Free State's Brendan Venter. Transvaal players either never transgressed, or were never punished, and I must say that, as a journalist covering the Boks in those early days under Christie, that was the impression I was left with too. As it turns out, Mark Andrews can only agree.

"On that first end-of-year tour under Kitch, there was very clear favouritism for Transvaal players. They could joke and play around and he would laugh with them, but he wasn't like that with the rest of us," says Andrews. "He got rid of a lot of Natal players, and made an example of James and Juba. I wondered at the time if he would have done that with a Transvaal player. I was never comfortable with him and never felt part of the inner circle. I think the other players from outside Transvaal felt the same way. I know [that], James, André Joubert [and I] always felt like we were on the outside.

"Kitch had a stick-in-the-mud approach. He said at the outset that he would be democratic and that decisions would be made by getting a two-thirds majority. But two-thirds of the team were Transvaal players, so we always ended up doing what they wanted to do."

Christie held Monday training sessions in the build-up to his first match in charge of the Boks, which formed part of a two-Test home series against Argentina, before the end-of-year tour to Wales, Scotland and Ireland would commence. According to Christie, the players had not been fit in New Zealand, and he was determined to fix that. As he recorded in his book, at the end of four weeks he wanted the squad to have "graduated from a group of rookies into a squad of hardened professionals who no longer hated the sergeant but instead revered him".

Christie had initially thought that he could carry on coaching Transvaal while coaching the Boks, but he soon realised that this was impossible when he came onto the field to talk to his players during a Currie Cup game against Free State and the Free Staters looked at him accusingly.

When Transvaal followed their previous year's triumph at Kings Park by thrashing Free State in a high-scoring, one-sided Currie Cup final at the Springbok Park cricket field, Christie was not their coach. Ray Mordt, whom Christie had wanted as his Springbok assistant coach, had taken charge of Transvaal on his departure. Christie could not use Mordt at national level due to an IRB regulation that prevented people who had been involved in rugby league from coaching a national rugby union team. Mordt had played the 13-man code for Wigan. So instead of Mordt, Christie chose Gysie Pienaar as his assistant, much for the sake of continuity.

Christie's first squads were dominated by Transvaal players, and some rugby scribes accused him of selecting "Vaal Boks".

"As a coach you are obviously going to pick players you can trust, and it may well follow that you are more likely to trust the players you know best," Christie conceded.

But this had not been a luxury afforded to Ian McIntosh. In fact, McIntosh would have liked to have selected a few more Natal players, but his fellow selectors would not allow it. One of those players was Gary Teichmann, who did, in fact, make Christie's first national tour squad, and for his willingness to play out of position on the flank on that tour, he was rewarded with his one solitary Springbok cap during Christie's tenure nearly a year later.

Christie laid down the ground rules in a team meeting at the end of his first training session at the Wanderers. He gave each player a piece of paper, which read, "Springboks – what we need to win", and listed 20 points that Christie felt would make the Boks great. He wrote afterwards that he thought the non-Transvaal players were not as wary of him after that session.

The first Test of the Christie era was played against Argentina in Port Elizabeth in early October 1994. I bumped into Transvaal prop Balie Swart in the lift of the Kings Beach Holiday Inn on the morning of the game, and he could not curb his enthusiasm for the abilities of the "new coach". Obviously Christie was going to get more out of the Transvaal players than McIntosh had managed to.

The Boks won 42-22 at the old Boet Erasmus, but it was an underwhelming performance that didn't exactly send the fans home raving about the new dispensation. In fact, there hadn't been that much between the teams until quite late in the game.

It was after that game that James Small got involved in an altercation with a Springbok wave-skier, Ian McLeod, at the aptly named Barney's Tavern on the Port Elizabeth beachfront. It had allegedly been sparked by McLeod's girlfriend pinching Small on the bottom, and the wave-skier then getting upset when the Springbok wing reacted badly to it. I didn't witness the incident, but I was there for most of the evening. I had a drink with Small and Joel Stransky and could assess the general mood, which was quite convivial and not at all tense.

So I was shocked when it was announced the next day that Small would not be considered for the overseas tour because of what had happened at Barney's. Judging from the reaction, the public were as outraged as I was at the move by the Bok management, and then to top it all, Small nearly got me into trouble when he told a Johannesburg media conference that I had been at Barney's when the incident happened.

"Gavin Rich was there, ask him; he will tell you [that] the whole thing has been blown out of all proportion," Small told the press. My colleagues then wanted to know why I had not written about the incident. Sorry, but I have never written about what rugby players get up to in their private time; it's not my style, and to this day I still don't see how it is relevant to my job, which is to report on rugby.

But I did vigorously defend Small, certainly in the Cape newspapers, where I was now working, and I agreed with him that an investigation should have been launched into the incident instead of him just summarily being axed from the squad.

At the very least, they could have asked McLeod what had transpired. In fact, he was quoted in the media, saying: "It was an incident that happened on a pavement and [it] should have been left on the pavement."

The Springbok management's overreaction to the incident could probably be blamed on events during the New Zealand tour, when a big fuss had been made of the players' partying (again I was there, and again I think it was blown out of proportion). On top of that, Jannie Engelbrecht, who was still the Bok manager, didn't have any love to spare for Small, and Small, in an interview I did with him years later, indicated to me in no uncertain terms that he had no love for the Springbok manager at that time either. He felt that Engelbrecht had hung him out to dry when he should have defended him after the incident in Hamilton that saw him cited on the New Zealand tour. "Small is beyond rehabilitation," Engelbrecht said. He mentioned that some members of the New Zealand public had reported a number of incidents to him in which Small had been involved.

I agreed, and I still agree, with Mike Shafto, whose article in the *Weekend Star* appeared on the morning of the Johannesburg Test against Argentina. He suggested that Small was caught in the crossfire of the feud between Louis Luyt and Engelbrecht. The Bok manager was trying to prove that he wasn't lax on discipline, as Luyt had alleged during their public spat.

The Springboks won the Test 46-26, but again, it was neither an inspiring result nor a good performance. Dan Retief, writing in the *Sunday Times*, was particularly blunt: "Boks simply not good enough."

But they would be good enough once they got overseas, and it was in Wales, Scotland and Ireland that the real building towards the World Cup triumph the following year would begin, although I am not sure I fully agree with Louis Luyt's version of events in *Walking Proud*, where he described the 1994 Springbok tour of the United Kingdom as the "rebirth of South Africa as a formidable force in international rugby". In his opinion, this "timely turnaround" was due to the work of Kitch Christie. McIntosh had had a "disastrous" New Zealand tour, and it was Luyt's job to find a suitable replacement.

And he says that the same experts who had criticised his decision to replace McIntosh with Christie as a "blatant act of provincialism and a display of impulsiveness" now considered it "a stroke of genius".

But of course, Luyt says, it was neither provincialism nor impulse that had motivated his decision. It was "a simple act of necessity". According to him, even Engelbrecht had asked him to find a substitute for McIntosh, as had many others, though they still pretended to support him in public. In the end, Luyt claims, his own personal feelings had nothing to do with his decision.

Where Luyt was wrong was in his assumption that the turnaround was all due to Christie. Players who were on that tour were quite open about the fact that most of the drills they did were those of Ian McIntosh.

Says Brendan Venter: "I think we had got to the point under McIntosh where we had started to understand his game and were starting to [feel] comfortable with it, and when he was sacked was probably the very moment we were about to really start flying under his coaching."

The Boks battled on the first leg of the tour, which was played in inclement weather, until they scored a big win over Swansea at St Helen's. Until then, the most memorable event had been the infamous Battle of the Gnoll, where the Boks and Neath had tried to beat the living daylights out of each other. My abiding memory of that game, apart from the animosity of the crowd, the incredibly cramped stands and the overflowing press box, was of Tiaan Strauss running the length of the field to help a teammate who had been set upon by some of the Neath players.

What was noticeable after the game was that Christie refused to condemn his men. According to Edward Griffiths, who wrote the Christie book and was on tour as media liaison officer, at team talks Christie often mentioned that he wanted the opposition to feel physically "scared" of the Springboks.

But the overseas media quickly forgot to focus on the Boks' physicality when they exploded into form on what happened to be Guy Fawkes Day, running up a 78-7 win over Swansea. Steve Bale of the *Independent* described the Bok victory as "the most conclusive achievement by any touring team to have ever visited these islands".

Ian McIntosh later told me that he saw his game plan coming together that day – Hennie le Roux was at last playing the game the way he'd asked him to play it. And André Joubert scored 38 points at the same ground where, decades before, Garry Sobers had clobbered six sixes in an over off Malcolm Nash.

The next day the Boks boarded a jet-prop aircraft, the media boarded another and off we went, over Cardiff Bay, on the next leg of our journey, which was to be the first of my many visits to Scotland. The tour started off in Peebles in the Borders district, a town that my colleagues and I referred to as "the waiting room to heaven" because of all the old-age homes and the elderly people who lived there.

Although he had seen his team click just the night before, Christie was looking decidedly glum when we pitched for a Sunday-evening press conference at the team hotel. Gerbrand Grobler, the talented fullback who had played under Christie at both Transvaal and Northern Transvaal, was on life support back in South Africa after a motor accident, and would pass away the following day. Christie had a very human side to him and his emotion was clearly evident that night.

It was at this juncture of the trip that the tour nearly unravelled in a way that was to dictate Christie's management decisions at the World Cup the following year. Christie had decided François Pienaar and Tiaan Strauss could not play in the same team, and while Joel Stransky had seemed to be his preferred flyhalf at the start of the tour, Hennie le Roux's willingness to play a more direct game against Swansea had put him back into contention for the No. 10 spot.

So Stransky and Strauss were dropped from the first-choice team and, as Rudolf Straeuli was excelling at No. 8, with Ruben Kruger and Pienaar as the flanks, from then on the tour group was split into two different teams. After a while, it became obvious that cliques were forming within the squad.

It was a demoralising situation for the dirt-trackers, and their noses were obviously out of joint. We kept bumping into them in various pubs and pool bars, and it was clear for all to see that they were miserable. The whole situation, and the way he had handled it, was a valuable lesson for Christie to learn. During the World Cup, he would make sure that every player in the squad got a chance to play in a match.

The midweek team that played Scotland A at Melrose was obviously not going to be the same team that would play against Scotland at Murrayfield, which was confirmed by the late Duncan Hodge drop goal that condemned the Boks to their first tour defeat.

The match was followed by an interesting development that told us a lot about Kitch Christie, the coach. When we arrived in Glasgow ahead of the next game, I spotted lock Drikus Hattingh, who was as approachable and friendly off the field as he was angry and over-robust on it, all dressed up and carrying his suitcase, checking out of the team hotel. I asked him where he was off to, and his simple response was, "Home."

He muttered something about a sore stomach, but he didn't look like he was ill. Later, Christie explained that he was fed up with some players' lack of commitment – Hattingh had been poor in the tour matches – and when Hattingh mentioned a sore stomach, Christie asked if he would like to go home. When Hattingh said he would, Christie sent him on his way, which clearly conveyed the message that the coach wouldn't take any nonsense from his players.

The Boks went on to score wins against minor opposition in Glasgow, in appalling wet conditions – so much so that Christie muttered afterwards how glad he was that his parents had left Scotland – as well as in Aberdeen.

They then smashed Scotland 34-10 at Murrayfield in a game that was the birth of Joost van der Westhuizen as an attacking threat and, arguably, the Boks as a world rugby force in the post-isolation era.

Former England lock Paul Ackford, writing in the *Sunday Telegraph*, was certainly a lot less negative about the quality of Springbok rugby than he had been in Paris two years earlier. "If they carry on getting better, the Springboks are in danger of starting the World Cup as firm favourites," he wrote. "South Africa at last has a side which does justice to the torrent of boasts which flow from their partisan supporters."

Stephen Jones was even more positive: "It's official. South Africa are awesome." But the wittiest line came from former Welsh international and British Lion John Taylor in the *Mail on Sunday*: "Scotland planned a party to celebrate the completion of the new palace of Murrayfied, but again they had to settle for a wake."

But, as he had after the big win over Swansea, Christie refused to get carried away, and at the press conference he dished out all the phrases we were to become so familiar with over the next year. One of them was that the Boks had left "points on the table".

The next Test was against Wales at Cardiff Arms Park, where the pouring rain prevented the Boks from being quite as effective as they had been in Edinburgh. But they still scored three tries to nil and prevailed 20-12.

After a 54-19 romp over a Combined Irish Provinces team at Ravenhill in Belfast, where the Boks were told to let their hair down and play it off the cuff, it was on to Dublin, where they expected to do much the same against a strong Barbarians team. However, the Barbarians didn't enter into the Baa-Baas spirit and a surprised Bok team ended up losing 15-23.

Early on during the tour, Christie, referring to some of my articles, had accused me of being an "Ian Mac man", so I wondered what he was going to say as he turned around to talk to me as I followed him and Pienaar into the arrivals hall at Johannesburg International Airport. It was a déjà vu moment for me, as I had trailed in McIntosh and Pienaar's footsteps at the same venue just four months earlier, when we returned from New Zealand.

"There was a *Saturday Star* on the plane and I read your article," Christie said to me. "I take back what I said. You've become very positive, and thanks for the praise. Mark my words, we'll win the World Cup next year."

At that stage, after a rather successful tour, I saw no reason to disagree with him.

8

Shades of MCD ...
and a World Cup title

"So, do I see a red face sitting there at the back of the room?"

It was Kitch Christie, directing his question at me during the build-up to the World Cup final. The Springboks had completely confounded my prediction that "buck manure will drop out of the sky above Ellis Park on the day of the final if the Boks are there".

Christie was always straight with you, which I appreciated. I took his ribbing in good humour. But there had been many occasions during the year leading up to that point where it seemed that a World Cup triumph was an unrealistic prospect, primarily because of Christie's unconventional methods. For one, running players up and down hills in the manner of the old-school training directives of the legendary former Bulls coach, Brigadier Buurman van Zyl, seemed the height of folly at a time when most nations were embarking on a more scientific approach to training and conditioning. Indeed, looking back nearly 20 years after the fact, and remembering what some of the players had told me about Christie's Spartan-like training sessions, it is easy to see him as a precursor to Rudolf Straeuli.

The only difference between Christie and Straeuli, who played for him at that World Cup and was a big admirer of his approach, may have been that Christie had the talent and a depth of leadership within the squad that offset his unconventional approach. Certainly not all the players felt comfortable with his preparations for the World Cup, particularly with his intense emphasis on discipline and hard physical training.

"[Christie] was very old school in his fitness [regime]," says Mark Andrews. "Mac would tell you ahead of a session what you were going to do and [for how long]. Kitch would never tell us, and he would drive us and drive us and we would never know when he was going to stop. I am not sure if it was the intention, but his method probably prepared us psychologically for the World Cup final, when we ended up playing extra time. We knew [that] physically we could go more than 80 minutes.

"We did a huge amount of fitness [training] at Silvermine, the military base in Cape Town, and in the World Cup final week he had us running up a hill next to the field at Megawatt Park. Because we won the World Cup, there was a perception that his old-school approach had been correct, but only five of us were still playing rugby three years [later].

"Many of the players got injured and their careers [were cut short], and I think part of that was [because of] Kitch's training methods. I don't believe what he did was sustainable. I am not sure that we would have carried on winning if he had remained the coach after 1995. He would have had to have had a huge playing pool."

Christie's big selection poser was how to fit all the players vying for positions into a squad of 26. At the start of the season, before Uli Schmidt's retirement due to a neck injury, Christie was sure of 19 of the 26 places. James Small was back in the mix; François Pienaar even mentioned him in a column he wrote for the *Sunday Times* after an early-season training camp.

"James Small, in particular, was looking fantastic. Judging by his tan he has been running on the beach, and I must say it was good to have him around again."

Interestingly, Pienaar referred to Christie as "Mr Christie" throughout the article. Not even the captain could get away with calling him Kitch.

Schmidt's retirement heralded a search for a new hooker. James Dalton selected himself, but Christie wasn't interested in Natal's experienced John Allan. Instead, he brought criticism upon himself when he selected Transvaal B hooker Chris Rossouw for the first Test of the year, against Samoa at Ellis Park.

"Of course it was a gamble, but I had seen Chris play and I knew he had the potential to fit in with the pattern we wanted to play," Christie explained. Rossouw ended up scoring a try on his debut in the 60-8 massacre of Samoa and never looked back. (Christie even invited Transvaal under-20 scrumhalf Bennie Nortje to a training session, which further perturbed the rest of the rugby-playing provinces.)

The Bok performance against Samoa was outstanding, even though Samoa were under-strength, and it was a perfect way to round off the Test-match preparations for the World Cup. Now there were only two matches against provincial opposition still to come.

Hennie le Roux was selected ahead of Joel Stransky for the Samoa game, but fate played a hand when Brendan Venter was injured, forcing Christie to move Le Roux to centre and bring Stransky in at flyhalf. It had, in fact, been his selection for the first game he was in charge, against Argentina in Port Elizabeth, because, like his predecessor, Ian McIntosh, Christie saw Le Roux as a potential inside centre.

Says McIntosh: "It was interesting for me to see that selection, as I had tried to get the selectors to go for Hennie le Roux as a centre, and not a flyhalf, for the previous year's tour to New Zealand, with Joel being my first-choice No.10."

Indeed. With Stransky and Le Roux calling the shots in the crucial fly-half/inside centre decision-making axis at the back, the Bok backs showed what might have happened in New Zealand the previous year if McIntosh had had his way.

As Christie said, it was just "one of those things." Stransky suddenly clicked in the way the Bok coach had been hoping he would click, and that was that.

Stransky's form was a tribute to Christie's straight-talking attitude with the players. He had challenged Stransky when he dropped him in Peebles on the previous tour by telling him that he was the best footballer in the squad and that it was up to him whether he wanted to play a major role in the World Cup or not.

By the time the Samoan game came along, Morné du Plessis, the former Springbok captain who was revered around the rugby world for his states-manlike presence, had assumed the role of manager. Jannie Engelbrecht had been living on borrowed time on the previous tour, and speculation was rife that Edward Griffiths had been appointed as the media liaison officer for that tour specifically to spy on Engelbrecht at the behest of Louis Luyt. By the time the World Cup year came around, Griffiths was fulfilling two functions – he was still the Bok media liaison, but also the SARFU chief executive.

Du Plessis was to play a massive role within the World Cup group. While Christie and Engelbrecht had never really gelled as a combination, Du Plessis immediately impressed Christie, particularly with the humility he exhibited in going about his business.

With Du Plessis as manager, Christie as coach, Gysie Pienaar as assistant coach, Rudi Joubert as technical analyst, Dave Waterston and Hennie Bekker as additional analysts, and Evan Speechley and Frans Verster as physiotherapist and doctor respectively, the Bok World Cup management team was complete.

All of the people who worked in that management team mentioned the family atmosphere that prevailed, which spread to the players once the World Cup kicked off. What is important to note, though, particularly with regard to the problems that some of the future Springbok coaches were to experience, was the unwavering support Luyt gave to the group, and to Christie in particular. And the CEO of SARFU was with the team as the media liaison person.

"In making any kind of study of the Springbok coaches, you really do need to take into consideration the other people who formed the crucial partnership without which every coach is lost and stands alone," Rudolf Straeuli said when I interviewed him about his years in the top job. "The coach is backed up by the chief executive and the president, and much of what happens during his reign is determined by the support he gets, and the expectations, of those two."

The winning trio of 1995 would, of course, eventually split up, but that was still in the future when the Boks gathered in Cape Town at the start of an internal mini-tour that would lead up to the World Cup itself. It was a balmy day in early May when I drove through to the Woodstock Holiday Inn to interview Christie.

As usual, he emphasised the need for discipline in the team, and he singled out James Small and James Dalton as two players who would have to improve their on-field discipline. This incensed Small, who confronted me outside a Durban nightclub a few weeks later. He told me Christie denied giving me that story. But Fritz Joubert of *Die Burger* had also attended the interview and had written exactly what I had written.

The Cape rugby public was also incensed at the time, because the Bok coach had left some Western Province players out of the squad, and there was already some speculation, and vigorous debate, about local hero Tiaan Strauss's World Cup hopes.

The Bok squad's warm-up game against Western Province had the potential to add to the friction, but it was Christie's deliberate intention to put the players through the wringer. And he got his wish, for the Newlands crowd was firmly behind the blue-and-white hoops. The Springboks had to dig deep before winning through a late Joel Stransky drop goal. Stransky was a Province player by then and being booed on his home ground would have been an unnerving experience for him.

Tiaan Strauss led Province against the shadow Boks in a match that was seen as his last chance to force his way into consideration for the Bok team. He hadn't started a Test under Christie since the Argentina series the year before, but few would have anticipated that he would not make the final squad at all, particularly when he put in such an inspiring performance in this match.

But for Christie, the similarity between Strauss and François Pienaar's playing styles was just too much, plus there was the fact that they were both strong leaders with forceful characters.

As Christie later explained: "There was no doubt in my mind that Tiaan was among the leading players in the country. But I was not picking a World Cup squad made up of the best 26 players in the country. I was gathering a Springbok squad that would combine to win the World Cup. I needed 26 players who would form an effective unit.

In his autobiography, Christie said that although he had no doubt that Strauss was among the leading players in the country, he was not picking a World Cup squad made up of the best 26 players in the country; he wanted a Springbok squad that would combine to win the World Cup. He had to have 26 players who would form a cohesive and effective unit.

Christie's biggest concern, however, remained the fact that Strauss was too much like Pienaar in too many ways. As loose forwards, they were too similar, and both were inspirational leaders. Christie could have chosen the easy option and included Strauss in the squad, but instead he reached the "difficult conclusion" that there was no room for him and François in the same squad. Christie knew the team needed to be united behind one captain.

Instead of Tiaan Strauss, Christie selected Robbie Brink, and some saw his selection as a sop to the Province fans, who were embittered by the way in which Strauss had been treated.

"I thought it was Leon Schuster on the phone. I got this call ... and my immediate reaction was that it was a prankster," Brink said about his surprise inclusion in the squad.

Quite surprisingly, along with Strauss and Gary Teichmann, Ian Macdonald, a Transvaal player who had played a lot of good rugby under Christie, was also out of the mix, and no explanation was ever given for his omission.

For the next three weeks, Christie concentrated entirely on the mental and physical preparation of the players. He ignored the public's accusation that he was being provincialistic in his selections and squad members' claims that, at least initially, provincialism was rife within the group as well.

This was borne out by an incident that occurred on the night of the squad announcement, when Balie Swart castigated me for a column I had written about Christie's "provincialism". However, Western Province coach Alan Zondagh later told me that the Province players in the Bok squad had agreed with what I'd written, and some of the provincial coaches who were in touch with their players in the Bok camp confirmed that they had complained of provincialism at the start of the Boks' World Cup campaign.

But Christie had his plan, and it worked out well for him. There were setbacks along the way, none more so than when Chester Williams was injured. His likeable face had beamed from nearly every lamppost in South Africa in the build-up to the World Cup, proclaiming, on behalf of South African Airways, that "The waiting is almost over". As the only black player in the squad representing the new South Africa, his loss was massive, but he would make a remarkable comeback to the team after his recovery.

In the meantime, Christie's training methods continued to astound. Morné du Plessis admitted in Christie's book that he often winced when the coach asked the players to do 10×100-metre sprints. Although his methods seemed to contradict the theories of modern sports science, on and on Christie ran the players. Even after the World Cup welcoming lunch in Cape Town, held in a massive winter downpour, the players were made to train.

The high-road/low-road scenario that the Boks faced in the opening game against the Wallabies has been well documented, but to recap: whichever team lost that game would be drawn to play either New Zealand or England in the play-offs, while the victor would play against easier opposition on the way to the final.

On the eve of the kick-off, Du Plessis informed the media that the players had been told they were living through a defining moment in their lives, while Christie, in his media conference, singled out the Aussie line-out genius John Eales as the biggest threat to his team's chances of victory.

By the time the opening game arrived, patriotism had swept the country. Christie related in his book that he even heard people chanting, "Kitch! Kitch! Kitch!" when he emerged from the Newlands tunnel to assess the conditions.

The Boks gave the country what it so badly wanted by beating Australia 27-18, with Stransky playing a blinder and Pieter Hendriks running around David Campese to produce a try that probably remains the most replayed Springbok try ever scored.

Forming a huddle with the players after the game, Christie delivered his post-match speech, and described it as one of the finest performances he had ever seen. But he said he would not be telling anyone else that. "Let's stay humble," he cautioned.

But there would be many pitfalls and hiccups on the high road ... In one instance, the so-called Green team, or second-stringers, put up a sorry performance against Romania, yet Christie opted to select the same team for the tougher match against Canada in Port Elizabeth. His critics wondered whether he was losing his mind. The Boks could still get blown out of the World Cup if they lost, so Christie was taking a massive risk. But the man had learnt his lesson in Scotland the year before, and was determined that every player would feel that he was involved in the World Cup campaign.

Christie did display some common sense, though, when he reinstated François Pienaar as the captain against Canada – Adriaan Richter, who had led against Romania, was retained at No. 8. And it was a good thing he did, too, as it was a difficult evening from start to finish. Apart from the blustery conditions and the sputtering floodlights that temporarily plunged the old stadium into darkness, a weird mood had settled on the crowd. The people of Port Elizabeth had "adopted" Canada, and while it wouldn't perhaps be accurate to say that the Boks were viewed as the enemy, the crowd had a lot of sympathy for the underdogs.

In some ways, the Canadians played like dogs, too; they had no more games to play after facing the Springboks and would lose nothing if some of their players were cited. That attitude may have induced the furious fracas that broke out in the 70th minute and resulted in James Dalton, as well as the Canadian duo of Gareth Rees and Rod Snow, being sent off.

Along with my media colleagues, I had to wait around Boet Erasmus until the early hours of the morning for the verdict of the subsequent disciplinary hearing. We finally heard that all the players who had been sent off were banned for 30 days, which meant the end of the World Cup for Dalton.

Then Pieter Hendriks was cited, making Johannesburg, where we were based for the build-up to the quarter-final against West Samoa, a fun place to be the following week. The Port Elizabeth fiasco seemed to be all-pervasive; Christie felt that Dalton had been treated unfairly, but radio personality Jeremy Mansfield joked with his morning listeners on 702 that Dalton was a crybaby after his emotional media appearance following the hearing. In an interview with Jenny Crwys-Williams later that day, an emotional Dalton explained how gut-wrenching it was to see your dream snuffed out by something that had been both so silly and avoidable.

For a while after the fiasco, and perhaps understandably, the Boks seemed to retreat back into the Dark Ages. They were no longer as transparent with the media and the public as they had been, and a tense atmosphere seemed to have settled on the squad.

The mood in the camp deteriorated further when skipper Pienaar, along with some of the other players, broke the team curfew after a visit to the Fish River Sun casino. According to some of Pienaar's teammates, the captain had allowed his anger about the Canada fracas to distract his attention from the team's goal, and he even became withdrawn for a while.

Fortunately the Springbok show got back on track once Christie summoned Pienaar for a chat in the hotel bar and they cleared the air over a few pints of Guinness. Christie knew he had to have "cappy" onside if the Boks' World Cup campaign was going to be a success. "We had to get the thing moving again. If we didn't, no one else would," Christie said about his meeting with Pienaar.

Christie even told the squad that he had wanted to walk away from the tournament because of all the drama. "But," he continued, "we can't do that. The fact is that we stand today three matches away from winning the World Cup in front of our own fans. We are lucky people, and we have to get out there and win that Cup. Stuff the referees, stuff all of the Rugby World Cup directors, stuff the press, stuff the Canadians. I don't care about any of them. But I do care about this squad, and it is time for this squad to stand up and be counted."

For Chester Williams, it was a case of better late than never when Hendriks was suspended for a dangerous challenge on Canadian wing Winston Stanley, which sparked the fight that led to all the trouble. More than one Springbok from that era has told me that Hendriks was financially persuaded not to appeal his suspension, as Williams's presence in the team would better serve to unite the nation.

Over the next few days the Boks blew off some steam by playing golf and enjoying some R & R, with Samoa suffering the consequences in the form of a four-try World Cup debut for Williams en route to a 42-14 Springbok victory in the quarter-finals. But it wasn't all good news, as fullback André Joubert broke his hand during the match, adding to a fairly lengthy injury list with the semi-final against France in Durban looming the following Saturday.

In an effort to be ready for the match, Joubert spent two sessions in a decompression chamber and was fitted with a glove flown in especially from Ireland. But Joubert's injury wasn't the only big news of the week. Christie was about to take a gamble that I doubt any other Bok coach would have been prepared to take at such a critical juncture.

While driving from Johannesburg to Pretoria to attend a training session, I received a call from someone who told me that Mark Andrews, instead of Rudolf Straeuli, was training at No. 8. I thought it was a joke, but on my arrival at the practice ground it was clear that this was no joke. These were the days before the internet, and while driving back to Johannesburg at 120 km/h after the practice, I quickly dictated a late final-edition story to the *Daily News* sports editor Gary Lemke for the Independent Group's evening editions.

As Mark Andrews remembers, "Funnily enough, that was the only time that I ever felt comfortable with Kitch, and knew that he believed in me. I told him that I couldn't play at No. 8, and he told me I would be fantastic."

Straeuli remembers the moment thus: "For me, rugby has always been about the team, not the individual, and while I had done well on the end-of-year tour the previous season, I knew I wasn't playing my best rugby in 1995, so I accepted [that I should be dropped]."

The semi-final day was bizarre for everyone involved. A Durban deluge threatened the very existence of the game, as the tournament organisers considered abandoning the match. Everyone had stories to tell – one journalist was travelling from Johannesburg to Durban in a Boeing 747 that was twice struck by lightning while in a holding pattern over Harrismith.

The pounding rain and an uncovered press box prompted some of us media guys to leave the stadium at half-time and head off to the media centre in a nearby soccer stadium in order to protect our laptop computers. It was a surreal experience sitting in a room with a few fellow reporters, isolated from the noise of the crowd, as the clock wound down to the final whistle and the confirmation of a 19-15 win that booked Christie's team their place in the final. It was an extremely closely fought game and the French still claim that Abdel Benazzi should have been awarded a try, which would have won France the game.

That night I had to make my way to Cape Town for the Sunday semi-final between England and the All Blacks, and I left the Welsh rugby legend Gerald Davies, who had asked me for a lift, sitting in the car outside my parents' house in Durban while I made a hasty departure for the airport. My day only ended when I landed in Cape Town at 3 a.m. ahead of a match that will forever be remembered as "The Jonah Lomu Show".

Lomu's one-man demolition of England was *the* individual performance of the World Cup, but the Boks tried to put it out of their minds as they headed to Sun City, where they would spend a few days regrouping, away from all the media demands.

It was there, far from the madding crowd, that Christie tried to come up with a plan that might have resulted in a different team lifting the 1995 Rugby World Cup. The coach might, in fact, even have displayed a mild form of MCD.

Lomu's performance must have made a very big impression on Christie, as he suddenly didn't seem to have much confidence in the Boks' existing game plan or their ability to beat New Zealand in the final. He started looking for the X-factor and, in doing so, hatched a plan that would have resulted in the Boks playing the fast, off-the-cuff rugby they had played in Belfast the year before, and which had led to a big victory.

Christie called it the "Brains Game", and it involved executing every move at double the pace, tapping penalties and running the ball deep from inside the team's own half.

"We have the skills to execute this game plan," Christie told the players.

But the Ravenshill game in Belfast in November 1994 had been a midweek match against a provincial team. Would that game plan work in a high-pressure situation such as the World Cup final?

Brendan Venter argued that a loose game would play right into New Zealand's hands, and future Bok coach Rudolf Straeuli warned how stupid the Boks would look if they gave away soft tries on such an important occasion.

Recalls Venter: "I remember that very clearly; it was probably the only time that Kitch ever discussed tactics with the wider group and not just with François and some of the other Transvaal players he was close to. He called it the Brains Game, and I remember how he sold it to us. He looked at François and said something about him having a law degree, and then compared him to his direct opponent. Then he would go through the group, pointing to Rudolf Straeuli, who [also] had a law degree. He said to us that we could out-think the All Blacks.

"But what his plan didn't take into account was that the All Blacks had great game-breakers like Glen Osborne and Frank Bunce in their team. They would kill us if we made mistakes, which we were sure to do because Kitch's plan was all about quick line-outs and tap penalties."

Nevertheless, the new plan was reluctantly adopted, and only after several poor training sessions was Christie convinced that he was barking up the wrong tree.

"The Transvaal players loved Kitch so much that they didn't have the heart to tell him his plan wouldn't work," says Venter. "I remember Balie Swart taking a quick kick that didn't work out and the reserve team, of which I was a part, scoring. I think Balie might have done that on purpose to show Kitch the folly of the plan. No one needed to say anything; we just reverted to Plan A."

And Plan A worked. It was an incredibly tense day, and the atmosphere that pervaded the scene seemed to favour the Springboks' more percentage-based style of play. Many fans arrived at the stadium expecting it to be a one-sided game, but it quickly became apparent that the Boks were up to the challenge and that it would be closer than expected.

In his final speech to the players on the day of the final, Christie conveyed absolute confidence that they would win – and that confidence was translated into a strong forward display coupled with a highly physical and aggressive defensive effort that just never allowed Jonah Lomu to be the factor he had been in the semi-final.

Mark Andrews is probably right, too – the way Christie had driven his players in training, never telling them when the ordeal was going to end, probably did help them in a final that just went on and on. It wouldn't be fair to say that the All Blacks wilted in the final stages of the game, and they could even have won it in the last minutes of normal time had Andrew Mehrtens not been off target with a drop-goal attempt.

But the Boks, with so much riding on the game and boosted by seeing Madiba wear Pienaar's No. 6 Springbok jersey before the kick-off, were resilient and determined, and they showed great composure in extra time. In training, Christie had spoken to Joel Stransky about possibly attempting a drop goal in the final, and when the opportunity presented itself, he let rip – the ball sailing high and handsome through the uprights to spark a joyous celebration.

It was, as François Pienaar said afterwards, a victory for the "43 million [who stood] behind us".

9

Money, the root of all evil

Much of what followed after that epic day at Ellis Park, when South Africa won the Rugby World Cup for the first time, was about nation building, and "selling" rugby, the Springboks and sport in general as a unifier of the people.

Fortunately for Kitch Christie, he had astute people with political nous working with him. When you have Edward Griffiths, an ace wordsmith and ideas man, and Morné du Plessis, respected for his wisdom and diplomacy, on your team, there shouldn't be much need to extend your responsibilities beyond the field of rugby. According to Griffiths, Christie never wanted much to do with what he referred to as "sideshows".

Some of the Bok coaches who succeeded Christie never quite enjoyed the same level of support he did, nor benefitted from the same level of leadership or public relations expertise. For some, it would be their ultimate undoing, while others had their campaigns derailed when they were dragged into controversies that no coach from any other country would have had to face.

In the aftermath of the World Cup, while the Springboks swept around the country on a roadshow, which started with a ticker-tape parade in Johannesburg, the quiet and unassuming Christie was weighing up his own rugby future. He was determined to leave the game at the top, and at the post-match press conference following the World Cup final he said that he would no longer be involved with the Springboks. He wanted to return to coaching Transvaal, a deal he had struck with Louis Luyt when he had accepted the national coaching position in September 1994.

Euphoria might have swept the nation in the days after the Springboks' World Cup triumph, but the media were already speculating about Christie's future and his possible successor. When the Boks escaped to the Lost City for a few days to unwind, some of the senior role players within the group started campaigning for Christie to stay on as coach. They felt he was not quite finished with the job, and in the end they convinced the World Cup–winning coach to stay on.

And so Christie was the man at the helm when the Springbok squad reconvened at the start of the week that would lead to a one-off Test against Wales at Ellis Park. However, Christie immediately sensed that the atmosphere had changed; the group wasn't the same happy family they had been during the World Cup.

And in truth, everything *was* different, for there had been an announcement on the eve of the World Cup final that changed the face of rugby union forever. When the US$555-million deal between the Rupert Murdoch–owned News Corporation and the three main southern hemisphere rugby nations – South Africa, New Zealand and Australia (SANZAR) – was unveiled to the media at Ellis Park that Friday morning in June, it signalled the end of the old amateur ethos that still underpinned the game. It would be naive to pretend that money hadn't been in the game for a long time already, but not to the extent that it would dominate from that moment onwards.

South African rugby, and the Springbok squad in particular, was now at the centre of a global war between two rival factions wrestling for control of the top players in the union code. The deal with Murdoch had been struck in an attempt to beat off the threat posed by Super League, but unbeknown to the southern hemisphere partners at the time, a concerned group headed by a Sydney-based, South African–born lawyer called Geoff Levy and former Australian administrator Ross Turnbull had been recruiting players with promises of a new competition and major contracts.

Ironically, most of the Boks had signed these contracts while at the Lost City getaway where Christie was persuaded to stay on as coach. However, perhaps because his players didn't want him to be caught in the crossfire between themselves and Luyt, the Boks didn't confide in their coach like the Wallabies and All Blacks did in theirs at the time.

As his biographer, Edward Griffiths, noted, Christie's relationship with François Pienaar deteriorated as a result of the secrets that were kept from him. According to Griffiths, Christie was highly irritated when he found out that Pienaar had been meeting with Turnbull, whose cause he championed with the Springboks, behind his back, especially during the critical weeks of the World Cup. Christie felt that his captain should have trusted him and kept him informed of developments.

In *Rainbow Warrior*, Pienaar contended that they had kept Kitch in the dark for his own sake, and no one else's. But Christie's paranoia, if that was what it was, was not misplaced. Harry Viljoen, who had coached Transvaal before him, was heavily involved with the Turnbull group and in close contact with the players. So it wasn't unreasonable to assume that if the World Rugby Corporation did get off the ground, Viljoen might be installed as the rebel Bok coach.

In the end, the whole WRC deal fell flat when an irate Luyt promised Pienaar that he would better Turnbull's offer. When Pienaar told him that he was being paid R1 million in commission to sign up Springbok players, Luyt offered him the same plus an additional, symbolic one cent – or so it is said – and Pienaar accepted.

Pienaar's about-turn on Turnbull did not go down well with all of his colleagues, some of whom are still resentful years later. It didn't sit well with the overseas players either, as without the world champions, the WRC deal was off.

I interviewed Wallaby captain Phil Kearns when he was out injured during the following season's inaugural Tri-Nations tournament. The Boks weren't doing well, and Kearns ascribed it to the extra effort the New Zealanders and Wallabies were putting in to get back at Pienaar.

But Luyt's was the most significant nose that was put out of joint. The Bok players had forced him into a situation that he intensely disliked. His SANZAR partners were urging him to do something that he most emphatically did not want to do – negotiate.

"We have other players back home as good, if not better, than the current Springboks," Luyt told Newscorp, but they wanted the world champions. Luyt was impelled to cough up far more than he wanted to, and the World Cup Bok squad (with the exception of Chester Williams, who chose to remain a free agent) signed lucrative contracts that were to have a profound influence on South African rugby for the next couple of years.

Some of the events that occurred during the stand-off between the various interested parties intensely annoyed the SARFU administrators. In one instance, the Transvaal team, which consisted mostly of Boks, effectively went on an impromptu strike and refused to train before a Currie Cup game. Luyt refused to believe that Christie wasn't a party to what was happening, and accused him of colluding with the players.

So when Christie started the build-up to the Welsh Test, his relationship with two of the people he had relied on so heavily in the past, Pienaar and Luyt, had become trying, to say the least.

According to Christie, Pienaar had been behind the entire Bok World Cup squad signing the optional contracts with Turnbull, and the coach believed he had no right to "sell" his team. Christie felt that they had built the team together, and it seemed to him as if Pienaar was leaving him behind and selling his side to the highest bidder.

Christie foresaw problems with the World Cup contracts, as the new players who had been selected for the team to play against Wales – Gary Teichmann and Jacques Olivier – were not contracted and would only be paid match fees. The rest of the team was getting exorbitant amounts of money.

"I could see the situation was going to cause problems for years to come," Christie said.

The Boks won the Test against Wales 40-11, and lock Kobus Wiese was one of the first "professional players" to incur one of the penalties ushered in by professionalism when he was fined a rumoured R60 000 for knocking out Welsh lock Derwyn Jones early on in the game. Afterwards it was said that Christie had instructed his players to "deal with Jones", who was the Welsh line-out kingpin, or "sort him out".

Teichmann had been selected to play in that Test, chiefly because Christie was repaying him for agreeing to play out of position on the previous end-of-year tour, and he acquitted himself well. However, the Bok coach's charity didn't extend to the tour to Rome and London that would conclude a momentous year for South African rugby. Teichmann learnt that he had been left out of the touring squad soon after leading Natal to a third Currie Cup trophy in a wet Durban final against Western Province.

But Tommie Laubscher, Toks van der Linde, Fritz van Heerden and, later, Willie Meyer were added from outside the World Cup group. Ray Carlson, a Natal player-coach in the mid-1970s, was brought in as an assistant coach. He hadn't coached senior provincial rugby for years, so this was another of Christie's left-field appointments, in the same vein as playing Mark Andrews at No. 8 – a ploy that was not continued after the World Cup.

The potent Bok scrum won them the game against Italy, but they were well short of a gallop, and then, on arrival in London the next day, they went straight into a press conference. One of the first questions Pienaar was asked was what he thought of Mike Catt saying that he was an "overrated" player. I remember Pienaar's eyes popping wide open on hearing the insult, but Christie was delighted when he chatted with some of us afterwards.

"I love it," he said. "I thought I was going to battle to motivate the guys ahead of this game, but it looks like Catt has just provided all the motivation we need."

On a clear autumn afternoon, the Boks beat England 24-14, the team turning in one of their finest performances of the year. Perhaps the score even flattered the vanquished, as Joel Stransky had an off day with his place-kicking boot and the referee didn't allow a perfectly good Chester Williams try. The Boks had proved their championship status by winning against a big team away from home. It was a perfect end to the year.

Unfortunately, the events that unfolded after Christie returned home would eventually bring a flat and low-key end to his illustrious coaching career. Whether these events can be attributed to Luyt valuing Christie too highly, or as a consequence of the stand-off between Luyt and the players, Christie was the one who lost out in the end. However, even if Luyt's initial intentions were honourable, Christie, as an unbeaten World Cup–winning coach, deserved better than the treatment he received from his former benefactor.

Christie had intended to coach the Boks into 1996, according to the agreement he had made at the Lost City, but Luyt wanted him to also coach Transvaal. Luyt asked Christie to consider it, even if he only took the team to the end of the Super 12 campaign, when he could return to the Boks. Christie agreed, but the decision was not universally popular around the country. Quite justifiably, many felt there was a conflict of interest.

"I was reluctant," said Christie, "but I wanted to stay actively involved in the game for the first six months of the year before the Boks were due to play, and I felt I owed Doc Luyt for originally giving me the chance to coach Transvaal." He added that he had accepted the job because Luyt had asked him, and that he would not have taken it on otherwise.

But the atmosphere at Transvaal had changed with the advent of professionalism. It wasn't the same family environment any more, and Christie later claimed that he saw the writing on the wall when his team lost a pre-season game to André Markgraaff's Griquas. They then went on to lose their three overseas games in the Super 12, a tour during which Christie suffered from a bad dose of flu.

The illness, according to Edward Griffiths, was just flu, not cancer, although the many years of chemotherapy had probably compromised Christie's resistance to disease. But it was while he was suffering from flu that Luyt, who had already appointed Markgraaff as Christie's assistant at the Boks, pounced.

Christie recalled in his autobiography that Louis Luyt had effectively asked him to resign from both positions. "Everyone was talking about how sick I was and how I would be stupid to carry on coaching, but I could certainly have carried on. I didn't put up a fight at the time because I was tired and under the weather. Maybe it was the right decision. Maybe it wasn't. But I can't honestly say I resigned out of my own free will."

Christie went on to say that he was under the impression that Louis Luyt wanted to appoint André Markgraaff as the Springbok coach as soon as possible. He, Christie, didn't think that Markgraaff wanted to be merely the assistant. "He wanted his chance and I understood his impatience," Christie said.

Markgraaff had been told that he would succeed Christie after the All Black tour, but Luyt fast-tracked the handover. Christie's health did suddenly deteriorate after that, and Griffiths wondered whether summarily being axed from both coaching positions may not have had something to do with it. The coach would have had less time to sit at home and be ill, Griffiths said in Christie's book, if he had the chance to remain active and positive.

It was an abrupt end to the career of South Africa's first World Cup–winning, and most successful, coach.

We can forever speculate on what might have happened if Christie had retained his health, but of course we will never know. As Mark Andrews said, Christie's way, with its emphasis on fitness and discipline, might have been good for a particular time, but it may not have been sustainable over an extended period. Christie also had the luxury – if you could call it that – of coaching the Boks in one-off games, and a truer test of his coaching skills would have been set when he had to coach the side in a series with return fixtures. And his team never played New Zealand or Australia outside of South Africa.

But regardless of what the future may have had in store for Christie – he passed away in 1998 – no one can take away his achievement and the place he will always have in the hearts of South Africans. After all, he had coached the team that, one year into the new democracy and however briefly, had united the country.

In South Africa, it seems rugby will always be more than just a game.

10

On a hiding to nothing

There were times in 1996 when it appeared as if South African rugby was determined to undo the nation building of the year before. There were even suggestions that a conservative bloc in rugby was trying to wrestle back some sort of control for the Afrikaners. André Markgraaff, South Africa's fourth post-isolation coach, outwardly fitted the stereotype of the white Afrikaans male, and he was often described as "old school" and "autocratic".

But we need to be clear on one issue whenever Markgraaff is the subject of debate: to accuse him of being the coach who broke up the World Cup–winning team is simply not fair. A combination of factors, not least of them the loss of form of the players who had made up the team, can be blamed for that.

I was one of Markgraaff's biggest critics in 1996. By his own admission, he made a lot of mistakes during his tenure as Bok coach. But the splintering of the World Cup team had preceded his arrival; it had probably started in the months immediately after the World Cup.

The Transvaal team, which included many of the World Cup winners (François Pienaar being just one), didn't win the 1995 Currie Cup; in fact, they didn't even come second. Natal and Western Province played in the final in Durban. And when Province played Transvaal at Newlands, they beat them comprehensively. A few Province players who had not been selected for the World Cup made their point in that match – Tommie Laubscher, the big West Coast farmer, among them.

Kitch Christie had not selected Laubscher because he didn't think he was fit enough. In the first scrum at Newlands, Laubscher eyeballed Balie Swart, his direct opponent on the day and the man who had switched from tighthead to loose-head prop for the World Cup, which effectively kept Laubscher out of the squad.

"Balie," he said, "we've seen you scrum at the World Cup, but now let's see if you can handle the Currie Cup."

Swart had done outstandingly well at the World Cup, but he couldn't handle Laubscher, and Transvaal, or "the World Cup team" as many referred to them, couldn't handle Province. Nor could they handle the following year's Super 12; their foray into the first SANZAR competition was a disaster, and they ended near the bottom of the log. More damningly, with Christie as coach, François Pienaar's team never came close to winning a single game overseas, losing most of them by big margins.

So Pienaar may not have been right to suggest, as he did in *Rainbow Warrior*, that Markgraaff's tenure as Bok coach might have turned out differently if he'd just stuck to what had worked the year before. When Peter de Villiers took over another World Cup–winning team 12 years later and got off to a shaky start, he reverted to the style of his predecessor and achieved some initial successes as a result. But it was different in 1996 – the players in that team were on average much older than the Class of 2008.

Recalling those events today, Markgraaff reckons the biggest mistake he made was to ignore his gut feel that the Transvaal era had come to an end.

"My biggest regret was not dropping François [before the international season had even started], as he was not playing well and never followed my instructions, which I believe had also been the case [when he was playing under] Ian McIntosh. I could have gone with Gary Teichmann straight away. He impressed me with his captaincy of Natal and the calls he made in the line-outs and from the scrums. I didn't know him from a bar of soap, and he was English-speaking, so it was not as if I was backing Afrikaans interests like some people said I was. Natal had become the form team by 1996, and after playing in the final of the Super 12, they went on to easily win the Currie Cup.

"They played some brilliant games in that Super 12, and I wanted to base my style on [their game]. If I'd had the guts to go with my hunch from the beginning, I would have had Teichmann as my captain and Dick Muir as my vice-captain. Muir, with Japie Mulder on his outside, would have been a brilliant choice, especially with his rugby brain and the way he attacked the gain line. Later, under Nick Mallett, he proved that he could play international rugby and he would have been [ideal] for the type of game I wanted to play."

Markgraaff believes that Teichmann was done a massive injustice by South African rugby. "He should have been in the 1995 World Cup squad, and of course he should never have been dropped before the 1999 World Cup either," Markgraaff says.

He is adamant that several of the World Cup squad from the year before had reached their sell-by dates by 1996.

"Sometimes you reach the pinnacle of your career and then afterwards it is all downhill, and I felt there were several players I'd inherited from 1995 who weren't really up to it any more. Balie Swart was one, but there were others.

"People forget that Transvaal lost all their away games that year in the Super 12. They lost seven of their 11 games and won just three, and they finished 10th out of the 12 teams. They never shaped in that year's Currie Cup either. So by sticking with the World Cup winners, I wasn't choosing my team on form."

Markgraaff set up an informal committee, which included some of his former Western Province teammates like Nick Mallett and Divan Serfontein, to assess the players' form. At the trials, held in Pretoria, they helped Markgraaff identify the talent, and afterwards everyone agreed that Pienaar was not one of the in-form South African loose forwards.

"But I never took any notice of that view, as I thought I had to have him as the [captain] after what he had [achieved] the year before. I picked on sentiment when I first started out as Bok coach, and that was my big mistake."

Although Markgraaff hadn't coached at Super 12 level, one should not assume that he was appointed as the Springbok coach only because of the friends he had in the SARFU boardroom. Yes, he was a senior-ranking member of the SARFU executive, and yes, perhaps it was true what Christie had claimed, that Louis Luyt "owed" Markgraaff for obtaining the backing of the smaller unions in his quest for the presidency. But it is emphatically untrue, Markgraaff says, that he pushed Christie out of his job in his haste to be the head Springbok coach after he had already been appointed as Christie's assistant.

Markgraaff recalls: "In April of that year, Johan Claassen, who was on the SARFU exco, [phoned me]. Although I was a member of the executive myself, a management meeting had taken place at which I was not present. Claassen told me to expect a call from Louis Luyt.

"Luyt told me that Kitch was very ill in hospital, and the executive had decided that [he] must step down. In any case, Kitch had indicated to [Luyt] that he was not going to carry on, and it was unfair to expect a guy so ill in hospital to be ready to coach the Boks just a few months later.

"I was not excited about the prospect of taking over the role of head coach at that stage. We were going to be playing the All Blacks five times in the space of a few weeks, and the last thing any sensible coach would want to do is take over after a World Cup–winning year, when you would be on a hiding to nothing. I was already on the national selection panel and an assistant coach, and I was satisfied with that. The plan was for me to take over when the squad went to Argentina later in 1996, or even the following year.

"I cannot vouch for what Luyt said to Kitch in the hospital, and what Kitch said to Louis. Maybe Louis forced Kitch out; I don't know. It had nothing to do with me. But I knew it wasn't the right time to be taking over. So when newspapers started speculating later in the year that I had pushed Kitch out, I was furious. It was such a load of nonsense. That All Black side was one of the best teams ever and they should have won the World Cup the year before. I definitely wasn't in a hurry to play them in my first series as coach."

Although he hadn't coached at Super 10 or Super 12 level, Markgraaff was an experienced coach in his own right, and had spent several years coaching Griquas into punching above their weight. Accepting that Christie wasn't really fit to continue and factoring out previous coaches Ian McIntosh and John Williams, Markgraaff seemed as good a choice as any.

"I started coaching in 1987 in my final year as a player at Pirates in Kimberley, and then coached Griquas for the first time in 1988. Although I played much of my rugby for Western Province and also for South West Africa after leaving Stellenbosch, I've always had a strong emotional involvement with Griquas. Perhaps my biggest regret in rugby was that we didn't win the Currie Cup in 1998, when I felt we had a team that could do so. We got knocked out in the semi-final."

When you listen to Markgraaff speak, it becomes evident that a lot of his rugby personality evolved from his commitment to Griquas and his continual battle to ensure that union's survival. Griquas may even have defined his reputation in South African rugby. He is known as a political animal, but a lot of his politics was geared towards keeping Griquas afloat.

"I have never received a cent out of the game, unlike the modern administrators, who seem to be a lot more money-driven. For me, it was a passion, and I invested a lot of energy and emotion in Griquas. I even continued to coach them when I was coaching the Springboks," Markgraaff explains.

So committed was Markgraaff to the Griquas' cause that he drove to Kimberley from Johannesburg, where the Boks were preparing to play the final Test of the 1996 series against the All Blacks, to coach Griquas the night before they would play the New Zealanders in a tour match. Known by his players as a bit of an insomniac, Markgraaff says he was asleep the moment his head hit the pillow after arriving back at the team hotel in Joburg in the early hours of the morning.

Had Springbok captain François Pienaar not intervened, Markgraaff might have been working with the Boks alongside Kitch Christie before the end of 1995.

"Kitch first approached me to be a Bok assistant coach before the end-of-year trip to Italy and England in 1995," recalls Markgraaff. "To me, Kitch was one of the few honest people in South African rugby. More than 95 per cent of them weren't honest at all, but Kitch was very straight and direct, and what you saw was what you got. He asked me to come and meet him in Hermanus between the World Cup and that end-of-year tour, and we found we agreed on a lot of things.

"He was eager to get me involved, and I had agreed to it, but before anything could be finalised, he [dropped] the idea because of an objection from François Pienaar. That's not in any book, but that's what happened. So my [issues] with François had already started towards the end of 1995. Kitch and I got on well, and we would have had a good working relationship."

Regardless of the real reasons for Christie's hasty exit, Markgraaff was on a hiding to nothing when he took over. While the public, and obviously the World Cup players themselves, wanted to continue on a similar path to the one that had brought them success in 1995, it was possible only in theory and not in reality.

Since the Webb Ellis trophy had been lifted amid much euphoria at Ellis Park the previous June, the internecine conflict over the World Cup contracts, and the huge disparity between what was being earned by those on contracts and the new Bok players, caused a hangover that wasn't easy to cure. Indeed, the World Cup contract issue, and the exorbitant amount of money spent on the World Cup winners, was to have a negative impact on the Boks, and South African rugby as a whole, for at least the next two to three years.

"A lot of the problems started with the money. Suddenly you had some players earning almost R2 million. And they didn't have to do anything to earn it," says Markgraaff. "When we boarded the aircraft to fly to Sydney for the Tri-Nations, we still had to give letters to the players guaranteeing them medical insurance and other things not yet put in place by SARFU. Their minds were not on the rugby. Players were complaining that some of them were earning less than someone like Robbie Brink, who was sitting at home.

"I was continually involved in meetings, both with the non-contracted players who wanted a deal [that was] more equitable with the World Cup–contracted guys, and with the contracted players who felt SARFU wasn't [honouring] some of its promises. I remember having a series of meetings at [the] Burgers Park Hotel in Pretoria when we gathered for our first camp. Rugby seemed [to be] the last thing on anyone's mind."

The Springbok World Cup group had decided to opt out of the Turnbull/Packer deal, which rivalled that of Rupert Murdoch's Newscorp, a decision that did not go down badly just with overseas players – most of South Africa's provincial players had committed themselves to Turnbull too, and they also felt they'd been sold down the line. Some of those players later became Springboks, and their deals were not as lucrative as those of the players who, in their minds, had "sold out" to Luyt.

Once Markgraaff was installed as Bok coach, he and Pienaar met for the first time at the Sunnyside Park Hotel in Johannesburg. Pienaar warned that the contract situation with the Bok players had to be sorted out, and was initially encouraged by Markgraaff's willingness to help.

But the relationship between them soured almost immediately when Luyt told Pienaar that Markgraaff had accused him of bad-mouthing Ray Mordt to a group of bankers. Mordt had recently been appointed as Markgraaff's assistant coach. Luyt alleged that this was the reason why Mordt did not attend Pienaar's wedding, even though the invitations had been sent out three months in advance.

It led to a showdown between Pienaar, Mordt and Markgraaff on the day the Boks gathered at the Pretoria Holiday Inn ahead of Markgraaff's first Test in charge, which was effectively a Tri-Nations warm-up game, against Fiji at Loftus.

Markgraaff admitted he'd had that conversation with Luyt, but denied that he'd mentioned any names. He said he had spoken about the team in general, and suggested the entire situation had arisen from a silly misunderstanding.

Already, even at that early stage, it was apparent that there wouldn't be the same level of understanding between Pienaar and Markgraaff as there had been between Pienaar and Christie.

Pienaar's nose was further put out of joint when the selections for the first Test of the year were made. Henry Honiball came into the side ahead of World Cup winner Joel Stransky, and Pienaar noted in his book that it was clear that World Cup reputations meant nothing any more.

But should they have? I took the side of the World Cup players at the time, and Markgraaff was severely criticised each time he dropped a star from 1995, but with the benefit of hindsight and an additional 17 years of experience in writing about the sport, it is possible to speculate that perhaps the Transvaal and Springbok group of that era had quite naturally come to the end of its cycle. Very few of those players were in form after the World Cup, and to Markgraaff, setting plans in place for the new international season, the abysmal Transvaal Super 12 performance proved that he couldn't just press on with what had worked in 1995.

The Boks beat Fiji 43-18, but it was considered an underwhelming performance ahead of the away leg of the first-ever Tri-Nations, which was to start a few days later in Wellington, with a match between New Zealand and Australia. The game had taken place midweek, and the next day I headed off to New Zealand and that historic first match. Clearly the newspapers had more money back then than they do now.

For a man who had only ever coached a minor union, Markgraaff was quite bombastic ahead of the Springboks' Tri-Nations campaign. "We will play rugby the world has never seen before," he told the media.

But sitting at the old dilapidated Athletic Park watching Jonah Lomu and the All Blacks demolish Australia on a chilly afternoon, I was under no illusions about the huge challenge the new coach would face. Add to that the deep hurt New Zealand was still feeling after the 1995 World Cup result, and it made the Boks' task even more daunting. In fact, it became increasingly clear to me during the weekend I spent in the nation's capital that the Kiwis wanted revenge, especially given the many aggressive questions I had to answer about Suzy, the phantom waitress who had allegedly "poisoned" the All Blacks before the RWC final.

Christie was not the only World Cup–winning coach who had exited the scene since the 1995 event. The ARU had jettisoned Bob Dwyer, who had guided the 1991 Wallabies to the crown in England. On the flight from Wellington to Sydney, where I was to arrive just in time to meet up with the Boks as they flew in from South Africa, I happened to sit next to Dwyer's brother, whose name escapes me now.

"I think a lot of South Africans were surprised they dropped Bob," I said after we had made our introductions.

"I think a lot of us were surprised too," Bob's brother said as the Air New Zealand 767 banked to the right and set off on its bumpy course across the airspace above the Tasman Sea. "It certainly doesn't look like we've made an improvement on yesterday's evidence. How is your mob shaping up?" I wasn't sure quite what to tell him.

It was to be an even bumpier ride for Markgraaff, Pienaar and the Springboks over the next month or so. I remember that after the Test in Sydney, which the Wallabies won 21-16, I asked François Pienaar a question, and then had to look sideways in order to follow his gaze. He had received a bang to the head during the game and was cross-eyed. I wonder whether he even remembers that press conference.

But Pienaar definitely recalls what had preceded that game, as he wrote about it in his book. Apparently, in the build-up to the match, Markgraaff had handed him a piece of paper on which he had written down the game plan.

"[He] wanted us to take quick penalties, to throw quick line-outs, to punt the ball deep into their half rather than into touch and, if we won a penalty in their half, to kick for a line-out in the corner rather than kick for the posts."

Pienaar was uncomfortable trying a new strategy in such an important game, but he pledged his support, although he confided to manager Morné du Plessis that Markgraaff's game plan was unsound. Du Plessis was sympathetic, but told him that he couldn't meddle in the coach's affairs.

"I did want to change the game," Markgraaff says. "What François didn't appear to appreciate was that there had been a massive change in how rugby was played since the World Cup. In the Super 12, the Sharks had been the South African team who had showed an aptitude for adapting, and I wanted to base a lot around their style. François was all about kicking the ball deep and then squeezing the opposition with suffocating defence. I thought that strategy had become outdated. And the Transvaal results in the Super 12 may have shown that."

The captain said that when the Boks got to Christchurch for their first match against the All Blacks since the World Cup, Markgraaff was incessantly talking up the opposition. Pienaar felt this was the wrong approach to take with the players and that all it did was expose Markgraaff's inexperience.

Pienaar was right that Markgraaff was inexperienced at that level, and in those early days he was also old school. And this does not come from Pienaar, who was perhaps used to Kitch Christie's fairly old-school approach to training, but from Mark Andrews, who was a graduate of the more modern Natal system.

"I have very fond memories of Markgraaff, and he was very much a players' coach," says Andrews. "But he wasn't very scientific or statistically astute in those early days, and he was quite old school in his methods. For instance, he would drive us forever in the scrums."

In his book *For the Record*, Teichmann mentions how his heart would sink whenever Markgraaff ordered the setting of 100 scrums in a training session the week before a Test match. According to Teichmann, Markgraaff was dogmatic and inflexible in the beginning. "My first impression of Markgraaff was not a positive one. He seemed to have graduated from the old school of South African coaches, where you were taught that if it was good enough for Oubaas Markotter and Danie Craven, it was good enough for you. [They] had been great men in their day, but it was our day now."

Markgraaff was often portrayed as someone who was passionate, but who at times struggled to make up his mind. Both Pienaar and Mark Keohane, the rugby writer, wrote that he would sometimes leave players in the dark until the last minute about what was expected of them. (Keohane would work with Markgraaff under Harry Viljoen in later years.)

I saw evidence of this in the week building up to the Christchurch Test, when Markgraaff was vacillating for several days over his scrumhalf selection. As is invariably the case in New Zealand, the weather forecast predicted that it would be wet on match day, and I remember getting involved in a conversation in the hotel foyer with Markgraaff, assistant coach Ray Mordt and Keohane.

I can't remember exactly what was said, but I know both Keohane and I agreed that Johan Roux, with his kicking game, would be a better wet-weather option than Joost van der Westhuizen, and his selection would also lend an element of surprise.

In the end, Markgraaff did select Roux, but unfortunately the game wasn't won or lost at halfback. Actually, the Springboks had their opportunities to win the match, and I remember sitting in the press box afterwards, thinking that the South Africans had looked the better team for long periods of play. But the same problem that had haunted their tour to New Zealand two years earlier made an unwelcome return – ill-discipline. And it cost them dearly.

This was the game in which John Allan head-butted Sean Fitzpatrick in the first scrum, and the Boks gave away several idiotic penalties. In one crucial instance, the All Blacks were awarded a penalty because Pieter Hendriks had been guilty of a late charge against Christian Cullen, which cost the Boks three points when they were pressing for the win in the last minutes of the game. The Boks lost 11-15.

In his book, Pienaar mentions that, after the game, he went to Morné du Plessis and complained bitterly about Markgraaff. "It's his fault. You know that. This is all the coach's fault. We should be winning these matches. This is bullshit."

To rub salt in the South Africans' wounds, after the final whistle had blown, they were witness to the Kiwis' joyous and over-the-top celebrations. Perhaps they felt that to some extent the result had avenged their defeat in the World Cup. I wasn't there to see it, but I can only imagine that a month or so later the celebrations must have been even more rapturous, when the All Blacks celebrated their first ever series win over the Springboks in South Africa.

But before that series could kick off, there were still two more Tri-Nations games back home. The first one was the clash against Australia in Bloemfontein, a match in which Pienaar did not follow the coach's instructions, or so he claims in his book. The Boks won 25-19, and Joel Stransky at flyhalf played a starring role. Pienaar says he had instructed Stransky to kick for touch rather than into space, and the territorial dominance created by his kicking resulted in the Boks leading 16-3 at the break.

However, Markgraaff contests this. He says that the instructions he issued were the ones that were carried out. "We always intended to play for territory that day, as we knew how important it was for us just to get the win after the two losses overseas."

But Pienaar sensed that Markgraaff wasn't happy with him afterwards, and if it is true that he didn't follow the coach's instructions, maybe Markgraaff had a right to be upset. It certainly explains why, unbeknown to Pienaar, the media and the public, he was entering the last week of his Test career.

But all of this was overshadowed by a furore that erupted after the match, and which would result in probably the most disappointing period of my more than two decades of writing about the national team. In one crazy week, so much of what had been positive about 1995, in terms of nation building, was eroded.

It started when Markgraaff selected the Northern Transvaal hooker, Henry Tromp, who had been imprisoned for killing a black farm labourer. Morné du Plessis was most unhappy with Tromp's inclusion and, had Edward Griffiths, the Springbok media liaison and SARFU chief executive from the year before, still been involved with the Springboks, he would have been upset too.

Louis Luyt had fired Griffiths earlier in the year. The SARFU president had sent a fax from his office at Ellis Park to the SARFU headquarters in Cape Town informing the chief executive that his services would no longer be required, and with Christie being replaced at much the same time, it was the beginning of what turned out to be a purge.

The Tromp issue was less of a problem for me than the controversy that blew up the day after that Tri-Nations win against the Wallabies in Bloemfontein (it would turn out to be the Boks' only win of the series).

Morné du Plessis had gathered a few of the reporters who were departing from Bloemfontein airport and issued a statement condemning those fans who had waved the old South African flag during the match. I viewed Tromp as yet another victim of our apartheid past, but the old flag was another issue entirely – it was a symbol of apartheid when the Springboks were supposed to be representing a nation that had waved that abhorrent part of its history goodbye.

And then François Pienaar threw in his penny's worth, seemingly publicly opposing Du Plessis by saying that people could wave whatever flag they liked. SARFU, or at least some its employees, defended Pienaar, vapidly pointing out that "After all, he's just a boytjie from Witbank." But Pienaar's words refuted the image he had created for himself when he'd famously told television reporter David van der Sandt, "[We did it] not just for 60 000, but for 43 million" moments after the World Cup final.

I deliberately didn't interview Morné du Plessis for this book, as I reckoned he would just be his usual diplomatic self and not want to rock the boat. However, I did interview him later that same year and I know that he was deeply hurt by those events. The newly burnished Springbok image took another knock at a press conference before the next Test, against the All Blacks.

I asked Du Plessis a question relating to the flag issue, which prompted the new media liaison, Alex Broun, who had replaced Griffiths, to intervene. This is what he said: "I would just like to make it clear that anything that Morné says here is not representative of the views of SARFU."

A bemused silence engulfed the room. Du Plessis, highly embarrassed, looked away, and I asked Broun to explain what he meant. What *was* SARFU's line on the old flag then? After all, the country did have a new flag, and the Boks were supposed to be representing the *new* South Africa. Come on, Alex, explain yourself. But of course, he couldn't. Broun might have been a nice guy, but he wasn't equipped to deal with politically related questions. He was an Australian who had come to South Africa for the first time to attend the previous year's World Cup and had liked it so much, he decided to stay.

But the next week, in Durban, I bumped into the new SARFU chief executive Rian Oberholzer at an SA Breweries function. Rian would make a lot of enemies during his tenure at SARFU, but I was mostly a fan. He was often caught between a rock and a hard place trying to sort out the demands of rival factions and ending up satisfying no one. But he was an astute administrator, and his quest to transform rugby was sincere and unrelenting.

However, at the SAB function that evening, he and I had a casual chat that developed into quite a debate, fuelled by the sponsor's excellent product. His response to my questions about the flag issue was quite lame.

SARFU, he said, could not be seen to be siding with Morné, as it would alienate their target market. I assumed that he was referring to the white Afrikaner.

11

Dropping an icon

If I was a bit ambivalent about Markgraaff in the first part of 1996, I became less so in the build-up to the final Tri-Nations Test, against the All Blacks in Cape Town. The buck stops with the Springbok coach, and whereas rugby had unified the country little more than 12 months before, it now appeared to be retreating back into the laager – and at a rapid rate!

The Minister of Sport, Steve Tshwete, shared my perception. He felt impelled to issue a statement in which he said that many South Africans, "mostly from the black communities", did not believe the sport had moved into the new era. He also told the *Sunday Times* that there was a growing feeling that unity was nothing but a ruse "to take white rugby back into the international arena".

On the morning of the Newlands Test, Alex Broun's comment that SARFU did not share Morné du Plessis' view on the flag-waving incident was front-page news in the Cape Town newspapers. But a far less political but no less contentious issue hogged the headlines in the week following the Test. James Small had been spotted at a nightclub in the small hours of the morning in the build-up to the game, and his transgression was reported to the Springbok management.

In those days, if you wanted to wave a red rag at this bull, all you had to do was drop Small or discipline him. To others he might have seemed undisciplined and difficult, but I always thought he was just different and that he'd behave himself if his coaches and management treated him intelligently and sensitively.

Small had won me over on the first post-isolation Springbok tour of 1992. He shared my dislike of flying – in fact, he was far worse than me. So instead of flying from Beziers to Paris, he and I managed to get a lift in the car of a Romanian journalist, Chris Thau.

As it turned out, Chris's driving made both of us wonder whether we'd made the right call ... But what I remember most vividly about that trip was Small weeping when the car radio played Eric Clapton's "Tears in Heaven", a song he had written for his son, who had fallen to his death from the 53rd floor of a New York apartment block. Later, when Small came to Durban to play for Natal, I always marvelled at the special way he had with kids.

So when Markgraaff disciplined Small by dropping him for the three-Test series against the All Blacks, I reacted with considerable vehemence.

"How would Markgraaff deal with Eric Cantona?" I asked in one of my columns. I argued that the coach's inability to deal with a talented yet maverick character showed up a weak spot in *him* and not the player.

At the time, I was under the impression that Small had broken curfew earlier in the week before the Test. But Markgraaff corrected me when I interviewed him 17 years later.

"No, it was the morning of the game. He was out at a nightclub at 6 a.m. on the morning of the game," Markgraaff insists. "I won't mention their names, but some of James's teammates came to me to tell me how angry they were."

At the time, reports indicated that Small had been out until 2 a.m. and not 6 a.m., but nevertheless, even I would have to admit that staying out that late was unacceptable on the morning of a Test match. Still, there was no denying that Small was missed in the series against the All Blacks. Due to his omission and other players being injured, the three-quarter line was too inexperienced to stand up to the powerful and pacy New Zealanders.

The All Blacks had already wrapped up the Tri-Nations by the time they arrived in Cape Town, but with the three-match series still to come – there would be a Springbok/All Black Test match on four consecutive Saturdays – many saw the final game of the tournament as the start of a four-match rubber.

The Boks led 18-6 after the first half an hour, but fell away badly after that. The All Blacks' intense rucking allowed them to dominate at the breakdown, and they eventually won the game 29-18.

In the aftermath of the match, much was made of Os du Randt's parting comment as he left the field of play, apparently injured – "*Ek is gatvol* (I've had enough)."

Afterwards, Markgraaff was convinced that Du Randt wasn't the only Bok player who'd had a bellyful. "There were actually two Boks who opted to get onto stretchers in that Test rather than play the full 80 minutes," he remembers today.

In his book, Pienaar claimed that Theo van Rensburg had heard from former teammates within the squad that Markgraaff had accused him [Pienaar] of faking an injury when he was replaced early in the second half, and Markgraaff doesn't deny it.

"I never said it publicly at the time because I felt I couldn't, but I would have said it to my best friends, my family and people close to me, and I still say it today that he faked the injury. I didn't say it to François, but I knew he thought that. [You just have to] watch the video of the game. There you see François, walking and walking, a long way behind the play. He didn't get touched, and then suddenly he sat down [before] getting on a stretcher.

"He apologised to me, phoned me on the Sunday night to say sorry for what [had] happened and that he was now motivated to play the All Blacks [in the series] and would play for me and the team and not let me down. He told me he was fit and ready to play. He never himself said he had faked the injury, but we both knew what he was apologising for, and I know it was the truth because I saw it happen.

"But the next day [when I arrived at] the Beverly Hills Hotel in Umhlanga Rocks to start the preparation for the first Test of the series at Kings Park, the team doctor Frans Verster told me François had contacted him and said [that] his [GP] had booked him off for six weeks. It was the exact opposite of what he had told me just the night before, when he said he was ready to play and there was nothing wrong with him."

Gary Teichmann had taken over the captaincy armband after Pienaar left the field. Officially, he had sustained a concussion after trying to tackle Sean Fitzpatrick. The legendary World Cup–winning captain would never lead the Boks again, and he may have realised as much that evening when he returned to the Newlands change room from the medical room and found Louis Luyt sitting with his arm around Teichmann. Markgraaff also seemed indifferent to Pienaar's presence and didn't inquire about his injury.

Markgraaff, so many years later, shows no remorse.

"I've had to sit with this blight on my character because I dropped a player whom everyone [considered to be] untouchable, but I know what happened. And yes, I was furious at him after the game. Shouldn't I have been?"

Pienaar was ruled out of the series against the All Blacks, and Teichmann took over the reins. The No. 8 could not have assumed leadership at a more difficult time, with controversies raging on several fronts, and with a Test series against the All Blacks looming. In his autobiography, he reflected that he did not inherit a happy side. The players were constantly being distracted by the "broad divisions created by World Cup contracts and other things".

It wouldn't be the first or the last time that distractions derailed the Boks. After his stint as the Boks' media liaison/special advisor, Mark Keohane explained to me just how much heavier the off-field workload is when the team is playing at home. The many functions and signing sessions the players are expected to attend are all intensely energy sapping.

And in 1996 there was also the added distraction of the flag controversy.

It is small wonder then that Teichmann didn't initially want the job of captain. Besides being put off by all the off-field controversies, he wanted the opportunity to play himself into international level first and become a permanent fixture in the team. But he reluctantly accepted the captaincy when he was told that there was no one else.

The All Blacks won the first Test in Durban 23-19 after leading 18-9 at half-time. It was an odd game – although the score seemed close, the Boks seldom looked as if they might actually win the match.

The Springbok defeat concluded a week that had started off with the news that Small, who was withdrawn from the team for the Durban game, had been cleared by a disciplinary hearing conducted in an office under the main grandstand of Kings Park. He was cleared in part because it emerged that Morné du Plessis had been aware that he was leaving the hotel and had allowed it. But while SARFU cleared Small, Markgraaff stuck to his guns. He made it clear that Small would not take part in the series when he wasn't included in the 23-man squad for the second Test, in Pretoria.

On the flight to Johannesburg on the sombre, overcast Sunday that followed, some of the Kiwi journalists asked me if I had been at the same Kings Park game as them. In their opinion, I was writing far too positively about the Boks. And the Boks were under massive pressure going into the Pretoria Test. It had been only a year since they had won the World Cup, and here they were on the brink of losing their first ever series against the All Blacks on home soil.

In the second half of the second Test, the All Blacks looked desperately fatigued, but they nevertheless hung on for a gutsy win that made history. I still remember the clever drop goal the All Black No. 8, Zinzan Brooke, snapped over in the dying minutes for his team to win 33-27.

Afterwards, in *For the Record*, Teichmann described his own team's performance as a "heroic effort", despite the six-point loss. "In my view, we'd lost because, despite all our enthusiasm and effort, we did not truly believe we could beat the All Blacks," he said. "Our inadequate administration, the World Cup contracts and the climate of controversy that have dogged us ... all sowed seeds of doubt and confusion in our team. As a result, we lacked the conviction and arrogance that sets winners apart."

Kimberley is usually one of my more enjoyable stopovers on the rugby circuit, but not so much when the All Blacks visited the town for a tour match before the final Test at Ellis Park. By then I was convinced that Markgraaff was a disaster as Bok coach.

Kimberley was Markgraaff's home town, and the locals considered him a hero. He was president of the Griqualand West Rugby Union, and still involved with the coaching of the team, and the match against the All Blacks was Markgraaff's opportunity to back his claim that he was a top-level coach. And to a certain extent he managed to do that, as Griquas held the All Blacks to a draw and earned themselves the right to be seen as the most successful provincial team to have played the visitors.

Hurrying away from the ground through the car park after the match, I was waylaid by a group of Griquas fans, who enquired about my laptop. When I told them I was a rugby writer, I quickly realised it was a stupid thing to do.

"*So jy is een van die veraaiers?* (So you are one of the traitors?)" snarled a big Afrikaans gentleman as he moved towards me.

I quickly weighed up my options and decided I didn't really have the inclination to stop for a chat. So I hot-footed it to my hired car and sought the sanctuary of my hotel. The *Diamond Fields Advertiser* was one of the smaller newspapers in the Independent Group stable, but as the only English-medium paper, it was big in Kimberley. And splashed all across its pages were my so-called anti-Markgraaff sentiments.

While driving back to Johannesburg the next day, a colleague rang me on my cellphone.

"I'm just giving you a heads-up. Markgraaff's been telling everyone he's looking for you. He told me he's going to *dônner* [hit] you if he sees you," he said.

I resolved to sort out any issues Markgraaff might have with me when I next saw him, but I was nonetheless pleased to be staying in Sandton and not at the Sunnyside Park Hotel, where the Boks were located. Breakfast isn't an enjoyable experience when you have the Springbok coach staring daggers at you.

At the time I thought that Markgraaff wasn't gracious enough in defeat, which was partly why I felt enmity towards him. And after winning the final Test, at Ellis Park, 32-22 over a fatigued All Black team, he was a little *too* cock-a-hoop for a coach whose team had lost three of the four matches they'd played against them in South Africa, and four out of the five games in total against them in 1996.

Nevertheless, having resolved to sort out my differences with the coach, I approached Alex Broun before the Ellis Park game to set up a meeting. Markgraaff had won the Test and was thus not as angry as he had clearly been in the week leading up to the match. At least he never looked like he wanted to *dônner* me.

We met in one of the vacant rooms in the stadium after the post-match press conference, and Markgraaff said that some of the players had told him they wanted to distance themselves from some of the things I had written, especially my suggestions that the squad wasn't harmonious. I wasn't going to argue, and after much finger-wagging and a few "I told you so's" from Markgraaff, the meeting ended.

As I left the room and headed towards the media area, a concerned-looking Barry Glasspool of *The Star* approached me to ask what it had all been about. He thought Markgraaff had hijacked me into the meeting, and was surprised when I told him that I had asked the coach to meet with me.

The next time I heard from Markgraaff, albeit indirectly, was a few months later in Argentina, and it had to do with a column I had written in September. I got a call from Nick Mallett, who had by then been seconded into Markgraaff's management set-up as assistant coach.

"I just want to congratulate you on having the guts to be the only person who has been honest about François Pienaar," Mallett told me. "I told André the other day that you were the only person who backed him [on the issue], and he nearly died of shock. He said that you were the media person that was most anti him."

I wasn't sure about being "anti" Markgraaff; I thought I was just being objective, whether I was backing him or criticising him. In my research for this book, I couldn't find the column Mallett was referring to at the time, but I remember that I wrote that Pienaar wasn't in form and hadn't been since the

World Cup. However, I hope that I wasn't too acerbic, as rugby is not an empirical science – a lot is open to interpretation and opinion. And Pienaar did deserve a more fitting exit after leading the team to World Cup glory the year before.

However, while part of me thinks Markgraaff should have prepared an exit strategy for the captain if he was determined to get rid of him, he had thought of firing Pienaar since early in the season. So maybe he had bowed to sentimentality enough by then.

"When he [Pienaar] didn't pitch at the Beverly Hills Hotel on that Monday morning after telling me he was sorry, that was when I decided he would not be part of my team any more," Markgraaff told me.

Perhaps things would have turned out differently for Pienaar if Morné du Plessis had been allowed to perform the same function he had fulfilled for Christie. By all accounts, Du Plessis had shown great diplomacy whenever a situation called for it. He might well have come up with an acceptable exit strategy, or he could have galvanised Pienaar into pulling out all the stops for his coach. Clearly, Pienaar was not as committed as he should have been, which was obvious from what he said subsequently.

But Du Plessis had not been happy in the Bok management group since the flag controversy, and it didn't come as a great surprise when, just before the end of the All Black series, he announced that he was going to step down. The Boks dedicated their victory in the final Test to him.

It has often been assumed that Markgraaff had had a hand in Du Plessis' departure, and perhaps the former Bok captain did struggle with Markgraaff's management style. But Markgraaff vehemently denies that he'd wanted Du Plessis out. On the contrary, he needed Morné to perform the political and ceremonial duties for which he didn't care much.

"Morné played an extremely important role and I wanted him to continue," Markgraaff insists. "I was very happy with Morné and felt he was the right man for me, but Rian Oberholzer came to me in Joburg and said he wanted to change the whole system of South African rugby. In fact, I recently [saw] him at a soccer match in Cape Town and he is still [maintaining] his view that the structure of world rugby needs to change, that there should be managers and not coaches.

"He told me [at the time] that they were going to make the coach the manager of the team. So for that end-of-year tour, I was the manager and not the coach. I went to see Louis Luyt in his office, and I told him I felt bad about Morné. But Luyt told me that he saw the manager as an honorary job and Morné wanted R50 000 a month, which SARFU couldn't afford."

After Du Plessis' departure from the Springbok management team, there was effectively no one within the group who could represent Pienaar's interests. Pienaar's own perception was that perhaps he was too strong for Markgraaff, which many in the media agreed with at the time. I wasn't one of them, though.

"François Pienaar is not a part of my vision for the future," Markgraaff was quoted as saying in the Sunday papers the next day. According to him, if Pienaar wasn't dropped, he was going to withdraw from the squad anyway.

"When we were on our way to the team announcement, [Pienaar] phoned Ray Mordt, who was sitting next to me in the Kombi, to say that he was withdrawing from the squad to Argentina."

Markgraaff then bravely – or perhaps stupidly – attracted even more censure by selecting one of his Griquas players, Theo Oosthuizen, into the squad. As Oosthuizen was coming to the end of his career, it could hardly be said that he would form a part of any "vision for the future" either.

The reaction from the media and public was quick and vehement, with 95 per cent of the 60 000 respondents to a *Sunday Times* poll saying it was wrong to drop Pienaar. Radio personality Darren Scott, then presenting the drive-time show on 5FM, doctored a popular song of the time and played it on his show. Part of the lyrics went like this: "No Pienaar ... how bizarre ..."

It was bizarre to almost everyone, and as a result Markgraaff felt isolated. It was reported that he even received death threats at the time. "It was one of those situations that develops when a person is revered by everyone for something he has done and he becomes almost untouchable, but sooner or later a change would have had to be made," Markgraaff explains.

In his book, Pienaar says that he wishes he and Markgraaff had enjoyed a better understanding from the outset. "I had wanted to help him settle [in] as an international coach, but he appeared unwilling to listen to any views or opinions. Was he too proud or too insecure to learn from an experienced captain? Why could he not have arrived and been happy to build on the foundations of 1995?" Pienaar writes.

But the man who took over from Pienaar is not so convinced that the 1995 template would have worked in 1996. As Gary Teichmann says in *For the Record*: "François wanted to carry on the momentum from 1995 into 1996, but although he would never have admitted it at the time, this was not possible. A new coach means a new start, new structures and new levels of trust. You have to build from the ground floor. There are no short cuts."

At the time of Pienaar's axing, Teichmann was more of a Markgraaff fan than he had been at the start of the year. "As [Markgraaff] settled [in], he started to listen to his players, taking on board what they were thinking and taking it upon himself to advance their cause. The contrast between his attitude at the start of the year and at the end of it was striking."

The contrast *was* striking, and not just to the players. Markgraaff appeared determined to make up for the mistakes he had made earlier in the year, and the fact that the shadow cast by Pienaar's axing was so quickly erased once the Boks went on tour should be seen as a tribute to his willingness to do whatever was necessary to get the Boks back on the winning track.

Contrary to what Pienaar had assumed, and unlike many other coaches, Markgraaff was not averse to bringing strong personalities into his team, as he appointed Nick Mallett as an assistant coach for the tour to Argentina, France and Wales. He also called in Natal's Hugh Reece-Edwards and his former Western Province teammate, Carel du Plessis, as the other assistant coaches.

"I rated Mallett," Markgraaff says. "Yes, he was a strong character, but I believe in having strong characters who challenge you. I also wanted to play Ian McIntosh's game. I was a big admirer of [his style of rugby], with a few variations. That was why I brought in Reece-Edwards. I thought he could [introduce] elements of Mac's game. I knew Mac was furious with me, and he let me know about it. But the way I saw it, I was coaching the Boks, the national team, and everything [should be done] for the good of the national team. Surely that is also what is good for the country?"

Markgraaff says he assembled the group with succession planning in mind, and he may have played an unwitting role in determining who would coach the side the following year – but more on that later.

Regardless of the way in which Pienaar was axed, on the tour it quickly became apparent that he wasn't missed. The atmosphere seemed transformed. And it could all be attributed to changes Markgraaff had made to his management style.

"Of all the Springbok coaches for whom I played," Mark Andrews says, "Markgraaff was the one who was most in tune with us and with how to get what we wanted from SARFU. Compared to later coaches, [he insulated us the] most from admin-related problems [so that] we could just get on with playing rugby."

Of course, Mallett's arrival in particular would have helped drive many of the changes in management style, but Markgraaff at least deserves credit for recognising that change was necessary. Mallett, for example, was the one who suggested that the coaches fly in economy class and the players in business class. He also suggested treating the media to a braai in Mendoza. I wasn't in Argentina for the event, having timed my arrival to coincide with the first game, but my colleagues who attended it said it had been a great day.

And the players, according to Teichmann, appreciated being treated like adults, a positive change from earlier in the year. His theory was that, in South Africa, Markgraaff had been a little too sensitive to criticism, but in Argentina, and later in France, where he couldn't read the newspapers, he felt less pressure.

Whatever the reason, it was a great tour. Everything was far more relaxed than had been the case earlier in 1996, and the positive match results no doubt helped.

The two Tests against Argentina were played at the same stadium in Buenos Aires on successive Saturdays, with midweek matches against regional teams in between. The Boks won both Tests comfortably, the first 46-15, and the second 44-21.

Henry Honiball was now a fixture at No. 10 and impacting positively on the Bok playing pattern. The two Tests in France that followed were also a success, particularly the first one, in Bordeaux. It was a wet-weather game, and with Kobus Wiese leading the charge from the second row, the Boks raced into a 19-6 half-time lead before eventually winning 22-12.

France could easily have won the second Test, in Paris at the old Parc des Princes Stadium, when they laid siege to the South African try line in the dying minutes, but the Springboks' outstanding defence saved the day. Christophe Lamaison only just missed with a drop-goal attempt as the Boks scraped home 13-12 for a 2-0 series win, which Teichmann regarded as an apt response to Markgraaff's critics.

The Boks were staying at the Concorde Lafayette, the same hotel where I had once spent my entire weekly tour budget on a round of sandwiches for colleagues who had popped into my room for a late-night party. Mark Andrews recalls Markgraaff doing something similar on the night the Boks' clinched the series, only he spent a small fortune on beer, not food.

"There was a problem with our beer supply from SAB, so he forked out from his own pocket and bought us four cases of beer to share. I think [the bill] came to about R12 000, which was a lot of money in those days. I hope

SARFU paid that money back [to him], because Markies really splashed out on the players that night as his way of saying thank you for a great tour."

In the build-up to the last Test of the tour, against Wales in Cardiff, Markgraaff effectively gave the players the week off. The Welsh rugby writers saw this as arrogance, but it was an astute move, as Markgraaff could see how tired the guys were after a long year. Later Springbok coaches would use the same tactic on the end-of-year tours to the northern hemisphere.

The Boks responded with a convincing 37-20 win over the Welsh, which was a fitting end to a successful tour. It also conveyed a positive message ahead of the British & Irish Lions series that would take place the following year. Of course, this was what we thought at the time ... However, other nefarious matters were afoot. I remember being invited to join in the celebrations in a suite at the team hotel and noticing that Markgraaff seemed strangely subdued. Was it a portent of things to come?

Markgraaff recalls: "During the Argentina leg of that tour, Carel du Plessis came to me and asked me if I was sure that I had not been taped saying something that would be bad for me and the team. I didn't know what the hell he was talking about. His wife worked for Independent Newspapers and she had seen a letter that had been written to Tony O'Reilly (the owner of the company) by the lawyers for the Bester brothers, Piet and André, who played for Griquas. But I knew nothing about it at the time. It was only when we were in Bordeaux before the first French Test that an attorney in Kimberley called me to say that the Bester brothers wanted R750 000 each or they were going to publish the transcript of a damaging tape-recording [in which] I had allegedly made racist comments.

"I didn't remember [having] a conversation [in which I'd made] racist remarks, so I ignored it and said [that] I would sort it out when I got home. What had happened was that earlier in 1996 most of the Griquas players had decided that they did not want to stay on contract if Piet and André were still contracted to the union. They weren't popular.

"Even though I was the Springbok coach by then, it was my responsibility to inform them of the decision, and they made it obvious [that] they weren't happy. Then, just before the end-of-year tour, André Bester made an appointment to see me. I thought he was coming over to fight with me, but he surprised me by being really friendly, making comments about politics and drawing me into conversations about dropping François Pienaar and other [stuff].

"He said things like, 'Did you see what Mululeki George said about you?'
Then I got the letter from the lawyers, the one that I was contacted about. It
was worded in a way that they thought would protect them from accusations
of blackmail, but it *was* blackmail."

Markgraaff said he didn't want to receive faxes about the matter at the team
hotel, so he asked his lawyers to postpone proceedings until he got back from
the tour.

"When I got back and saw it for the blatant blackmail attempt that it was,
I had various options, one of which was to go to the police. But [no matter
what I decided to do], it was not going to avoid a problem. I went to Rian
Oberholzer and suggested we [inform] the executive of SA Rugby about the
story. I wanted to open it up to the executive to see what we could do about
it. I wanted to make an appointment with Muleleki George.

"But Rian was strongly opposed to that. He said if I did that, I would be
dead. I wanted us to deal with it as a group, because I didn't believe that the
tape was genuine and felt it had been tampered with. I didn't believe I had
said the things that I was told I had said. I am definitely not a racist. [But]
Rian refused to take it up. He said he disagreed with my strategy."

After Oberholzer told him that the battle was his alone, Markgraaff
approached Luyt directly.

"He took me to Fanie Cilliers, a top lawyer, and when he went through
the tape he said it was a load of bullshit."

But the saga was acquiring a life of its own. Markgraaff heard that Brian
van Rooyen, at that stage a disgruntled rugby official at the Lions, was on his
way to Edward Griffiths, then chief executive at SABC's Topsport, to sell him
the transcript of the tape.

"There were a lot of rumours flying around, [and] all the attorneys [were]
trying to put the different parties under pressure," recalls Markgraaff. "The
[Besters] were always [after] the money, but I resolved quite early on that even
if it meant I was going to go down, they weren't going to get a cent from me.
They were very bitter, and I knew them well. I thought [even] if there was a
proper settlement, they would [still] try to find a way to leak the stories to
make [some] money."

As Markgraaff remembers it, the *Sunday Times* was the first newspaper
to publish anything on the race-tape allegations in a short article inside the
paper. It alleged that a top rugby official had been accused of making racist

comments. The first time Markgraaff's name was linked to the tape was in a massive front-page story in the *Cape Times*. Mark Keohane, who was then still working for *SA Sports Illustrated* magazine, had written it in a freelance capacity, though his name did not appear in the byline.

"Everyone thought I would fight it, but the next day I resigned," says Markgraaff. "I didn't feel I had an option. But I did take the tape to Dr Len Jansen, an expert in the field of voice recordings. His verdict was that the tape had been tampered with. It cost me a lot of money, but at least it proved what I had suspected."

Although Markgraaff does not deny that he may have used the dreaded "K word" in the conversation, he is adamant he did not use it in the context the tape purported.

"If you were living in the Northern Cape 17 years ago and you knew the person I was talking to, then [perhaps] it is possible that you might have used the word once in conversation when you [were] drawn in and they were using it. But saying it 20 times in one sentence is laughable. I can't deny saying it because maybe I said it, but I also can't say [that] I said it.

"People who know me today will tell you that it is not me. My family and I aren't racists, and we weren't [then] either."

Indeed, people who know Markgraaff and who worked with him then and subsequently have vouched for him on that score.

In his book, Teichmann said that he had wanted to support Markgraaff, but that Rian Oberholzer stopped him from doing so. Oberholzer told Teichmann that Markgraaff had become "too hot to handle".

But Teichmann remembers Markgraaff as a brave coach who knew what he wanted.

"I have respect for him as a coach, and a man, and always enjoy seeing him in and around the rugby world. Each time I meet him, I can't help but wonder what we might have achieved if that fateful tape had never been made. My view is that we would have sustained the progress."

12

The Prince of Blunders

Everyone, including the players, thought Nick Mallett would be the man to take over after André Markgraaff's resignation, as he had been the dominant assistant coach on the end-of-year tour in 1996. So when he was overlooked for Carel du Plessis, I smelt a rat.

On the day of Du Plessis' appointment, *The Argus* ran a front-page story I had written in which I suggested that South African rugby was retreating back into the laager. However, once the article had been edited, it seemed to imply that Du Plessis was a *verkrampte* choice. I felt embarrassed, as I knew enough about him to know that he and his family were anything but. His brother, Michael, had made himself unpopular with the ruling classes a few years earlier when he refused to stand to attention during the singing of "Die Stem" before a Springbok match, and while I wasn't sure Carel shared all of Michael's views, the acorn seldom falls far from the tree.

More than that, from a rugby viewpoint, Du Plessis was the exact opposite of a conservative choice. He was one of just three Bok coaches (the others were Harry Viljoen and Peter de Villiers) who would, at least initially, advocate moving away from the so-called traditional approach of physical dominance. In fact, he was the only one of that trio who never compromised his beliefs when the media and the rugby public, who demanded success at all costs, heavily criticised the new strategy. It might have been why his stay in the job was so brief.

The point I was making in that front-page article wasn't that Du Plessis was conservative, but that the people who had selected him had opted for the safer and more traditional coaching option – apart from Du Plessis being Afrikaans, he had graduated from Stellenbosch University and was a soft-spoken, thoughtful and undemonstrative man.

Mallett was English-speaking, but, more importantly, he was also a product of the University of Cape Town and Cambridge University, and as such was perceived as a liberal. And then there was his reputation for being an outspoken hothead ... After Markgraaff, SA Rugby were probably going to be over-cautious in their choice of a new coach, which may be why Gary Teichmann said of Du Plessis' selection: "[SARFU] appointed the man, not the coach."

Of course, as a coach, Du Plessis had no track record to speak of.

Says Du Plessis: "After my retirement [from rugby] in 1989, I worked on a casual basis in a sort of advisory capacity for the University of the Western Cape for a bit, but my only exposure to a top-level coaching environment was when I worked as technical advisor with the Springboks in 1996."

It has always been one of rugby's big mysteries how Du Plessis could have been appointed as head coach of the Springboks with so little experience. He had been a celebrated player and a great Springbok, and will always be remembered as the "Prince of Wings" – but the Springbok coach? He wasn't ready, which the people who appointed him should have known. It was thought that Louis Luyt, the SARFU president, might have spearheaded Du Plessis' appointment, as his huge regard for him had been obvious when Luyt lured him and his brother Michael to Johannesburg to play for Transvaal in 1987.

Du Plessis is not so sure. "That might have had something to do with it, but I really have no clue. SA Rugby approached me, and [only] the chief executive, Rian Oberholzer, [was involved in] the negotiation process."

Later that year, Nick Mallett would meet with Luyt and André Markgraaff to start negotiating his takeover from Du Plessis. At that meeting, Luyt and Markgraaff had a little side conversation that Mallett sensed might have embarrassed Markgraaff. He recounts: "Louis asked André why he had wanted Carel to be the Springbok coach, instead of me, if he had never rated him."

But Markgraaff has a perfectly plausible explanation, which may clear up the 16-year-old mystery.

"I would never have backed Carel as the head coach; I never saw him [in that role]. Nick has taken what Luyt said out of context. I had sold Carel to Luyt as a member of the management team the year before on the basis that Carel was good at what he did, which was coaching attack. Carel would still make an excellent attack coach if he were employed with that degree of specialisation today.

"I think people misunderstood me ... The previous year I'd sold SARFU the concept of succession planning. I believed that the next coach should come from my management, [as he would have built some experience]. This had originally been the intention [when I was appointed to assist] Kitch too.

"I never had any input in the appointment of my successor. After the race-tape saga, I just wanted to get out of rugby, which I did for about three months."

Markgraaff reckons that the SARFU executive decided against Mallett because of a negative report Johan Claassen, the SARFU representative on the 1996 tour, had written about him.

"Nick was seen as a hothead, and Claassen was highly critical of Nick in [that] report ... In one instance, when the crowd was booing our players, Nick made rude gestures at the spectators. So the 14 presidents were left with Carel as the [only other] option. He was the only guy left from the previous year's management whom they wanted. It was yet another example of botching up the coaching appointment. [The process] just wasn't scientific and thorough enough."

I'll say. Du Plessis may be a clever man, but unless you radically wanted to reinvent your approach to rugby, it is best to stay away from him. Only if you want things changed do you appoint someone like Du Plessis.

But, as usual, the people running the game didn't really have a clue what they were seeking in the coach. For starters, they didn't even ask Du Plessis about his rugby philosophy.

"I did speak to the chief executive, Rian Oberholzer, about my philosophy when I first became involved [in 1996], but there was never a formal selection process or rugby committee to whom I had to [punt] my approach," says Du Plessis.

Had there been such a process, Du Plessis would have been spared his early dismissal, as those who had appointed him would have had to support his efforts at changing the game. Or, alternatively, they would not have appointed him at all, sparing South African rugby the pain that was to follow.

So while the media would often accuse Du Plessis of being "blind" to the errors of his ways, it wasn't he who couldn't see, but the administrators who had appointed him. After all, they had employed a man who wanted to make substantial changes to the way the Boks played the game, but were not prepared to give that process the time it needed.

"I did perceive that there was a need to take a fresh look at the Springbok style of play," Du Plessis recalls. "This is oversimplifying it, but what I was [trying] to do was to improve the individual skills levels of the players and incorporate that into a team environment. I wanted us to have more options and variation on attack and better-equipped players. I wanted to improve the skills levels of the players so that they could play the game I thought they were capable of playing.

"I have never relied on the convenience of hindsight. If I did, I might say now that perhaps I should have looked more closely at *how* I was going to introduce changes into a team environment. If the members of the team are going to perceive it as a change, then you have to avoid a situation where that change creates uncertainty."

Du Plessis says now that if he had the time over again, he would probably continue on the path Markgraaff had started and phase in his changes subtly and slowly.

"But at that time I was convinced that the changes weren't as radical as some people were making them out to be. In my mind [they were] just subtle changes, [like] a change in the way of thinking. A lot of people laughed when Mark Andrews was quoted as saying he was being taught how to sidestep, but that wasn't really what I was trying to do.

"I had no intention [of turning] Mark into Danie Gerber. All I [wanted] was a greater awareness of where to run at the tackler; in other words, to run at his arms and not necessarily at his body. It is true that I was not a fan of just playing direct rugby all the time. Of course you have to be direct. But I thought we needed to vary our points of attack, and to operate off a split-field attack.

"I felt we needed to move away from thinking that we should take the ball up all the time, and that we should always take it up through the one and two channels. That works if you have players [who are dominating physically], but I felt that to properly manipulate opposing defences, you had to offer more than that.

"I felt – and I still feel – that we had a massive talent pool in this country and the players had the ability to do a lot more than what they were producing on the field."

In other words, he wanted to take Springbok rugby to a new level, a theme and a goal that have recurred with subsequent coaches, but without ever being fully achieved.

"Looking back, it was ambitious of me to think we could change things in the time that was available. We had a week with the team before the opening match against Tonga, and then, a week later, it was the opening game of the series against the British & Irish Lions."

Listening to Du Plessis talk during our 2013 interview, I could understand why he may have struggled to impose his philosophy on the players in 1997. The man is obviously very intelligent, but he struggles to convey his ideas. I made far more sense of what he was trying to say once I played the interview back on the tape-recorder, but his players would not have had that luxury. Far from being gobbledy-gook, as one player described Du Plessis' theoretical sessions in 1997, I could now understand why some of his supporters call him a genius.

At the time of his appointment, I predicted that Du Plessis would either be a spectacular success or a resounding failure, mainly because he didn't have any head coaching experience but had been highly regarded as a thinking player during his rugby career. I resolved to give him a chance to prove himself either way.

Soon after he was appointed, Du Plessis and his assistant coach, former Springbok teammate Gert Smal, accompanied a media party on a three-day bus trip to the Boland to assess its union's development initiatives. The fresh-faced, clean-cut Du Plessis and the imposing but genial Smal both struck me as honest, humble, down-to-earth and decent human beings.

Du Plessis' first task as Bok coach was to reappoint Gary Teichmann as his captain, and Teichmann wrote in his book that he had felt positive after their first meeting, over breakfast, at the Elangeni Hotel on the Durban beachfront. But once the players convened at a training camp, Teichmann quickly realised that the guys were struggling to follow Du Plessis in his theoretical sessions.

Being brilliant doesn't automatically enable you to successfully impart your knowledge, which is probably why so many of the top coaches (New Zealand's Graham Henry, Mallett, McIntosh, Jake White, etc.) were teachers first. Although Teichmann respected Du Plessis' intelligence, he wanted the coach to "dumb down" for the players.

Sixteen years later, Du Plessis stresses that he was not exactly teaching the players rocket science. But the proof of the pudding is in the eating, and although the Boks won the opening game against Tonga comfortably enough, the players themselves were a confused bunch by the time the first Test against the Lions came upon them.

The players were not only perplexed by the "weird drills" they were made to do, but also felt that both Du Plessis and Smal were unfamiliar with modern coaching trends. Smal, for instance, made the forwards practise against a scrum machine for hours, which was like going back to the Dark Ages.

"[That] was the time when I felt the most lost [with the Boks]," recalls Mark Andrews. "Carel was technically very good, particularly when it came to running lines and [showing one] how to swerve, but everything was very backline-orientated and it just felt like there wasn't any substance to [what] we were doing.

"There was no understanding of where we had to be and [how] the game [would flow] as there [had been] under Ian McIntosh. Under Carel, everything was fragmented. We were asked to look at various video clips, but they were never edited to form a holistic picture. It was all theory. We were sitting in video sessions for two hours not knowing what Carel was trying to get across. I remember having to wake up André Venter because he fell asleep."

According to Teichmann, the result was that the players were not at all adequately prepared for an iconic series that would be a once-in-a-lifetime experience.

And indeed, the Lions were gaining impressive momentum as the series drew nearer. In the weeks leading up to the first match, they had the time and the opportunity against provincial opponents to fine-tune their game and find their perfect combinations.

And the Boks probably weren't helped by the high expectations of the media and the public, who expected them to canter over the Lions. In fact, most of us regarded the series as just a warm-up to the Tri-Nations ...

"We weren't complacent, but the public were, and it did feel like everyone was expecting us to win easily," Du Plessis says.

I remember attending a welcoming party for the Lions at the Beverly Hills Hotel in Umhlanga Rocks at the start of the tour. I was one of several local journalists who had been lined up to be interviewed on our expectations of the series. I said that the Boks might lose one of the three Tests, and my prediction was considered the most sobering of all the reporters' views! All my fellow scribes thought it was going to be plain sailing for the Boks, although one of my Afrikaans colleagues was a bit of a *skelm* – he tipped the Boks to win 3-0 publicly, but made a tidy sum on the side by betting at the bookmakers on a series win for the Lions.

What did the ace Lions goal-kicker Neil Jenkins think? I couldn't be sure, but the Welshman had a broad grin on his face as he knocked back several glasses of red wine in quick succession before his team was rushed off to a training session after the lunch-time function.

Two guys who weren't smiling were World Cup winners Kobus Wiese and Hennie le Roux. Du Plessis had left out a few of the established Springboks from the first squad, and included some real bolters out of nowhere, such as the Free Stater Edrich Lubbe. But the most fuss was made about the exclusion of Wiese and Le Roux, who reacted by saying that they might follow François Pienaar and Joel Stransky overseas.

"I was disappointed by their reaction," Du Plessis said at a press conference. "I told both players before the announcement that they were going to be left out and [that] I hoped to talk to both of them in more detail some time in the future ... They must concentrate on working on their strengths."

Clearly Wiese wasn't learning to sidestep. Or perhaps Louis Luyt was behind their omission from the team ... Reports doing the rounds suggested that Wiese and Le Roux may have been dropped because of an ongoing dispute they were having with their union, which by then was known as the Gauteng Lions. After all, politics has never been far away from most of the controversial decisions that have blotted the South African rugby landscape.

But some of the players Du Plessis brought into the squad would prove inspired selections. For some of them, it was the beginning of a long association with the Springbok jersey. Pieter Rossouw and Percy Montgomery became Boks because of Du Plessis when neither of them had played Super 12 that year, as Western Province had finished outside the top four South African teams in the previous season's Currie Cup.

Province, coached by Harry Viljoen and playing the sort of rugby Du Plessis appreciated, did win the Bankfin Night Series and, in the regular domestic season, would go on to win the Currie Cup outright for the first time since 1986. However, Montgomery's selection was contentious, as Du Plessis had selected him to play at outside centre, and he wasn't considered physical enough for that position. His selection into the midfield also fuelled the perception that defence was an afterthought for Du Plessis.

While the Boks warmed up with a 74-10 win over a weak Tonga at Newlands, the Lions hammered Natal 42-12 in Durban in their last Saturday match before the first Test. The Natalians may have been without some of their Boks, but the Currie Cup champions still had enough star players for the score line to serve as a loud warning for the national team.

With Henry Honiball at flyhalf for the first game of the series, one might have thought that Du Plessis was planning on playing the Natal game, but that was not the case. Honiball stood far too deep at Newlands, which took him completely out of the game. It was flyhalf rugby from a forgotten era.

"Carel wanted us to play a very outdated style of rugby, standing deep and running the ball to the wings," remembers Andrews. "I think that was the problem – he had played in a different era and didn't seem to realise that the game had moved on."

But it was still a close game, and the Boks even looked like they were in control at certain stages, but they were outdone by a brilliant late solo try by Lions scrumhalf Matt Dawson, followed by another try, by left wing Matt Tait, to make the game safe for the Lions (25-16).

The next morning, as I prepared to fly to Durban for the next Test, the Springbok supporters at Cape Town airport were in a funereal mood, the atmosphere exacerbated by the newspaper headlines, which mostly carried a doomsday theme. The old-fashioned rugby the Boks had played had motivated me to write a front-page article for the *Weekend Argus* in which I slammed SA Rugby for their decision to appoint an inexperienced coach who was set on playing an outdated style. And this was after only the first Test.

However, Gary Teichmann brought a bit of perspective to the matter when the Boks started their training the following week.

"It wasn't us who wrote the Lions off and gave them no chance," he said to me after commenting on the sense of melodrama that seemed to have engulfed the South African media. Perhaps the reason I had predicted a Bok win was because I wasn't aware of just how poorly they were being managed. In his book, Teichmann wrote that the Springboks turned on each other after the defeat. And in truth there was a lot going on behind the scenes at the time.

As Dan Retief wrote in the *Sunday Times*: "From president Louis Luyt – who botched the initial contracts – down, there is jealousy of the World Cup players' contracts, and these Springboks feel themselves both set upon and victimised. Perversely, the contracts also lead to problems with new players in the squad who are dissatisfied by what is an unequal payment structure."

Teichmann said he felt "exposed" by the lack of support he got from the team management. Du Plessis and Gert Smal were quiet by nature, and manager Arthob Petersen was not the sort of person who could take hold of the situation.

"Professional sports teams lean heavily on their management to create the right mood within the camp and ... to allow each individual player to fix his mind solely on playing the game. I simply believe the Springbok teams of 1996 and 1997 were not afforded these circumstances," Teichmann wrote.

Injuries and panic selections forced a change to the make-up of the South African three-quarter line for the Durban Test, with Percy Montgomery coming in at outside centre alongside Danie van Schalkwyk.

The irony of that dark night at Kings Park was that the Boks did play a lot better than they had in Cape Town. They even scored three tries to none, but they just couldn't nail their goal kicks. By contrast, Neil Jenkins slotted everything, and then came the Jeremy Guscott drop goal that clinched the series for the Lions with one Test still to play.

The South African goal-kicking might have been atrocious, but Teichmann was at least partly to blame for not deciding ahead of time who his front-line goal-kicker would be. In the end there were six attempts at goal, with Henry Honiball, André Joubert and Percy Montgomery all missing two each.

Looking back from the vantage point provided by 16 years of retrospection, Du Plessis feels it was those missed kicks that ultimately sealed his fate.

"I am told my message wasn't getting through to the players, but I don't see it like that," he says. "The results were the problem, not the game we were playing. If you are not successful, you cannot initiate anything new, as losing undermines confidence. If you are winning, then people don't question your playing style and you can get on with it. But we lost that game, and we really shouldn't have. We played a lot better than in Cape Town and were just let down by terrible kicking and by some 50/50 calls that went against us."

And blaming the 50/50 calls is not just sour grapes from a vanquished coach. After the game, several rugby writers criticised the referee, Frenchman Didier Mene, for missing a number of crucial incidents during the 80 minutes.

The Boks went on to win the dead-rubber final Test at Ellis Park quite comfortably, but the Lions were out on their feet by then and their job was done.

Late that night at Vertigo, an old nightspot in the suburb of Illovo that I used to frequent, I bumped into some English journalists.

Over the booming music, Nick Cain, with his deep English accent, shouted, "We did you, we did you!"

"Come on, admit it," he continued when I didn't respond, "we did you, we did you, we did you ..."

They did "do" us, indeed. For his trouble, I held up Cain's partying for two hours as I moaned about Carel du Plessis, the bizarre selections and the coaching decisions that had stymied the Boks. Even though the Boks had won comfortably at Ellis Park and had scored more tries in the series than the Lions, that didn't matter to my good friends from the United Kingdom. They "did" us!

But let Teichmann have the final word on that Lions series: "Quite simply, the Boks in that series were out-thought, out-coached and out-managed."

Okay, maybe not. Let's rather leave the last word to André Markgraaff, Du Plessis' predecessor, who had this to say to the *Sunday Tribune*: "The whole problem lies in the constant changing of coaches."

Quite right, too. Enough progress had been made on the end-of-year tour in 1996 to suggest that, had Markgraaff stayed on, the Boks would have won 3-0 against the Lions. Markgraaff had cooked his own goose, as it were, but at the very least more thought should have gone into his replacement. And if it was going to be Du Plessis, with his ideas about bringing in a new game, then SARFU should have guaranteed him the time he needed to get it right.

When Henry Honiball was dropped for the final Test against the Lions, Markgraaff told the media that he thought it was a crazy decision. And Nick Mallett agreed with him.

"I feel helluva sorry for some players, particularly Honiball, who has been asked to do a job that is completely different to that which he was asked to do when he first became a Springbok," said Mallett.

The pain wasn't over yet. The Tri-Nations still lay ahead, and things would get worse before they got better. There were, however, some encouraging signs when the Boks led most of the way against the All Blacks at Ellis Park before succumbing in the dying stages of the game. Again, it was a small margin that would impact big-time on how much longer Du Plessis would remain the Bok coach.

"We were unlucky not to win against New Zealand in the first Tri-Nations Test," Du Plessis remembers. "I thought the guys had a different vibe before that game and I felt [that they] were starting to understand my game and were beginning to execute [my] plan. Again, though, we didn't get the result, and then we played really badly when we travelled. Our defence was just really poor against Australia in Brisbane. We let some silly tries in."

The score in that match was 33-22 to Australia, but only some late points by the Boks brought some respectability to the scoreboard. At one stage during the first half, the Boks were trailing 3-19.

That tour was a disaster for reasons other than just the results. The coaches were new to touring, and protocols and logistics were a mess from start to finish. By the time we'd flown over the Tasman Sea to Auckland, the mismanagement had become intolerable for the players.

In his book, Teichmann says he felt he was starting to lose the players' support because he was routinely ignored whenever he raised issues with the management. Had Du Plessis stayed on after the Tri-Nations, Teichmann would have stepped down, and Andrews confirms he would not have been alone: "By the end of that year's Tri-Nations, Teich, Henry Honiball and I had decided that our Springbok careers were over."

The team only arrived in Auckland on the Thursday before the Saturday Test, which will not seem unusual now, as it has become common practice not just for the Boks, but also the South African Super Rugby sides, to postpone their arrival in New Zealand as much as possible when they have to fly in from Australia. What was "inexcusable, farcical and unacceptable", according to Teichmann, was the fact that there was a level of maladministration that he felt "would have had most club teams raising their voices in complaint".

In Auckland, Teichmann objected when the entire squad was expected to attend the first press conference, which was completely unnecessary. And when the Boks arrived at Eden Park for a practice, they discovered there were no floodlights because the Bok management had forgotten to schedule the session. Then, on match-day, they left the hotel too late and arrived at Eden Park only 25 minutes before kick-off. Teichmann had to drop his bag and proceed immediately to the toss of the coin. There wasn't even time for a team talk.

Considering the chaotic lead-up to the kick-off, the Boks started remarkably well. They took an early 10-0 lead, but then Ruben Kruger broke his ankle and André Venter was sent off after an incident involving Sean Fitzpatrick. Although the Boks were still in the game in the first half – at least on the scoreboard – the All Blacks ran away with it in the second to win 55-35. It was the first time the Boks had ever conceded 50 points or more, while the All Blacks scored a record eight tries against them.

"That New Zealand Test was a horrible experience to sit through," remembers Du Plessis. "Whether it was justifiable that we were reduced to 14 men is debatable. André was sent off just before half-time, so retaining momentum was a challenge. And with Ruben also off the field, it meant we had to play a hooker on the flank.

"The win against Australia after that was a better reflection of [our capabilities]. In that match, our execution was perfect and I felt that the new players had started to settle down and were gaining in confidence."

The match Du Plessis is referring to is, of course, the 61-22 win over the Wallabies at Loftus on a memorable August evening. Before that game, I had written an open letter to Du Plessis in my column, asking him to see the writing on the wall and step down for the good of South African rugby.

After the victory over Australia, a few people approached me and asked what I had to say now that the Boks had won so handsomely. I let them listen to a radio interview I had done from the press box in which I pronounced that Du Plessis had coached the Springboks for the last time. Someone at SARFU had tipped me off that, win or lose, it would be the end of Du Plessis. And a phone call confirmed that to be the case even after the Aussies were routed.

The SARFU executive had at last cottoned on to the fact that Du Plessis had brought with him a package that they hadn't asked for.

A week or two later I was at a corporate breakfast at the Mount Nelson Hotel in Cape Town where SARFU chief executive Rian Oberholzer was the guest speaker. Afterwards I walked with him to his car, and he confirmed that he would be attending an executive meeting that afternoon where the Du Plessis axing would be put in motion.

Oberholzer later told me that the subject of sacking Du Plessis had only come up as everyone was packing up to leave that meeting.

"Guys, are we happy with the coach?" Oberholzer asked the board.

Obviously everyone wasn't.

Was Du Plessis fired just as the Boks were about to soar under his tutelage? It's a debate that still continues 16 years later, but plenty of the Springboks who played against Australia that day have told me that the players had just decided to do it their way and to hell with Du Plessis and his grand plan. Ironically, in the process they may have showed the coach that a more direct playing approach could lead to a try-scoring avalanche, as Peter de Villiers would discover in a similar match against Australia 11 years later.

But don't forget that the Boks had conceded 55 points in their previous game. So on which of the two games do you judge the coach? Yes, there were mitigating circumstances in Auckland, but at a squad meeting after that game the players quite openly expressed their unhappiness with the management and the coaching.

According to Teichmann, James Small was the first player who spoke out, saying that the team had been let down by the management. Louis Luyt was in the room, and he immediately chided Small: "You should be careful when you talk about the people who are paying the mortgage on your house."

But Teichmann intervened, telling Luyt that Small was speaking on behalf of the entire group. Perhaps that was what inspired Luyt to call a meeting of coaches in Johannesburg, but more on that later.

As Mark Andrews pointed out, the fault lay not with Du Plessis, but with the people who had decided to appoint a coach with no experience. And when SARFU subpoenaed Andrews to give evidence at an arbitration hearing in Cape Town to settle a dispute between SARFU and the coaches, he told Rian Oberholzer as much.

"When Rian took me back to the airport," Andrews told me, "I said, you guys are to blame for all of this. How could you appoint a coach with no coaching experience to an international team? Yes, maybe Carel shouldn't have taken the job. But it's hard to turn a job like that down when it's offered to you.

"I don't think Carel was a good coach, and I don't think that at that stage of his career Gert was either, but they both worked incredibly hard and no one could fault their commitment. They used to slip a synopsis on the performance of each player under [our] doors at night. That took a lot of time, and they always seemed to be working. But in the end they just weren't ready for the job."

And SARFU wasn't ready for any radical changes to the way the Boks played the game. Du Plessis might not have had the opportunity to talk rugby philosophy before he was appointed, but he finally got his chance a few days before he was shown the door.

"I was aware [that SARFU] were looking to end my contract. I drew up a comprehensive management report in which I set out the problems as I saw them, and I mapped a way forward. But whether they took it seriously or not I am not sure, because it may well just have been their way of ensuring there was fair process," Du Plessis says. "I realise now that to achieve what I wanted to, I needed to have very strong allegiances within the system. You need to have people alongside you who share your vision. If your aim is to play 15-man running rugby, there are ways to get there, but you can't get there in week one. The players have to buy in, and you need guys alongside you in the management who buy in.

"I never had a problem with the pressure, as I knew what I was getting into. But on the day that I was trying to push my case for a continuation, I had everyone in my management team write reports, with the exception of the manager himself. Arthob Petersen was part of the SARFU executive, so he was effectively on the other side of the door, among the people wanting us out."

Du Plessis' conviction that the Boks were improving inspired him to make a proposal to SARFU: he would take the squad on the tour to Europe and they could re-evaluate him afterwards.

"I told them that if they were still unhappy after the tour I would happily walk away and there would be no further argument. I was that convinced that the Boks were coming right."

He never got his chance. Instead, he was involved in a protracted arbitration process that initially ruled in his favour and then against him when SARFU appealed the outcome.

"It was all technical stuff," says Du Plessis. "We were contracted until the World Cup, but Rian Oberholzer had signed off our contracts and the SARFU executive argued that he didn't have the [authority]."

Andrews was the only player who was subpoenaed to attend the arbitration hearing and, as far as I know, I was the only journalist. I'm not sure what the respective lawyers expected from me, but I only had this to say: I had been prepared to give the coach a chance at the outset, despite the fact that he had no coaching experience, but it was impossible to continue backing him once it became obvious that his inexperience posed an obstacle to the Boks' success.

On the day that Du Plessis was sacked, Mike Greenaway wrote a column in the *Cape Times* in which he called the coach "The Prince of Blunders".

But it was really SARFU who had blundered...

13

A good excuse for a crazy celebration

You'd think that the James Joyce pub would be in Ireland, but it was at this establishment in Paris where I experienced the most raucous and enjoyable post-match celebration ever with the Springboks.

The French had been well and truly smashed at Parc des Prince earlier that day, a game where even the locals appeared to be supporting the sublime mixture of force and class that was wiping out their team. After their 52-10 win, the Boks did a lap of honour to a standing ovation from the crowd.

It had been a stunning exhibition of attacking rugby, and it happened on the last occasion that Parc des Princes would be used as the home of French rugby. As I stood in the James Joyce pub watching the Springboks, their supporters and rugby journalists socialising with one another while downing copious amounts of alcohol – and a person I knew from Durban even shedding his clothes while singing along with the crowd – it was hard to equate the prevailing mood with what I had seen earlier in the year.

The Boks had been fragmented and uncertain after the series against the British & Irish Lions, and only found their feet in the last game of the Tri-Nations tournament that followed. Their on-field form had generally been so poor that I wrote rather sarcastically that their goal appeared to be to give some self-respect back to the opposition.

But here they were, just months later, smashing their way through Europe en route to an unbeaten tour that would break several records, with England due to reap the whirlwind in London just seven days after that crazy night at the James Joyce. The pub was conveniently just across the road from the

Concorde Lafayette, which was the Paris home of the Boks during the Markgraaff, Mallett and Harry Viljoen years.

Before they went out on the town that night, Mallett gave a speech that would become legendary to the Springbok players and management.

"Guys, whatever happens with this team, whatever we may or may not go on to achieve, I can tell you that we will always look back on this day with special affection. If any two of us happen to run into each other in 20 or 25 years' time, no matter where we will be or what we are doing then, we will be able to look back on this match and, suddenly, there will be a very powerful bond between us. We have shared something very important today. You must all enjoy it."

And enjoy it they did, both then and for most of the next year. Not until 12 months later, when he dropped André Venter for Bob Skinstad on the next northern hemisphere tour, did Mallett make a false step. By then the Boks had gone unbeaten for 15 months and were on the brink of a record.

Carel du Plessis was somewhat consoled by the perception that some of his work with the Boks was manifesting itself in that period, and it would appear naive to think that nothing from his tenure was carried over. But Mallett bluntly dismisses any suggestion that he had ridden on Du Plessis' coat-tails and had presided over a winning run that would have happened anyway.

"I thought the Boks played really well when they smashed Australia in that Loftus game," Mallett says now. "It was a fantastic win and they seemed liberated. So when I [became the Bok coach], I went to Durban to meet with Gary Teichmann. I asked him what he would like to keep [from that game], because I thought the team had been really brilliant. Gary surprised me with his response. He told me to change *everything*. He said the players had played it *their* way at Loftus. Gary was going to resign, and I also don't think he felt that Carel necessarily backed him."

When Mallett became the Springbok coach, the players considered it an appointment that should have been made much earlier in the year – after André Markgaaff's resignation, to be exact. Mallett, however, had publicly criticised Louis Luyt, and had even taken him on face to face. He felt he had cooked his goose with the SARFU president and did not expect to get the Bok job when Du Plessis was sacked.

"I had been coaching for 10 years both in France and South Africa by then, and when they appointed Carel, who had no coaching experience, I thought to myself that it showed they didn't really place proper value on the position of Springbok coach," recalls Mallett. "So I wrote an article in *SA Rugby* magazine saying exactly that. I also said that the SARFU executive was closer to 70 or 80 than 50 years of age, and I heard that also really pissed Luyt off.

"Then came that public relations job when Carel was coaching, when they called a whole lot of coaches together to discuss what was wrong with the Boks. I laid into Louis [there too], and I told him it was his fault, as he had appointed a coach with no experience. I repeated what I had written – that he clearly had no respect for the position of Springbok coach. It got quite heated and Rian Oberholzer had to step in to stop the argument.

"I think my attitude surprised a lot of people. The Afrikaans guys in those days had generally been brought up to believe they had to respect their elders no matter what, whereas as an English-speaker who had studied at an English university, I believed that you needed to debate things and question and challenge that which you thought was wrong."

Mallett's reputation as a bit of a hothead preceded that 2006 meeting. In fact, it preceded it by more than two decades. A big, robust and skilled No. 8 who had played a big role in Western Province's golden era, when they won several Currie Cups in succession (it was five eventually, but Mallett had left by then), Mallett felt piqued when he was left out of a Springbok squad that embarked on an internal tour following the cancellation of the scheduled 1985 series against the All Blacks. He had won his only two Bok caps in a series against the South American Jaguars the year before.

Then Mallett was selected in a Cape Barbarians team that beat the Boks at Newlands. Afterwards, he raised a two-finger salute to the administrators in the grandstand, a gesture that pitched him into controversy.

Shortly thereafter he decided to leave South Africa to play in France, where he was a successful player-coach and then coach before returning to South Africa in 1993 at the behest of the False Bay chairman Rob van der Valk. Van der Valk was later to become Mallett's logistics manager at the Springboks and would write a book, *Nick and I*, which Andy Colquhoun co-wrote, about his experiences with Mallett.

"Nick turned False Bay into a very successful and vibrant club, but he was hard-nosed and bullish and didn't suffer fools or stand on ceremony," Van der Valk wrote.

Van der Valk said that instead of the SARFU executive interviewing Mallett for the Bok job, it had been the other way round.

"It did turn out a bit like that," Mallett laughs, "but that was because when I finally got called into the meeting with the SARFU executive, I knew I was their only candidate. How I got into the reckoning at all was down to André Markgraaff's intervention. He called me and said that he just had to get me and Louis Luyt together for the good of South African rugby. He said that while I may not like Luyt, [he] was the only person who could make the change.

"I think André even paid for my flight, and we [met with] Louis in his office at Ellis Park. Louis said that I had to retract everything I had said, and of course I immediately got on my high horse and said, 'There's no way I will retract anything.'

"But André was [a] very good peacemaker, and I saw at that meeting why he was so good at SA rugby politics. He played up to Louis and fed his ego a bit by saying that he was the only guy who could make a change that would save the Springboks. After that, everything calmed down.

"It didn't necessarily mean that I was going to get the job, though, even though Rian Oberholzer phoned me and asked me to please submit an application for the position, as I had not done so yet. He told me that the landscape had changed since earlier in the year. I was called to a meeting with the SARFU executive in Johannesburg, and [I] flew up thinking that I was one of several candidates.

"When I arrived there, it took a long time for me to be called [in]. Initially I thought it was because there was another candidate that was doing well [in the interview], but it turned out that the Bok coaching job wasn't the most important thing on their agenda. They probably thought I would last for six months and then they would appoint another coach. There appeared to be a revolving-door policy at the time.

"I was initially a bit nervous, but after a while I realized that I was the only candidate. And then Anthony MacKaiser, the SARFU communications manager, asked me how to spell Hertfordshire, where I was born. He told me it was for the press release. So I knew I had the job before I even walked into the meeting. I am normally reasonably confident, but that day I was super-confident. I laid it down to the executive; I told them I wasn't going to hide behind selectors and I wouldn't take any interference from administrators."

A clause that would become very controversial later in his tenure was added to Mallett's contract with SARFU. Before he was appointed, nothing in the coach's contract stipulated that he would select the team only on merit.

"Ironically, the SARFU lawyer, under instruction from Rian, put that clause in," says Mallett. "They stressed that I must select the team only on merit. They considered me a long-haired UCT liberal, and I think they were scared that I might come in and just follow a transformation agenda."

After his appointment, Mallett travelled around the country speaking to key players, getting them onside. He met with the Natal contingent at the Elangeni, and as Mark Andrews recalls, Mallett had to pull out all the stops, as several of the players were disillusioned with the Springboks.

Mallett confirms this: "A lot of the top players were uncertain, but I asked them to commit to the Springboks and to make themselves available for the end-of-year tour. They all eventually did, with the exception of André Joubert, who said he was coming back from injury and was not sure he could make it. I told Juba that I thought he was a really great player, but that he must understand that it was probably going to be a very successful tour and that the player who [replaced him] might do well. If he did, I would find it hard to drop him afterwards. Juba said he understood that."

Justin Swart wore the No. 15 jersey in the first Test of the tour, against Italy in Bologna, but he was injured the following week, building up to the first Test against France, in Lyon. Mallett then selected Percy Montgomery, who had only played centre for the Boks up till then, and the former SACS pupil quickly proved to Mallett that his hunch was correct – fullback was his position. Joubert never got to play Test rugby again.

"I was convinced Percy would make a great fullback, and I told him that ahead of the tour. I also made it clear to André Snyman that I would move him back to centre from wing, where he had played out of position under Carel. Carel had dropped Henry Honiball, but I knew what I wanted from him and I made it clear to him that he was my first choice."

Mallett was also responsible for giving the veteran playmaker Dick Muir, who had captained Western Province to the Currie Cup title after moving to Cape Town from Durban, his only taste of Springbok rugby. It was a selection that Ian McIntosh had wanted to make four years earlier, but was prevented from doing by his selectors.

"I appreciated Dick's communication skills and fast hands," Mallett says. "He brought out the best in Henry Honiball, who wasn't a great communicator, and I think it's fair to say that Dick was the reason we scored so many tries on that first tour."

Tries they certainly did score – plenty of them. Only in the first Test against the French in Lyon did an opposition team even come close to the Boks on the scoreboard (36-32), but that was only after a late fight-back. The South Africans had been far ahead earlier in the game. The Boks outplayed Italy, France (twice), England and Scotland as they completed their best-ever northern hemisphere tour of the post-isolation era.

The last Test of the tour was against Scotland in Edinburgh. At a press conference before the game, Jim Telfer, who had been one of Ian McGeechan's assistant coaches on the Lions tour earlier in the year, spotted me and exclaimed: "Ach! I see we have South Africans in the room."

He came over afterwards for a chat and told me that some of the selections and tactics the South Africans had employed against the Lions had been nothing short of crazy.

"But I see you guys have sorted yourselves out and are playing to your strengths," he added.

He was right, and the Boks showed him just how much they had improved by accumulating 68 points against the Scots at Murrayfield, with James Small breaking the Bok record for aggregate tries and Percy Montgomery scoring a record number of points.

These were glory days for the Springboks, but none of the on-field successes would have been achieved without the changes Mallett had brought about off it.

Mallett differed from most of the other Bok coaches in that he was quite willing to engage with the media. As he was also based in Cape Town and was English-speaking, he perhaps read more of my articles than the Afrikaans-speaking coaches who read *Die Burger*, and we had a good relationship from the start.

Mallett and I had first spoken after the 1995 World Cup. I had been publicly ripped off about my hopelessly inaccurate prediction that the Boks would bomb in the tournament, and Mallett phoned to congratulate me on how well I had handled it. He also admitted that he had shared my view ahead of the World Cup.

On the media's recommendation, Mallett had appointed Alex Broun as his media liaison officer. And Van der Valk, as Mallett's logistics manager, ensured that there was no repeat of the shambles in Auckland three months previously. He worked tirelessly to ensure that Mallett, his players and his staff could concentrate solely on the playing side of things; he was in charge of everything else, with Arthob Petersen travelling as ceremonial manager.

Mallett also appointed Alan Solomons as his assistant coach, along with Peter de Villiers. He told Teichmann that he "had been told to appoint one [black] coach in the set-up, to give opportunities as part of development", but as De Villiers related in his autobiography, *Politically Incorrect*, perhaps SARFU and Mallett weren't honest enough with him about why he was there.

It led to the one unsavoury moment on the tour, when De Villiers threatened to abandon the Springbok party and fly home as they were departing Charles de Gaulle airport for the British leg of the trip. De Villiers, who saw himself as equal to Solomons in the pecking order (they were both appointed as assistant coaches), was eventually placated by Van der Valk, and in his own words, spent the rest of the tour doing coaching courses.

Solomons was actually more of a talking point at the time than De Villiers, as the press were alleging that the Boks were being run by a "UCT/Western Cape cartel". Solomons, the long-time coach of UCT, was the assistant coach to Harry Viljoen at WP at the time, and he'd initially turned Mallett down because he felt his loyalties should lie with Viljoen.

"I nearly fell over when Mallett told me he was appointing Solly," Van der Valk said. "I never had a clue they were close; they had been rival coaches at UCT and False Bay. But Mallett recognised that he didn't have the enthusiasm or the will to handle the small details of coaching. He wanted Solly's meticulousness."

Mallett had been expected to bring Hugh Reece-Edwards back as his assistant, as the pair had enjoyed a great relationship on the previous end-of-year tour under Markgraaff. But Mallett eventually decided against him because their rugby philosophies were too similar. Mallett knew Solomons's talents lay in providing the much-needed checks and balances that would make his own job easier.

"I knew I had to have people working with me whom I trusted. That was a non-negotiable. I had seen too many people getting shafted in the past, and you have to be absolutely tight as a coaching staff. Solly was a lawyer, so he understood the principle of having a fair debate. He never contradicted me in front of the players, but he would give his opinion."

On his return to South Africa after the superb end-of-year tour, with Springbok rugby on a high, Mallett had time to reflect on what had transpired in the initial months of his tenure for the first time since his appointment. He felt he had all the players onside. Whereas the English-speaking guys had thrived on his style from the outset, the Afrikaans players had, at least initially, been a bit circumspect because of his brusque, forthright manner. But by the end of the tour, they, too, had been won over, and that memorable evening in Paris was only one of several occasions when it was apparent just how united the squad was.

But the following year did not start well for the South African teams in the Super 12 campaign.

"The Sharks ended up getting into the semi-finals, but they only just managed it, and they stood alone among the South African teams," recalls Mallett. "I knew that my big challenge for the year would be to get the Boks to believe they could win in Australia and New Zealand. André Venter had said to me that he had never won in four years of playing Super Rugby in Australia and New Zealand."

The Boks enjoyed an easy warm-up to the Tri-Nations, as the clubs in England would not release their contracted players for national duty and both Wales and England came to South Africa with under-strength teams. Ireland also undertook a short tour of the country, but it did very little good and was mostly just plain bad and ugly.

Solomons had coached Western Province against Ireland in a horrible wet-weather fixture where nothing seemed to happen from beginning to end. Afterwards, he said: "I think Ireland must be sponsored by Kit-Kat, because they were always taking a break in this game." An ad was running at the time that invited chocolate-eaters to "Have a break, have a Kit-Kat".

The Boks won easily enough against the Irish in the first Test of the year, in Bloemfontein. Stefan Terblanche scored four tries on debut, and that weekend I discovered that perhaps Mallett was a bit more sensitive to media criticism than he let on. It was the early hours of the morning and I was drinking at the Mystik Boer, one of my favourite pubs, when I bumped into Bok technical advisor Jake White. He told me he had a message for me from Mallett.

"Nick wants to know if after Stefan's four tries you still think James Small was treated unfairly," said White.

It is true, and I have said it before: I have never spared a negative word for any coach who has ever dropped James Small. But I hadn't exactly launched a venomous acerbic assault on Mallett either. So, perhaps fuelled by a tad too much red wine, I found myself at the Bok hotel at 3 a.m. on a Sunday morning asking the night porter if he could please go and wake Mallett up. It's a good thing he refused to do it – probably more so for me than for Nick.

If there was aggression in the air at the Bok hotel, it was nothing compared to Loftus the following week. Some referred to it as a good old-fashioned Test match, with sporadic fighting and brawling punctuating the 80 minutes of a game that the Boks won comfortably enough, but where all the memories must surely be of the bruises.

I let the Irish have it in my match report the next day, calling them a disgrace, but in my recent interview with Mallett he implied that perhaps I had condemned the wrong team.

"Ireland were determined to play off the ball, and Gary [Teichmann] was *klapped* in a ruck towards the end of the Bloemfontein Test. So the following week it was pay-back time and we hit them with the full fury of our physical game, and they just couldn't handle it. I can recall Irish players just repeatedly coming off the field to be attended to.

"It was brutal. But in retrospect I think it served a purpose, as I think we picked up a hard edge in that game that served us well moving forward. There were no TMOs or assistant referees in those days, or some of our players would have been in trouble."

The Boks fell just short of posting a three-figure score against the hapless Welsh the following week, and something similar was expected against a weakened England team that had been beaten by something like 80 points in Australia. But the day of the match coincided with one of those Cape Town winter storms, and it turned into a game memorable only for the fiery personal duel between James Dalton and Robert Cockrill, which ended with the two players embracing each other. The Boks won 18-0.

Much more had been expected, so Peter Jackson of the *Daily Mail* started off the post-match press conference by asking Mallett if he was disappointed.

"Why should I be disappointed? Your team got naught," growled Mallett.

As it turned out, that game was the perfect dress rehearsal for the first Tri-Nations game, which took place in equally inclement weather conditions in Perth. The Boks played poorly that day, but fortunately the Wallabies' Matt Burke was even worse with his goal-kicking. The Boks won, not by much, but they won, and it was their first overseas Tri-Nations win.

"The Wallaby side was building under Rod Macqueen, but maybe we didn't realise it at the time. Our guys were just nervous of losing, and it was one of those games you just couldn't take by the balls," says Mallett, who reckons the result could easily have gone the other way were it not for the good relationship he had built up with the referees.

"I can remember Ollie le Roux falling over on the wrong side and Paddy O'Brien could so easily have called against us and given the Wallabies a chance of winning. But in the New Zealand papers they were saying we were a changed team, and I think that makes a difference to the perception of the referees. Rugby is so much about the odd call going your way, and I believe that went our way because of how we conducted ourselves on and off the field."

At the Monday video session, held in Wellington, Mallett gave his players a right bollocking.

"I really tore into them in that session; you would have thought they had lost. But then, at the end of it, I changed my tone and said, 'By the way, well done, guys; you're the first Springbok team to win a Tri-Nations Test overseas.' I also told them it was the mark of a good team when you win playing badly."

During the flight from Australia to New Zealand, Mallett had called Henry Honiball over and asked him to think of a move that he would find difficult to defend, which could perhaps be tried against the All Blacks at Athletic Park. That conversation gave rise to the try that Pieter Rossouw would score to clinch South Africa's first win on New Zealand soil since 1981.

"It was extraordinary, and that success was entirely down to Henry. You've got to get things 100 per cent spot on to win in New Zealand; you have to produce a Ricky Januarie moment, and that was one of them."

Mallett invited the media into the change room afterwards. By then, I had toured New Zealand several times and only ever seen the Boks lose, so my eyes must have been moist, because Mallett later said he had noticed how much the win meant to me.

The return game against the All Blacks in Durban was irrelevant to the Tri-Nations standings, as the Ellis Park Test against Australia the following week would be the decider. The players were therefore not very motivated in the first half, and Mallett found himself giving his Boks another bollocking when they trailed New Zealand 5-17 at half-time.

They responded magnificently, and with the aid of some clever and well-timed substitutions, the Boks completed one of the great comebacks of modern rugby to win the match in the dying minutes.

"I told them they had to run every ball after half-time. It was great to see how they responded under pressure."

It was the perfect platform for the final match in Johannesburg, where Joost van der Westhuizen was tasked with putting pressure on Stephen Larkham, who in those days was new to the flyhalf position and was standing too deep.

Larkham was to get his own back the following year, but on that day the plan worked a charm, and Van der Westhuizen played one of his finest games for the Boks. Mallett had reason to feel satisfied as he and the players celebrated South Africa's first Tri-Nations title after a comfortable 29-15 win.

As Mallett recalls: "Up till then I'd had no interference from the administrators, perhaps because we were winning, and the press were all supporting me. In those days, some of you guys were referring to me as St Nicholas, which was embarrassing, but they were good days."

But for how long ...?

14

A breakdown of trust

Nick Mallett's big chest was heaving as he listened to my question. It was a bright, even sunny afternoon in Cardiff, and he had just participated in a game of touch rugby with his team. He's always competitive, so he was pent up.

But I had a job to do. I was in Wales at the expense of the Independent Group, and the *Cape Times* was part of their stable. Louis Neethling, the sports editor, had called me in my hotel room in the Marriott before the training session and said that they wanted, as a matter of urgency, a reaction from the Springbok management to a political storm that had blown up back home.

Two black players, Breyton Paulse and Deon Kayser, had each scored a hat-trick of tries in a series against Italy back in South Africa, and yet only Paulse was on the tour. And even Paulse wasn't named in the team for the match against Wales, which was to be played in honour of the opening of the new Millennium Stadium on the Saturday. Neethling told me the ANC politicians back home were jumping up and down, wanting to know what was going on. So were some of the SARFU administrators.

"I will not be pushed around on this issue," Mallett gasped between breaths. "I feel very strongly about it."

And thus he started the speech that led to my story, which was run under the headline "Mallett Married to Merit", being published as the front-page lead in the *Cape Times* the next day. Reading the article now, and knowing the details of his contract, Mallett was not being unreasonable.

"There is no way I will ever take part in anything that can be construed as window dressing. The reason Kayser did not play in the Port Elizabeth Test and only came on as a replacement at Kings Park was that I did not feel he was quite ready for Test action. When he is, he will play. Every player in the team must know that he deserves his place and is strictly there on merit. I don't ever want to see Paulse or Kayser being in a position where they might feel they owe their place in the team to anything other than rugby ability. The fact [that] they are black must have nothing to do with their chances of playing for the Boks."

Perhaps it was my introductory line that got the politicians back home into such a lather: "Springbok coach Nick Mallett has a simple message for those who are dissatisfied with the lack of black representation in the national team: he will not be pushed around and told whom to select."

Both the administrators and the politicians like to think that they *can* tell a coach who to select. And boy, did they get jumpy after that story appeared. Britain is only one hour behind our time in summer, but it still felt way too early when my cellphone started buzzing. One of the first callers was Rian Oberholzer. He wanted to verify that I had quoted Nick accurately before taking any action himself. He'd been feeling the heat since early that morning.

"I had a call from John Ncinane [ANC MP and SARFU executive member] earlier, and he wanted to know what I was going to do about this," Oberholzer told me. "He said to me that 'When Nick Mallett was sitting in Constantia eating his bacon and eggs, my people were on Robben Island breaking stones.'"

I understood Oberholzer's plight. Even fellow SARFU employees, such as Sas Bailey, were criticising Mallett's stance publicly. The upshot was that, within 24 hours of the story hitting the streets, Mallett issued an apology, and Oberholzer flew to Cardiff to read the riot act to him and the team. He felt that everyone in the Bok squad should be apprised of SARFU's transformation policy.

Oberholzer has often been painted as the bad guy in the whole sorry saga, but I will always come up for him, because I knew that he was under tremendous pressure. He'd told me some time during the week that there would never again be an all-white Bok team, and I wrote it. Dan Retief somehow came up with a story that Sunday claiming that my information was incorrect, at the same time implying that Oberholzer had been misquoted. So it was my turn to make an angry call, to Oberholzer, who said he had told Retief no such thing, and reiterated what he had disclosed to me. And unless I've missed something somewhere, what Oberholzer said then has proved correct.

It was Mallett's first exposure to political pressure, and the first time that a Springbok coach had come under such pressure in an overt way. The events of 1998, when Louis Luyt lost his position as SARFU president, were partly to blame. Luyt had set the sequence of events in motion when he threatened to take the country's president, Nelson Mandela, to court to challenge his government's decision to set up a commission to investigate alleged racism in rugby. It would culminate in the SARFU board passing a vote of no confidence in Luyt's leadership.

The way in which Luyt had handled that controversy meant that rugby, and what was being done to promote transformation agendas, was attracting more intense scrutiny. When Luyt was removed from his position, Oberholzer became the man driving South African rugby.

"Louis only lasted for a short time during my reign," Mallett recalls, "and the one good thing was that he never interfered. He was like a supporter. He got incensed when the team didn't do well. But he left in early 1998 at a time when my team was yet to lose a Test.

"Once he was removed, the political stuff started happening. I knew that there was strong political pressure being brought to bear and I understood the drive for transformation. Rian was running [SARFU] and he was a good administrator who kept things going, but it must have been a very difficult job. He was used to Louis driving everything, and then suddenly *he* was, and he had to handle the political fallout after the whole Mandela issue.

"He was perhaps more savvy about politics, but I had been appointed to select [my team] on merit, and ironically it was Rian who had directed the lawyers to place that clause in my contract, perhaps because they thought I would want to select too many black players."

Oberholzer addressed the players before the Wales Test, and he made it clear that they were not immune to the realities of their own country. He was right, of course, but maybe he should have waited till after the Test. The defeat in Cardiff, the first ever to Wales, will forever be blamed on his interference.

Another enduring perception of that week in Cardiff is that it was the beginning of the end of Mallett's 1999 World Cup campaign. As Van der Valk said, Oberholzer's speech to the players in the build-up to the Test was rugby's equivalent of P.W. Botha's Rubicon speech in 1985. In other words, once his words were uttered, nothing could ever be the same again ... and there was no turning back.

But I think a proper analysis will show that the campaign had probably started veering off course long before that. The first false notes in Mallett's tenure had, in fact, been recorded in the weeks building up to a Test against England on a cold November afternoon a few months before.

It was at Twickenham that the unbeaten run of victories under Mallett came to an end, thus thwarting the quest for what would have been a record-winning sequence of 18 matches. The record of 17 consecutive Test victories still stands, and is shared by an All Black team of the 1960s.

Mallett's selections on that tour started to create uncertainty among the players and, in the end, would lead to the breakdown of the relationship between coach and players. And it all centred round his high regard for Bob Skinstad's talent.

"Bob had enjoyed a really good year in 1998 and he had helped us swing many games our way when he came on as a sub," Mallett explains. "He had been in outstanding form for Western Province at the end of the Currie Cup season. I had a one-on-one with him at the start of that tour where I told him he would be getting a lot of game time as a sub. He said he understood that, but he also made an interesting point. He said that he knew I was very loyal to the team and wanted to retain a winning team, but he asked how many of the games I would have won if he hadn't come on.

"He wasn't being arrogant at all. He was just making it clear that he didn't just want to be buttonholed as an impact player. He was making the point that he would like to get a chance to start, and I understood that."

After a less than convincing win over Wales at Wembley at the start of the tour, Mallett felt the time had come to make the call. In fact, he made a double call, as he brought both Skinstad and Christian Stewart into the starting team. Both players just happened to play for Western Province and were English-speaking, while the two players being dropped, André Venter and Franco Smith, were Afrikaans-speaking.

This was before the Test in Edinburgh against Scotland, and as a journalist I immediately sensed the disquiet that seemed to settle on the squad. Former Springbok hooker Uli Schmidt was on the tour as a television commentator, and he and I became quite friendly during that trip. He knew a few players in the squad really well, and he told me that they were not happy. The big bone of contention was Venter's axing – he had been a Springbok stalwart for some time.

Alan Solomons was the Stormers coach by then, which fuelled speculation that he was having too much influence on the Bok team. It was no secret that he and Skinstad, who by then had become his WP and Stormers captain, were extremely close.

As Mallett recalls: "I don't think it was a problem for the players when Solly was just the assistant coach at WP and the Stormers. But that may have changed when he became head coach of the Stormers. I am not saying Solly did anything wrong; just that the players from other provinces naturally started to get a bit resentful. Maybe the principle of having a Bok coach who was also coaching a franchise and a provincial team was wrong. For instance, I know Solly was eager to get Mark Andrews to move to Province, and that caused a massive rift with Ian McIntosh.

"I was never influenced by Solly, and he never put pressure on me. But he also would not have been doing his job if he didn't let me know his views on some things. He was an intelligent guy, and he saw that we had a problem with the freshness of the players on that tour. He wanted the best results for the team and would come at me with a counter-argument that we shouldn't carry on with the same team just because we were unbeaten."

The Bok players were tired on that tour, and it showed in their performances. The Test matches against Home Union opposition were not won nearly as convincingly as had been the case on the 1997 tour, and the possibility of a Grand Slam began to seem increasingly unlikely.

At the same time, the second-string team was winning all their games by massive margins.

"[On that tour], I should really have done what the All Blacks started doing years later, by playing two mixed teams. We had the talent to do it; our B team was excellent. I should have mixed and matched the selections and told the players that they would each play two Test matches."

In doing so, Mallett would have ensured that the players were fresh the following year, and it would also have given the Boks a better chance of beating England. Dropping Venter would then not have been seen as such a big deal, as it would have been part of a pre-agreed plan. And Mallett would not have had to face allegations that he was "anti-Afrikaans".

On that last point, Mallett could have helped his cause by not discussing the differences between the English and Afrikaans players quite so openly with the media.

"Look, you should never generalise, but at that time the English guys had better communication skills. I think I was construed to have said they are more intelligent, but that wasn't the case at all," Mallett says. "I would always pick an Afrikaans guy for his courage and durability. I would back an Afrikaans guy not to miss a tackle before I'd back an English player. But when it came to communication, I felt the Afrikaans players fell short, whereas the English guys excelled. The English players were more used to having their say, whereas the Afrikaans players had been brought up in a far more [authoritarian] school environment where you are taught to listen to your captain, your father and your church.

"But those times have changed, and now it's very different. When I coached a Barbarians team against the All Blacks a few years ago, some of the more recent Boks [were in my team], and I was amazed at how different [they were]."

Mallett was aware of the fact that some of the media people on that end-of-year tour thought he was biased against Afrikaners. And if he didn't know it, I could have told him. In Dublin, I had a heated discussion with the normally likeable Hennie Brandt of *Beeld*, who for some reason felt I should answer for Mallett's conduct.

We were in the hotel bar and we were loud enough for other people in the vicinity to stop what they were doing and stare at us. The situation was defused when I asked Hennie what *he* could do about it, and what he thought *I* could do about it. He looked at me, smiled, and said, "Well, there's probably nothing."

We carried on drinking without mentioning the subject again. It was obviously on Mallett's mind, though, for towards the end of the trip, when we were in London, Mike Greenaway and I were dancing through puddles en route to the team hotel in the West End when we suddenly heard a voice bark at us: "Hey, so are the *English* press out having fun in the rain?"

It was Mallett, who was smiling at us from a taxi.

But he wasn't smiling when, almost inevitably, his team relinquished their unbeaten record in the Twickenham gloom. Pieter Rossouw scored a try, but the team looked jaded and listless as a remarkable year came to an end in a most disappointing way (they lost 7-13). If Mallett was unhappy, some young South African lady, an expatriate living in London, was almost inconsolable. Standing next to me at the Harlequins club at Twickenham waiting for a drink, she was in a tearful telephone exchange with a boyfriend somewhere.

"Listen, baby, I'm not looking for shit with you, but that was a really stupid question. The Boks lost today, so how the hell do you think *I* might be feeling?" she wailed as the river of tears down her cheeks intensified. The passion that some South Africans have for rugby often exceeds the sensible.

Mallett was quickly made aware of that fact when a journalist told him that he would get hammered once he got back home. And he was, even though it was his first defeat in 17 starts. The uncertainties that had started to emerge from within the playing squad condemned Mallett to a fitful summer of introspection.

Was the team too old and was it time for a renewal? It was a fair question, for teams do operate in cycles. And the Bok first-choice team had by then played a lot of rugby together.

But it wasn't just the playing staff that Mallett was concerned about. The relationship between Alan Solomons and Jake White had also started to unravel. As White wrote in his book, one evening on tour he and Mallett were out, enjoying a beer, when the coach broached the subject of Venter and Skinstad, and told him that he was going to drop Venter. When he asked White for his opinion, he gave the coach a straight answer: "I think you're making a hell of a mistake. I think the team needs Venter."

Then, a while later, Solomons came in for a beer too, and Mallett told him that he was going to play Skinstad, but that White didn't think it was a good idea. White wrote that he could see Solomons didn't like the advice he had given.

With the benefit of knowing that White would go on to coach the Boks to World Cup glory, Mallett reckons that it worked out for the best when White left his management team.

"Jake [left] because of Solly, who gave me an ultimatum and said it was either him or Jake. I was in a difficult situation, but I chose Solly, because Jake was employed to be the video guy but wanted to be a coach. So I went to Rian to see if we could sort Jake out with the under-21 job. At least then he would be doing what he wanted to do."

It wasn't an inconsequential event for the players, though. Especially for the players from the north, as White was an ally in a Cape-dominated management team.

Interestingly, Heyneke Meyer replaced White in the management group. These days that would hardly elicit accusations of Cape bias, but at the time Meyer was assistant coach at the Stormers. Indeed, as the year wore on, the perception grew that the Boks were being run by what had become known as the Cape Cabal, and apparently even Mark Keohane and I were at times alleged to be a part of this select group because we supposedly supported the coaches and wrote pro-Cape stories.

Mallett spent the summer months mulling over the Teichmann/Skinstad conundrum, but by then he had resolved that if Skinstad was going to play, it would be at No. 8.

"I was very shaky on whether Gary would be able to make the World Cup, but I wasn't going to replace him straight after the Super 12, which is what he contended in his book," Mallett says. "What I wanted to do was give both Gary and Bob a chance to prove themselves during the pre-season Tests. As it turned out, though, they both ended up getting injured. Bob had a car accident in which his knee was injured, and Gary was suffering [from] 36 months of non-stop rugby.

"In retrospect, I was foolishly looking only at rugby-playing ability and not at how important the captaincy was in the South African context. In this country, if you have a good captain – like Teichmann, François Pienaar or John Smit – you must stick with them, even if they show a dip in form. The relationship between team and captain, and captain and coach, is extremely important here, which I realise now.

"And if you are not sure about the captain, the players get nervous and start feeling insecure, as I know my players did when my relationship with Gary started to break down. It all happened because of my concern about Gary's form. I even phoned Ian Mac and asked him to please not play Gary for the Sharks because he needed a six-week break. Mac's answer was that I coach the Boks and he coaches Natal."

Teichmann never felt secure during the1999 season, as Mallett would neither talk to nor confide in him as before. In the week building up to the Brisbane Test of that year's Tri-Nations, Teichmann even chided me for writing too much about the condition of the players.

"You're just fuelling Nick's concerns and making it easier for him to drop me," he told me. Teichmann was injured and not playing in that Test. I accompanied Teichmann and Mark Andrews to a pool hall across the road from the team hotel and let them have their say, and neither of them made any secret that they thought Mallett had lost the plot.

And in some ways, he had. Even before he axed Teichmann, he was not coping very well with events on and off the field.

Says Mallett: "That year, 1999, was really difficult, and that period when I was not coaching but only watching only added to the uncertainty. Skinstad was outstanding for the Stormers, who were top of the Super 12 [log] for much of the way. [The Boks] beat Italy, but you can't really gauge where you stand when you play against them. Then, after the Durban Test, where we won 101-0, the SARFU president criticised me for not playing Breyton Paulse and Deon Kayser in both Tests and not taking Deon on tour.

"A combination of [factors] sullied my relationship with SARFU. Up till then they had left me alone, but then they stopped leaving me alone. I didn't take kindly to it. After the big win over Italy, they offered to extend my contract by two years. With Rob and Solly present, I asked Rian Oberholzer to bring my contract to Wales when he came over and I would sign it then.

"But when he did come over, it wasn't for the contract. He came over to say that this would be the last all-white team. The players were very upset. Those guys had won all but one game for me over a period of two years; it was astounding that [SARFU] just didn't let me get on with it. That loss to Wales was without any doubt attributable to the attitude of the players.

"I wasn't aware of what the country wanted. I wasn't too politically aware at the time. I really thought transformation would happen from the schools upwards, instead of the other way round. I was facing the pressure of having to win while being told I was anti-Afrikaans, anti-black and even, on one occasion, anti-Christian.

"My [original] contract said I had the right to pick on merit, but [now] they were shifting the goalposts. Rian told me I could pick an all-white team, but I wouldn't have the support of SARFU or the Minister of Sport. It was a hell of a thing to put on the shoulders of a 42-year-old coach trying to do the best for his country."

The clause that gave Mallett sole charge of selection, on merit, was not in the contract he was offered in 1999. Instead, it had been replaced with a new clause that said Mallett must be "sensitive to the policies of SARFU".

Mallett and Oberholzer had a showdown about this in Cardiff, and it was ugly. Mallett claimed that Oberholzer was lying to him, as Oberholzer claimed never to have promised him an extension of the same contract. Van der Valk, however, reckons that the SARFU chief was caught between a rock and a hard place, as he had not been authorised to make Mallett any promises. Oberholzer declined the opportunity to give his side of the story when it was offered to him, but Van der Valk's gut feel is probably spot on. Remember, a similar thing had happened with Carel du Plessis' contract.

"I just couldn't believe Rian could lie with such a straight face. I kept telling him there were two guys who had heard him talking in Durban. I asked him how he could live with himself," says Mallett. "After that there was a complete break between me and the administrators. I told them to get on with administering rugby, which I told them they weren't doing particularly well."

The issue continued for weeks, and although the contentious matters were eventually settled in Mallett's favour, he never got back a cent from the R200 000 he spent on legal fees. It was hardly a working relationship conducive to success in a World Cup year.

After Wales, the Boks flew back to South Africa for a short break before departing for New Zealand for the start of the Tri-Nations. After a few days' leave in the UK, I flew to New Zealand from Heathrow – actually, the journey started in the Outer Hebrides – via Bangkok and Sydney.

About an hour out of Bangkok, the pilot of the Qantas 747 warned us that we were about to encounter "a little bit of weather". If that was a little bit of weather, I hope never to encounter "a lot" of weather. But it was still nothing compared to what the Boks experienced in New Zealand, where they lost 0-28 in Dunedin.

Afterwards, Mallett criticised his new halfback pairing of Dave von Hoesslin and Gaffie du Toit, but he admits now that he should never have done so.

"I spoke about the [lack of] experience of the halfbacks after that Dunedin Test, and then the next thing all the headlines were saying I [was blaming] Von Hoesslin and Du Toit for the defeat. I thought I was just stating the obvious, but I should never have done that, and I have learnt from that mistake."

As the rain fell on Dunedin in the week leading up the game, I was awoken early one morning by a New Zealand television crew who wanted to interview me about South African rugby. They set up their equipment in my room and I was asked several questions over a period of about 20 minutes. Most of what I said was middle-of-the-road stuff – I didn't think I was having a go at Mallett or the Springboks.

But that night, on the news, they ran just one sound bite: "Sometimes in South African rugby it does seem that saying a player is too small is a euphemism for saying he is too black."

Team manager Arthob Petersen saw me in the hotel bar. "The man is hopping mad at you," he said.

Alex Broun was more dramatic: "Gav, you've really done it this time," he whined.

I wanted to explain myself and I didn't care what time it was. I demanded that Broun allow me access to Mallett. Initially he advised against it, as he said that Mallett was too cross. But I insisted, and I eventually made my way up to Mallett's room, where he was chatting with Solomons and Van der Valk.

I told my side of the story and then shared some of my views, and it ended up being quite an interesting debate. The Bok management told me that they agreed with South Africa's opposition party, the Democratic Alliance (DA), who said that players should be selected on merit only. I reminded them that no matter what they thought, the DA wasn't the majority party and, as Springboks, they represented the whole of South Africa.

So we agreed to disagree on a few things. I suggested to Mallett that he appoint a sort of "political commissar" to help him navigate the minefields he would clearly start encountering from then on. He disagreed with me, so it was interesting when I interviewed him in Knysna in 2013 and he admitted that it had been a mistake not to have employed a liaison officer with more political nous to help him.

"Alex was good at what he did, but what I really needed was someone more senior who had greater understanding of South Africa and its politics. Andy Colquhoun is working as the strategic communications manager at SARU now, and someone in that position would have been perfect back then. It would have helped free up more of my time to do what I thought I had been employed to do – which was to coach a winning rugby team."

Not that Mallett was too confident that he was coaching a winning team at the time we met in his hotel room in 1999. After a while Van der Valk and Solomons took their leave and Nick and I carried on talking until the early hours of the morning. As I got ready to leave too, he asked me which team I thought would win the Test match. Aware that I was speaking to the Springbok coach, I thought I had to say *his* team had a chance.

But he scoffed at my reply.

"Not a chance. This team has been overplayed, and the young guys are too inexperienced. I think the All Blacks will win quite comfortably, and then I will have to start a clean-out."

It turned out just as he said it would.

15

It's tickets for the coach

Recalling the events of that time, Nick Mallett now considers his decision to leave Gary Teichmann out of the 1999 World Cup squad to have been wrong on a few fronts, and not just because the Springboks needed a good captain.

"Firstly, Bob Skinstad, the man I had wanted to bring in at No. 8 in [Teichmann's] place, was doubtful. I had sought medical opinion and was told Bob would be ready for the World Cup, but that proved to be optimistic. [Whenever the Boks are] successful, it is because [they] play with confidence and without self-doubt. That [much was evident] in my first few years [as coach], when Teichmann was captain. Everyone felt settled. But then I made decisions that undermined that confidence.

"I offered the captaincy to Rassie Erasmus. He was really my only choice as captain. I never imagined he would turn the captaincy down. But he did. And I never really had an alternative."

Joost van der Westhuizen was the only option left to Mallett.

"Joost was a fantastic rugby player, but as a captain, he and I were never on the same wavelength. It was the wrong decision all round. It was a rudderless team, unfortunately ..."

Mallett sparked a major media controversy when he dropped Teichmann. And because I'd had that conversation with Teichmann on the eve of the Brisbane Tri-Nations Test, I felt I had perhaps let him down in some way.

In my line of work, there's a fine boundary between what type of criticism is acceptable and what is not, and for a while I might have lost my head in the same way Mallett did. When the Boks lost to New Zealand at Loftus in the first game of the home leg of the Tri-Nations, I was too busy filing copy after the match to make it to the post-match cocktail party. However, Mike Greenaway conveyed the message that he had bumped into Nick's brother,

Dave, a man I have not met to this day, and apparently he was eager to see me as he felt my criticism of Nick was getting too personal.

Maybe he was right.

Teichmann's axing was officially announced at a SARFU press conference. Rian Oberholzer said that the Boks had been appalling and someone had to go. I asked the first question: "If that is the case, shouldn't the coach also have to go?"

Rian was unable to answer the question.

I wasn't the only one critising Mallett, though; his popularity was waning everywhere. According to Van der Valk, the Brisbane match, which a depleted Bok team lost 6-32, marked the moment when Mallett cut himself off from the rest of the management team. After that game, he was unapproachable – no one could talk to him or offer an opinion. The players no longer knew where they stood with him.

Mark Andrews remembers it as a particularly trying period: "I was incredibly impressed with Nick when he first took over. When he came in as the head coach, you immediately felt that he was going to build something special. He had amazing energy and a huge passion for the game. He was also highly intelligent. In fact, he was strong in all areas. My first year and a half under Nick was fantastic. You could argue and debate with him about aspects of second-row play. He was easy to play for. He was focused and driven, and had it together in all aspects of coaching.

"But then he had this brain fart and, brilliant as he had been, he suddenly became horrendous. He was arrogant, narcissistic and condescending. I suppose there is a fine line between arrogance and confidence. Nick crossed that line during this period. He just became a law unto himself. He verbally abused Percy Montgomery during a video session, calling him an airhead.

"I went to Teich and said, 'You have to stop this guy, he's breaking the team down.' Then I went to Nick himself. We were at the Crowne Plaza in Sandton. I said to him that he couldn't keep talking like [that], always swearing at us, and his response was that I shouldn't think I could tell him how he could or couldn't speak. Later, at a training session, we almost came to blows. It was a complete contrast to how he had been before. After that, our relationship broke down completely."

Today, Mallett takes any criticism of his behaviour back then on the chin. It's a period he regrets. Earlier in 1999, his sister, Jenny, had suddenly passed away, as did his father-in-law. At the time, Andrews heard about a story circulating in Cape Town that the death of Mallett's sister in particular had put a lot of strain on him and had impacted on his personality. Whatever had caused the personality change, today Mallett agrees that he had started to feel the pressure.

"It was just a really tough situation," he admits, "and different people handle pressure differently. My reaction was to fight back at anyone who disagreed with me on the basis that if I didn't respect their rugby opinion, why must I worry about what they think?

"I did feel cornered. My relationship with Rian Oberholzer had broken down. You can't rescue [a relationship] when you've told a guy he's a liar. And then there was the media. I had your support, as well as Mark Keohane's in my first years, but then I lost both of you. I just wanted someone in my corner pushing my case, but there was no one. I made mistakes, lots of mistakes. Some were of my own making; others were because of the pressure, because I felt backed into a corner.

"How do you survive when under such pressure? One of the things I most admired about Jake White was his ability to handle the pressure. What was extraordinary about him was that he wasn't confrontational in a conflict situation, or at least he didn't give that impression. He seemed to be able to listen to people and take what they were saying on board. I just immediately went on the attack."

As well as being on the receiving end of vitriolic criticism for dropping Teichmann, Mallett was also forced to focus on race issues. Every time he didn't select Breyton Paulse to start, the rumblings increased. And the criticism wasn't just coming from the media.

After Teichmann was dropped and before the Pretoria Test against the All Blacks, Mallett phoned Oberholzer, who told him he could pick his strongest team. Mallett therefore picked Stefan Terblanche, but then President Thabo Mbeki informed SARFU that he would attend the match and pay a visit to the squad. As a result, Oberholzer phoned Mallett and told him he would have to make a change. And so Terblanche was effectively selected and then dropped. The All Blacks won that Test 34-18, and they weren't even playing that well.

A scrappy but much-needed win over Australia in Cape Town followed, and the Boks then gathered for a two-week pre–World Cup training camp in Plettenberg Bay.

"I sensed [that] the players were unhappy to be without Gary Teichmann," Mallett recalls, "but we started to feel more like a united team again as we left for the World Cup, and I believe that if Henry Honiball had been available for the entire tournament, we might have done better than we did."

"Better" would have meant reaching the final, because the Boks came third. They were denied a place in the final only by a Stephen Larkham drop goal in the semi-final against the Wallabies at Twickenham, and that in extra time. It had, however, not been plain sailing up till that point. Mallett agrees that a night on the tiles after the Uruguay game had probably inspired the win over England in the quarter-final.

"You Are Bloody Useless", read the headline in newspapers back home after the dreadful Uruguay game in Glasgow. Mike Greenaway had heard Mallett letting rip at his troops from the coach's box. And they *were* bloody useless.

However, the Boks might just have needed some kind of release. I remember Ollie le Roux popping into the hotel bar and telling me that there was nothing some Red Bull and vodka couldn't put right. The Boks were going to spend the night on the town, and that is what they did.

"It was a big blow-out where the guys let their hair down, and I do think it brought everyone together," says Mallett. "The guys hadn't drunk any alcohol since the camp in Plett had finished six weeks earlier. I said to Rassie and the player leaders that maybe the guys should go out and have a big party, and they didn't need a second invitation. The management left the piss-up after about three or four beers, but I know the guys really let rip that night and it brought them together.

"The guys really acquitted themselves well in the quarter-final in Paris, which they needed to do because I think the referee, Jim Fleming, wanted England to win. At one stage, one of the southern hemisphere touch judges told André Venter, while we were standing behind the posts when England were attempting a kick, that we would have to spend as much of the game as possible in England territory, as the ref was determined to blow us off the park."

That, of course, was the match in which Jannie de Beer slotted five spectacular drop goals for the Springboks to beat England 44-21. De Beer was dubbed the "boot of God" when he was misquoted during the post-match press conference. He had said, "God gave us this victory," and the British media then reported that he had said God had "chosen" the Springboks to win the match. The real inspiration behind the drop goals, though, was closer to home: Mallett gives De Beer's Cheetahs teammate Brendan Venter much of the credit for the flyhalf's freaky match-winning performance.

"The squad spent a day playing golf, and I was in a four-ball with Brendan. I said to Brendan that I was having great trouble trying to figure out how to get Jannie to play my way. He was standing so deep and we were getting tackled behind the gain line.

"Brendan reminded me that De Beer was a great goal-kicker, and suggested maybe I shouldn't try to get him to play a game that he was unfamiliar with. He suggested instead that I should devise a game plan where we set targets for him and let him play to his strengths. Three or four of those drop goals came from set plays. After those five drop goals, the IRB wanted to change the laws of the game to prevent it from happening again."

De Beer's performance left Mallett in a quandary ahead of the semi-final against Australia. Henry Honiball, whom Mallett rated highly, was fit to play, and he was tempted to select the Natalian. But Honiball made up Mallett's mind for him by telling him that he had to stick with De Beer. Mallett was confounded by Honiball's sense of team spirit and sportsmanship, as indeed he was when De Beer, after the Boks had lost the semi-final, told Mallett that the team needed a cause to play for in the third/fourth-place play-off game, and that he should select Honiball.

"There was a missed opportunity for us in that semi-final that has never been spoken about," says Mallett. "I had told Joost that there would come a time when he would be able to throw a dummy and go right through. We had it all worked out how it would go from there and, sure enough, it happened just before the end of extra time. Joost threw a dummy, went through, drew the fullback and passed to Os. Had he passed to Pieter Rossouw, he would have scored.

"Instead Os tried to go on his own, and nine times out of 10 he would have just run over George Gregan, but Gregan just went straight for the ball and managed to dislodge it. Poor Os was distraught after that, and we had to console him in the change room, as the tears just poured down his face. That was when Jannie came up to me and thanked me for the opportunity and suggested I play Henry, who would not have played a World Cup match had he not started in the play-off game."

Breyton Paulse also started in that game, at fullback, and he scored a great individualistic try that helped the Boks beat the All Blacks in a second successive World Cup, albeit not at the stage of the competition where they would have liked to have done it.

The skipper, Joost van der Westhuizen, stared down the media at the press conference afterwards and reminded us all that we had said the Boks would fail. But after the success of 1995 it *was* a failure. And some players in the squad certainly felt they could have achieved a lot more had Mallett not chosen 1999 as the year to contract Mad Coaches Disease.

Mark Andrews, for one, is convinced that if Mallett had just stuck to what he was doing and retained Teichmann as his captain, the Boks would have won the World Cup.

As he puts it: "As much as Kitch coached above his ability for us to win the World Cup in 1995, so Mallett lost us the World Cup by going beneath his abilities in 1999. What makes it hard about Mallett is that he was so good and then he became so poor. Carel was never great and just shouldn't have been [in the job], so I have no ill feeling towards him. With Mallett it is so much harder because he had so much to offer, and when he went south, it felt like a betrayal."

However, third place in the World Cup, and a win over New Zealand in the last game, was enough to save Mallett his job. But he would have known at the start of 2000 that he faced a different challenge to any he'd had to handle up till then. With Henry Honiball retiring and Teichmann having left for Wales, 1999 was effectively the end of an era.

And Skinstad, the great young hope Mallett had been so excited about 12 months earlier, confirmed after the World Cup that he had returned to rugby too early and would not be able to play for a year.

South African rugby, it seemed, had gone over the crest of a hill, and Mallett would feel the effects of the trough that followed – as would the two coaches who succeeded him in quick succession.

"I have changed a lot since 1999," Mallett says now, "and there are a lot of things I would never do again, but even in 2000 I had learnt a lot from the mistakes I had made in 1999. I was a lot less critical of the players, and I knew that, from a talent viewpoint, we were up against it. I decided to turn it into a similar situation to the one I had faced at Boland in my first big job in South Africa. We were going into every game as the underdogs determined to make a point."

But Mallett also felt that it was an opportunity to develop a new way of playing, and he made no secret of how impressed he was with the Brumbies' style of play. So when he made the decision to relieve Joost van der Westhuizen of the captaincy, old Selbornian André Vos found himself taking the reins of a Springbok team that was starting out on yet another new path.

There was a regulation victory over Canada in East London at the start of the international season, with John Smit making his debut, and then it was on to Pretoria, where the Boks scraped home against England. The Boks had actually looked quite impressive in the first 20 minutes, indicating that they may be ready to run England off their feet, but injuries in the midfield robbed them of their momentum.

The following week they played England in Bloemfontein against the backdrop of the Hansie Cronjé match-fixing hearings, which were being broadcast on television. The constant revelations that emerged from that sordid affair deflected some of the attention from the Boks. But what did attract attention was the number of Stormers players in the team – there were 11 – which naturally drew a lot of criticism from the media up north.

And the criticism only intensified after England smashed the Bok forwards. The visitors actually deserved to win by more than their final score of 27-20. For some inexplicable reason I drove back to Cape Town from Bloemfontein the next day, and when I stopped in Colesberg for breakfast, I overheard a couple of farmers who were reading *Rapport* give vent to their anti-Mallett sentiments.

Apart from a brief respite when the Boks pulled off an excellent win over New Zealand at Ellis Park, Mallett would remain under both the media and the public's cosh for the next few months. At that time, the Independent Group decided that I needed a break, so I took the opportunity to head to the Algarve in Portugal instead of going on the away leg of the Tri-Nations, as I had the previous five years. While I was eating grilled sardines and drinking beer on the beach, I remember thinking that I probably wasn't missing anything.

I watched the Australian game on television, and it reminded me of the title of a Shakespeare play, *Much Ado about Nothing*. Although the Boks won a lot more possession than they were used to getting in an away Test, they went through phase after phase without gaining any territory or ever looking like they might break through the defence. Australia won comfortably.

By the time the Boks got to Ellis Park, rumours were again doing the rounds that Mallett was at the crossroads. But then the Springboks managed to pull off that great win against the All Blacks. Because of injuries, Robbie Fleck played at inside centre (he was normally an outside centre), and early on in the game it seemed as if he cut through the All Black defence every time he touched the ball. At one point the Boks led by 20 points before eventually winning 46-40.

Former All Black coach Laurie Mains, who was coaching the Lions and Cats at the time, observed rather tellingly that Mallett had learnt from his mistakes and appeared to be adjusting to a mix of the new way and the old.

But in South African rugby, you don't get a chance to learn from your mistakes for long if you hack off the administrators along the way … Mallett recalls that quite early in the year a journalist from *Rapport* had told him that word from the top had it that he would not be allowed to survive the season.

And then Mallett handed his enemies their opportunity. It happened after the Friday team photograph was taken in Durban ahead of the final Tri-Nations Test of 2000, against the Wallabies. In conversation with a supposed supporter, Mallett made a few off-the-cuff remarks about ticket prices, and then all hell broke loose.

As Mallett recalls: "At the start of 2000, I had been concerned that maybe I had lost the change room because of the Gary situation, but if that was the case, I felt that during the course of that season I won the players back. Ultimately, that's the most important thing for a coach. It's what you measure yourself by. I had wanted to introduce a Brumbies type of game, because in those days our defence wasn't great. Holding on to the ball was a way of minimising the opposition's attacking opportunities. I also felt the beginning of a four-year cycle [leading] to the next World Cup was the time to start something new, if that was your intention.

"It didn't go well initially, but I never expected it to. We were some way behind New Zealand and Australia by that time. But I felt we had started to find the right balance in the home leg of the Tri-Nations, and I will never forget the devastation I felt after the Stirling Mortlock kick in the last minute won the Durban game for the Wallabies.

"Joe Roff was holding the ball on the ground and Australia should never have been awarded the penalty that set up that kick, but by that stage [my exit] was already done and dusted.

"I had spoken to that person about the ticket prices, and when I saw the story the next day quoting me saying that the tickets were too expensive, I knew that I was done for. [The woman I spoke to] said she was a photographer, but [she] never took any notes when I spoke to her and she never asked if she could quote me, which I know is common practice among journalists.

"When I saw the story in the papers I phoned Rian, and he said don't worry about it, you have a game to prepare for. But at the cocktail party after the game you could see all the officials huddling in the corner. I told Solly and Rob that it was over."

And it was. Kim Robinson of the *Independent* never did identify herself as a reporter, and Mallett was going to argue at his disciplinary hearing that he thought he was having a private conversation. Rob van der Valk agreed that Mallett could only have been telling the truth when he said he didn't know he was talking to a reporter – he was far too savvy to have said something so controversial for public consumption.

Before the disciplinary hearing could take place, Mallett realised that the board wanted him gone, and he lost heart for the fight. We journalists waited to hear the outcome in the foyer of the Sport Science Institute building in Newlands, where the SARFU offices were at the time and where the hearing took place, but there was no air of anticipation. It had been made clear when we arrived that Mallett had agreed to resign.

Later that week I had a conversation with Corné Krige, who rated Mallett highly as a coach. His reaction to Mallett's departure was: "This is going to be chaos."

How right he was.

16

Recruited off a yacht

A few things made Harry Viljoen unique among Springbok coaches, not the least among them the fact that he negotiated his contract with SARFU from the deck of his own private yacht in the Mediterranean.

Viljoen, who made his fortune in the financial services industry, had enough money to pay the entire Bok management out of his own pocket if he wanted to. Many believed that his wealth was his biggest stumbling block to being a successful Springbok coach.

I met Viljoen in my first season of rugby writing in 1991, while watching a Transvaal captain's practice at Kings Park on the Friday before a match against Natal. We stood on the side of the field chatting, and I found him both friendly and personable.

According to Nick Mallett, Ian McIntosh was the only truly "modern" South African coach of that era, but in terms of what he achieved with his team, Viljoen wasn't too far off the mark. While McIntosh's Natal team was known for "direct rugby", the media described Transvaal's free-flowing approach as "total rugby".

Viljoen took Transvaal to two consecutive Currie Cup finals after they had been in the wilderness for years, and it's probably fair to say that he laid the foundations Kitch Christie would later build on to take the union to their first Currie Cup title in 21 years.

The former scrumhalf – Viljoen made his debut for Transvaal at the age of 19 – started coaching Natal in 1993, after Ian McIntosh had been appointed to coach the Boks. Although it was a remarkable season in terms of try-scoring records, with wings Cabous van der Westhuizen and James Small racking up unprecedented feats, the season is probably best remembered for the two defeats Natal suffered in the two domestic finals, the Currie Cup and the Lion Cup.

As Viljoen had also coached Transvaal to two successive Currie Cup finals, which they also lost, the stumble at the last hurdle in 1993 earned him the reputation of being a "nearly man". Or, to put it more bluntly, a choker... However, Viljoen shook himself of that reputation with a remarkable one-off season with Western Province in 1997, breaking an 11-year Currie Cup drought for Province while playing a revolutionary new type of rugby.

As he recalls: "That year, WP were the first team to show the benefits of playing with the ball up above the ground rather than going to the floor to set up the ruck, and I think it was the first time that pop-up passes were used in South Africa."

But just when Viljoen looked to be on the cusp of something special and Province on the brink of starting another golden era, a combination of factors led him to walk out on his deal with the union. He had disagreements with his assistant, Alan Solomons, and an injury epidemic cut a swathe through the Western Stormers camp (as they were known then).

Viljoen had also walked out quite suddenly on Natal, so when he was appointed as Springbok coach in October 2000, some people considered him a bit of a quitter. There was also the small matter of his wealth – unlike other coaches, he didn't really need a job in rugby. The man was a billionaire. I spoke to Corné Krige when Viljoen was appointed, and he also reckoned that Viljoen might not last the distance when the going got tough, as he simply didn't need the hassle.

It was a crazy time in South African rugby. The previous coach had been sacked for something as minor as criticising ticket prices to someone he did not know was a journalist. And then, in his place, SARFU appointed Viljoen, who hadn't coached for three years.

Viljoen was as surprised as most South African rugby fans when he was appointed to the top job in rugby: "I had kept up with the game by watching and speaking to my friends, such as [Wallaby coach] Rod Macqueen, but I spent those years developing my business [interests] and not thinking much about coaching or going back to rugby. When [I received] the call [asking] if I would be interested, I was taken by surprise.

"I had to think very hard about it. I had long discussions with my wife. She didn't want me to go back into rugby, as she felt we would lose our life again. But to me it was a challenge, and I felt if I could contribute in a positive way, I would like to do it. It is true [that] it was never about [the] money for me, and [SARFU and I] never even negotiated a contract."

So while Viljoen says he wanted to take up the challenge, it is clear that he wasn't exactly champing at the bit to be the Springbok coach. It is the crucial difference between him and the Springbok coaches who preceded and succeeded him, and it may explain why he remains the only Bok coach who quit of his own volition during his tenure rather than being fired or asked to resign.

Another unusual aspect to Viljoen's appointment was that the man behind it, SARFU chief executive Rian Oberholzer, must have had his reservations, too. According to André Markgraaff, at one stage Oberholzer was considering an option that, if implemented, would effectively have meant that the Springboks had three coaches.

"Rian wanted Harry to be one of three coaches, with the others being me and Laurie Mains. I told him it would never work," says Markgraaff. "I understand that he then approached Laurie, and Laurie told him the same thing. Then Rian came back to me and said that he wanted Harry, but that he had been out of the game for a bit, and would I be available to assist him. I was willing, but the next day a story broke in the media saying that I was effectively going to be the coach, and that Harry would just be the puppet.

"Naturally Harry got pissed off when he heard about that on his yacht in the Mediterranean. But he never called me to tell me how he felt. I didn't know he was cross with me. Then, about a month later, completely out of the blue, he phoned me on my farm and said he had spoken to Gideon Sam and it was okay to have me along. By then it was only a few days before the start of the tour to Argentina.

"I was the assistant coach, Jake White was the technical advisor, and Ian McIntosh was also there in an advisory capacity."

However, one appointment that confounded some and infuriated others was that of the controversial rugby writer Mark Keohane. Initially Viljoen had wanted Keohane as his media liaison man, but when some of the SARFU officials objected – most notably Keith Parkinson, who had not seen eye to eye with Keohane when he was Sharks president – that plan was shelved.

Parkinson gave Viljoen an ultimatum: he would back his appointment if he agreed not to keep Keohane. If Keohane was part of the package, then Parkinson, a powerful figure within the executive, would oppose Viljoen's appointment.

"Harry was [told] that if I was still involved, he would be on his own," Keohane said in his book, *Springbok Rugby Uncovered.*

Keohane was with Viljoen when he phoned Oberholzer on speakerphone to discuss Parkinson's ultimatum. Oberholzer suggested that Viljoen fire Keohane (who had already started working with Viljoen) and then re-employ him once he had been appointed as the Bok coach. But Keohane told Viljoen that he was either in or he was out, and Viljoen eventually said that he was a man of his word and would take the chance.

And he managed to get away with it, but, as Markgraaff recalls, only on the basis that Keohane would be seen as Viljoen's private assistant and not an official member of the Springbok management. "SARFU president Silas Nkanunu had agreed that Mark could be Harry's personal assistant, but not in an official capacity. You will remember [that] Freddie Hendricks was the media man on that trip to Argentina, Ireland and the UK. At that stage, Mark was paid by Harry and not by SARFU. But while he was always in the background in the beginning, the next thing he was in the front, sitting in team photographs dressed in a Springbok tracksuit. That wasn't what had been agreed to. I was very uncomfortable with it, and it is my view that Harry signed his [own] death warrant by appointing Mark."

At that point, as well as being a friend of Keohane's, I was also his colleague, as he was freelancing for the *Argus*. I was surprised when he told me that he was giving up rugby writing to join SARFU, and at the time I wondered if he was making the right move, because he had so many enemies both within the organisation and among the players.

I also remember feeling a bit disappointed. Mark and I had a chat the night after the Kings Park Test, which proved to be Mallett's last in charge. I was surprised when he seemed gleeful that Mallett was going to be sacked, as I didn't see how his departure could be a good thing for the Springboks. I also disagreed with Mark's view that Viljoen would be a good replacement. I felt rugby had changed a lot since Viljoen had last been involved. So when I heard Mark was going to be working with Harry, I felt that some of his behaviour may have been unethical in the closing stages of Mallett's tenure.

Why had Viljoen been so determined to appoint Keohane? Many thought it was because he wanted to keep his enemies close, and I had not disregarded that as a possibility either. In 1997, I had been one of the people a troubled Viljoen confided in when Keohane was criticising his coaching style on a daily basis in the *Cape Times*.

I can't remember what advice I gave him, as it wasn't a big issue to me and I don't like talking to coaches about my colleagues. But I do recall the about-turn the *Cape Times* made on Viljoen. Suddenly, after Keohane had mostly criticised the Province coach, he was drawn right into Viljoen's inner circle.

Keohane is my good friend, but as I once said to Dick Muir when he asked me about my relationship with Mark, being someone's friend doesn't mean you don't see their faults. Nevertheless, I jumped to Mark's defence, and quite vehemently so, when he walked away from the Springbok camp in 2003 because of a race-tape controversy and became a pariah. But there have also been times when I've just as aggressively pointed out his faults to him.

That said, I can understand why Viljoen appointed Keohane – and it didn't necessarily have anything to do with keeping one's enemies close. There is no one in rugby who better knows his way around the politics, or who better understands the nuances of the media's relationship with the sport, than Mark. And when I asked Viljoen why he had appointed Mark, it became clear that, unlike his predecessor, Mallett, he knew the value of having a political commissar by his side.

"Mark was very pro the black players and he helped me a heck of a lot when it came to avoiding the pitfalls presented by political demands and expectations," recalls Viljoen. "People criticised him, as there was a lot of politics between him and the rest of the press. Someone like Dan Retief seemed resentful of Mark working for the Springboks and just didn't like him at all. But Mark supported me and pushed me when it came to the selection of black players, always driving the point that we needed to transform and [had to assess] the abilities of the black players.

"I will say one thing about Mark. Give him a job [to do], and the next day it has been done 110 per cent, and in one-third of the time someone else would have done [it]. His issues with the press created a lot of problems for me, but he was like a working machine, and he often did everyone else's work [too]. I think Rian Oberholzer recognised that. Rian liked Mark a lot and [valued his input]."

Viljoen was right that elements of the press corps resented Keohane. Pettiness within the profession does occur, and there was a lot of it at the time. Yet Mark may not have helped his own cause. He tried almost too hard to convince the players and management that he was now one of them and no longer a member of the media. In his book, he writes about an article I had written about the Bok initiation ceremony at the start of the Argentina tour, which Joost took exception to. Mark took Joost's side against mine. Mark said that I understood what it was about, and he was right, so we remained friends. Others, though, were less forgiving.

In my opinion, Keohane was not a good media liaison person because, in his poacher-turned-gamekeeper transformation, he tried *too* hard to satisfy his new bosses. In that job, you need to strike a good balance between what is best for the Springboks and what is best for the media. I'm not sure Mark managed that.

Viljoen's first match in charge was played at the River Plate Stadium in Buenos Aires on a bright Sunday afternoon that, for me, followed a really heavy night's partying in that amazing city. It was a surreal experience, made even more so by the fact that Viljoen had instructed his men to play the entire 80 minutes without kicking the ball.

While I struggled to get the words of a popular song at the time, "Will the real Slim Shady please stand up", out of my head, the Boks were playing at a hundred miles an hour down on the pitch. Or at least until they eventually, and quite inevitably, ran out of steam, and were made to hang on in the last minutes amid a cacophonous din that ushered in a headache I was probably destined to have anyway, but that was hastened by several hours.

"So what did you think?" asked André Vos, the Bok captain, when we bumped into each other on the field after the game.

What did I think? "Um, interesting..."

At least Vos seemed to revel in the challenge of playing Viljoen's new running style of rugby. Viljoen's intention was to change the way the Boks thought about and played the game, and his instruction not to kick was his way of trying to cultivate a new consciousness in his men of what they were capable of. At the training camp and in the build-up to the game, he had each player carry a rugby ball wherever he went so that he could get used to handling it.

He also selected Danie Rossouw, a little-known player then just 20 years old, at the expense of Corné Krige in order to promote a style of play geared towards keeping the ball above the ground. Unfortunately Rossouw was injured in the first training session and was unable to tour.

During the Argentina game, Viljoen quickly realised that what had seemed good in theory wasn't necessarily so in practice, particularly when his assistants did not share his revolutionary views on how the game should be played.

"I thought André Markgraaff, sitting behind me in the coaching box, was going to have a heart attack," says Viljoen. "He was constantly going on about the need to kick, to change the approach. I kept saying that we must just keep going. I wanted us to develop the game. I did not intend for us to play like that [for the rest of our lives]. It was sunny in Argentina, and we could play a fast-paced game there. I wanted a fast game with [excellent] skills. But we ran out of steam.

"[During] my provincial coaching career, I realised that to play the game I wanted to play, the players needed to be supremely fit. I got that right at Transvaal. Markgraaff and I were just completely different characters, and maybe I [was] wrong [to have him as my] assistant. Don't get me wrong, I rated him highly, and he did bring value, but he was just a lot more conservative than I was and we had different ways of thinking.

"Once we got to the northern hemisphere for the next leg of the trip, we encountered wet, heavier fields, and our game started changing. We couldn't continue with what we had started in Argentina."

By the time the Boks returned to the northern hemisphere for what was to be Viljoen's last tour as Springbok coach 12 months later, his style had gone full circle, with Louis Koen, Braam van Straaten and Trevor Halstead standing next to each other in the backline and sending out a clear message that the objective was to kick the cover off the ball at every opportunity.

"When I got involved, defensive systems had become so strong that [I thought] we needed to move guys around the field, which meant we needed to have different attitudes to fitness and skills levels," says Viljoen. "Two weeks are the maximum a national coach gets with the players before a tour, which unfortunately isn't enough time to work on those things. And then, as soon as the Test matches arrive, the pressure is on and the players [revert back] to [their] old habits and everything falls flat."

Sound familiar? It's more or less the same problem that Carel du Plessis encountered in 1997. However, it would be wrong to equate Viljoen's intentions with that of Du Plessis four years earlier, as Viljoen had a much higher degree of specialisation in his management.

"I knew the changes to the modern game demanded better tactical kicking than had been the case in the past, and defence also had to be strong. In fact, defence was of critical importance. That is why I brought in Les Kiss and Lee Byrne from Australia later on."

If Viljoen's plans appear a bit crazy, perhaps we should consider what Jake White, who was one of Viljoen's assistant coaches on the first tour, had to say about him in his book, *In Black and White*: "There are many perceptions about Harry – most of them are inaccurate. He was way ahead of his time. He had a picture in his head about how the game should be played and about how professional rugby should be run. I enjoyed the tour immensely. I learnt many new things and was inspired by Harry's ideas and his constant search for change to the way we thought and operated. As well as the way the Boks were perceived. Harry was [all] for thinking outside of the box, and that was a good thing."

McIntosh was also there as an assistant, but he and Viljoen parted ways at the end of the tour, something that Viljoen now says he regrets.

"At the time I was all for breaking down the defensive wall by moving the ball around, and Mac, who felt we should take it up and play flat more, and I differed on that score," says Viljoen. "In retrospect, a mixture of what Mac wanted and what I wanted would have been a winning recipe."

McIntosh agrees with Viljoen. He was disappointed when Viljoen abandoned the blueprint McIntosh and a few other top coaches had drawn up as a guideline for the Springbok playing style going forward.

"People say we mustn't crash and bash, but why not if that is what we are good at?" McIntosh asks. "South African rugby requires a combination of power and flair, and not *too* much of either. It was Harry who scuppered the blueprint, but then his team was brilliant at the end of that first tour, when they finished off with a great win over the Barbarians in Cardiff. That was the blueprint South African rugby should have been looking for, [as] the game highlighted a combination of our strengths. I am not sure why Harry didn't stick with it. He made a big mistake by not doing so."

There were several reasons why Viljoen ended up moving away from the initial plan, and one of them was rooted in the match that preceded the Cardiff game. The Boks suffered their only Test loss of the tour against England at Twickenham, and were so comprehensively outplayed, it woke Viljoen up to the enormity of the challenge he faced if he wanted to win the World Cup.

"There were two really great teams that I saw play during the era that I coached," says Viljoen. "One of them was the Wallaby team that won the World Cup in 1999; the other was the England team that won the World Cup in 2003. Both of them built up over a period of years. We were well beaten by England at Twickenham; I was surprised at how strong they were. And I could see [that] they were building towards the 2003 World Cup.

"I was by then also coming to the realisation that I was going to struggle to find a flyhalf to play the game that I wanted to play. Percy Montgomery had worn the No. 10 against Argentina because there was no one else, but he was better at fullback and wasn't a long-term solution at flyhalf. Butch James was very young then and also had disciplinary problems.

"Louis Koen and Braam van Straaten were the two other flyhalves in the mix, but neither of them were players you could ask to play an all-embracing, running style of quick-paced rugby. I wanted to press on and see if we could perhaps find the answer to the flyhalf conundrum, but after that England game I was having serious doubts about our ability to win the World Cup."

Another factor had also come into play before the end of that tour: Viljoen had started to get jittery about the media. I was told that I had "irritated" him and his management when I failed to attend a meeting at which Viljoen had berated the press for their negative reporting.

Instead, my Independent Group colleague Liam del Carme and I had decided to remain in central London to enjoy a quiet last week of the tour rather than go out to Richmond, where the Boks were staying. Travelling out to Richmond to listen to Viljoen and his psychobabble (as I was referring to it by then) just didn't feel like a profitable way to spend the day. He was forever rabbiting on about the need for a positive environment, among other things. I also wasn't happy with what I perceived to be Mark Keohane's role in spearheading a campaign against "negative reporting". It just seemed too hypocritical.

I've always considered it my job to write it as I see it, and I knew that Mark knew that. But when a colleague later told me that most of the guys who had attended the meeting had rolled over to be tickled by Viljoen – in a figurative sense, of course – I wished I *had* been there to have my say.

Most of the management complaints were just petty. They even objected to the opening paragraph of my match report on the England Test. I'd written something like, "Come back, Nick Mallett, all is forgiven." A match report is supposed to convey the writer's opinion, and if you are a Springbok coach and can't tolerate criticism, go and find yourself another job.

Fortunately relations between the media and the Boks improved on the last night of the tour, though it had nothing to do with a public relations outreach on the part of the management. No, it was Joost van der Westhuizen who came walking into the hotel pub wearing a funny hat. He warmly embraced me and said something like, "I'm on holiday, you're on holiday ..." In effect, he was suggesting that we set the other issues aside for the time being.

Joost and I had our differences now and then, but generally we got on. I must have felt comfortable with him that evening, because I remember telling him that he should leave the Bulls and go and play for Boland, so that the Stormers might be able to use him as back-up to Dan van Zyl. "But only when Dan is injured," I said.

I knew there was quite a rivalry between him and Van Zyl, but Joost thought my joke was hilarious and kept calling people in the pub over so that I could repeat what I had told him.

Viljoen also turned up at some point and proceeded to convey all his complaints about the media to me, but the evening eventually ended on a good note. I left London the following day wondering how Viljoen was going to survive if he couldn't handle the minimal criticism he'd endured up till then. I was reminded of the lyrics of an old song: "You ain't seen nothin' yet ..."

Although I was mostly supportive of Viljoen the following year, that prediction did prove correct. However, there were many times when I felt that my colleagues were too critical, and even small-minded, about what Viljoen was trying to accomplish with the Boks. It was sad in a way, as McIntosh may have been right – that Cardiff game at the end of the tour had shown us how to play.

It was because of media pressure as much as anything else that we never saw Viljoen trying to recreate that game plan in 2001.

17

A complete about-turn

The frightening outbreaks of xenophobic violence that swept through some parts of South Africa in 2008 had been preceded seven years earlier by a less violent, but no less mindless, form of xenophobia. It threatened to undermine the start of what was to be Harry Viljoen's only full year in charge of the Springboks.

Viljoen was a great believer in incorporating as many disparate views and ideas in his management team as possible, and Australians Tim Lane, Michael Byrne and Les Kiss were all part of the group that gathered in Plettenberg Bay for a pre-season training camp in 2001. Feeling marginalised by the sheer number of advisors in the group, Jake White resigned, but he nevertheless understood Viljoen's goals. He, too, believed that a cross-pollination of views would benefit the Boks, and he would follow a similar path when he employed former Wallaby coach Eddie Jones as his assistant for the 2007 World Cup.

But the Aussie contingent of coaches didn't go down well elsewhere, particularly not with the Afrikaans media, who reacted as if Viljoen was guilty of treason for allowing foreigners to be part of the Springbok squad. This was but one of the stories simmering in the background during that training camp. Another issue was the inevitable early-season contract negotiations, which have perennially blighted almost every Springbok coach's build-up to a new season since the game turned professional in 1996.

"It was a very frustrating time for me," Viljoen recalls, "as people just didn't seem to understand what I was trying to do. I knew we had to [improve our kicking game], and the defence had to be strong. Les Kiss was one of the best defence coaches in the world. Lee Byrne, as a former Aussie Rules player, brought a different angle to the kicking, and the players appreciated it. We could feel the new energy in that training camp.

"But outside of the Bok squad everyone went beserk, and it wasn't just the media, but also the officials. I was attacked from all angles, and I felt like I had to spend all my time fighting to retain the Australians as part of the group. It was unnecessary and it drained my energy."

The contract saga that blows up every 12 months would have been equally draining, although it was not something that Viljoen dwelled on for long when I met him in 2013 at his palatial offices, Edge House, in Durbanville.

After the first tour, Viljoen had asked the senior players to come to Cape Town to discuss South African rugby issues and help him plot a way forward. They got together in January 2001. Viljoen explained that he wanted the players to have a greater say in the running of the side. But he also wanted to incentivise them, and he proposed a change to the contracting structure.

At that juncture, there were three salary bands – A-category players earned R700 000, B-category players R600 000 and C-category players R500 000 a season, while the win bonuses were worth between R5 000 and R10 000 per player per match, depending on the calibre of the opposition.

"That's where the business unit that I wanted to set up came in," Viljoen explains. "I wanted contracts to be separate; in other words, not run through the team structure. I wanted the players to start thinking for themselves. I wanted them to all have computers. I proposed that the Boks would have their own budget and the money saved reinvested in the squad."

But in order to incentivise the players, he wanted them to be paid on a match-by-match basis, with a bigger proportion of the payment on offer if they won their games. Viljoen explained to the players that a mediocre teammate could cost them money.

Viljoen met with the players on an individual basis and offered each of them non-negotiable options on their contracts. They were told that they would have to make a decision that day and not rely on their agents to do their thinking and negotiating for them. This is why the media later reported that the players had been "forced" to sign the contracts, and their unhappiness at the situation spilled over into the Plettenberg Bay training camp.

Not that it was all negative; in fact, an atmosphere prevailed that suggested something positive was happening for Bok rugby.

In his book *The Right Place at the Wrong Time*, Corné Krige recalls the events: "[Harry] came in and did exactly what he did at Western Province in 1997. He was very good at marketing. He put together a video presentation outlining what he wanted to do with Springbok rugby. He told the players that he required intelligent, business-like rugby players who would use their brains and be professional both on and off the field. He wanted the players to go to games dressed in suits. I think he had the right idea because he said, 'Let's run it as a business.'"

But Krige felt that Viljoen wasn't 100 per cent honest with the players and wasn't good at conveying what he wanted from them. For Mark Andrews, however, Viljoen's problem wasn't a lack of honesty, but not having a strong, stand-out leader in the Springbok group.

"Harry's biggest problem was that he was very naive, and he didn't appear to understand South African rugby politics and the back-stabbing that happens between SARFU and the unions," Andrews says. "He came in with the best intentions and coached for free while still running his billion-rand empire on the side. He gave lots of power to the senior players, but unfortunately there weren't great leaders in the side at the time. There were lots of guys who wanted the captaincy, and Harry ended up choosing André Vos just because there [was no one else]. Unfortunately, Vossie wasn't the stand-out No. 8 at the time, so it was difficult.

"[Harry] needed a really strong leader, and I did all I could as a senior player to [support] Vossie, but I felt that he was constantly being undermined by other guys. It seemed there were a whole lot of young guys all vying for the captaincy. Not all of them were leadership material.

"If Harry had the same strong leadership core that Nick Mallett had available to him, I reckon he would have done well. He would also have succeeded if he had come in earlier, such as 1997, when Carel du Plessis took over instead. He would have been more current then.

"It was a difficult period for me, as I was desperate for Harry to succeed, but I never felt he had the support of the players. We were in a rebuilding phase, but if Harry had coached when Carel did, he would have had players playing for him who had already become senior players. Unfortunately the minute the politics started, Harry just seemed to lose interest in the position."

Although not enough cause for Viljoen to lose heart completely, he definitely lost some confidence after the opening Test of the 2001 season. After the Plettenberg Bay camp, where the Boks had worked tirelessly on their structures and on the innovations introduced by the coaches, the squad moved to Johannesburg, where they were expected to beat a French team depleted by injury and the absence of some key players.

Not for the first time, however, would underestimating the French on the basis of their team sheet prove to be the Boks' undoing ... After a strong start the South Africans faded and were eventually beaten 23-32. And this at Ellis Park, which is supposedly their "fortress". The final score was flattering to the Boks.

"That Ellis Park game was a big setback. We had done mountains of work on structure, and when it didn't work out, I did start to doubt myself. We had started so well, with an early try to Breyton Paulse, but after that we just didn't measure up and the French pack took control," says Viljoen.

There was a constant difference of opinion between Viljoen and André Markgraaff on how the game should be approached, and after the defeat to France, Markgraaff started to get his way more often.

Viljoen recalls: "We beat the French in the second Test in Durban to tie the series, but to do [so] we relied much more on our physicality and started to dispense with some of the things we had worked on in Plettenberg Bay. It was a great pity that the pressure forced us to abandon so much of the stuff that we had been working on.

"But when you get beaten like that in a game you are confident you are going to win, it's inevitable [that] you [would] start [to lose] some confidence. I started to get sucked into being more conservative. The French had fielded big loose forwards against us. I realised we needed [to do] that too."

The 20-15 win in Durban saved some face for the Boks, but it was ugly, and certainly well short of a major confidence-booster for the Tri-Nations. Another warm-up game, against Italy in Port Elizabeth, lay ahead, but that week in the Eastern Cape won't be remembered for the game that was played on the Saturday. Instead, it is remembered for the events that sparked a change of captain and, later, a change to the management team. It was also the end of a Bok stalwart's international career.

I was still in Durban when the news began to leak that André Vos had been axed. Some of my colleagues in the rugby media told me about it, and they, in turn, had heard it from Mark Keohane. I wasn't on Mark's list of people to call that night, but, knowing him, he would have had a strategic reason for that.

This is what I wrote about the unfolding events in a Supersport.com column when I arrived in Port Elizabeth on the day after the news broke:

That there was to be some spin put on the event [of Vos's axing] became clear on Monday night, when coach Harry Viljoen's advisor Mark Keohane started phoning select journalists to "leak" the story. I was not one of the chosen ones, but from what I understand, his reasoning was that Viljoen wanted to get the news out before senior players "such as Rassie Erasmus" started leaking it themselves. Presumably the fear here was that these players may then have put their own spin on it, maybe a more truthful one.

The media were giving Viljoen a lot of flak after the loss to France in the opening match, and you can surmise my opinion on the matter from my opening paragraph in the same column: "François Pienaar, Gary Teichmann and now André Vos. Once again South African rugby gets to bid a premature farewell to a captain while the man the public would really like to see the back of is the confused and panic-stricken coach."

I also didn't spare the horses when I later revealed that the signs had been there from the beginning of the season that Viljoen might not be completely committed to Vos:

It's been almost impossible to get any sense out of Viljoen recently, but at the time of his first squad selection back in May, he was still relatively lucid. So when I asked at a press conference about the appointment of a captain and he replied that "Vossie will be in charge for the first three Tests", those were words which could easily have been interpreted as meaning, "I have not made up my mind about my captain."

Viljoen's apparent indecision was understandable, though. He'd always intended to make Bob Skinstad his captain, but as he was out injured that whole year, he had been unavailable for the first tour under Viljoen. And at the start of the 2001 international season, he was only just starting to play again.

Viljoen says there was another reason why he decided to appoint a new captain.

"André Markgraaff came to me after the Durban Test against France and said that he did not want to go any further with André Vos as a captain or as a player. I thought Vossie was a great leader and a fanstastic rugby player, but André didn't rate him," Viljoen says.

When I arrived at the Kings Beach Holiday Inn, where the Boks were staying, I saw Markgraaff and Rassie Erasmus sitting together, looking extremely surly and somber. Markgraaff and I had long since dropped the enmity that might have existed between us in 1996, and both he and Erasmus were normally hale and hearty in their greetings. Not that day.

"Hmmm," I thought after a brief chat, "guess who has their noses out of joint because Vos has been axed."

Little did I know then that Markgraaff had been instrumental in Vos's axing. Why he looked like someone who had just discovered a dead lizard in his half-eaten sandwich was for a completely different reason.

"André wanted Rassie as his captain; he wasn't keen on Bob at all," Viljoen claims. "I had always wanted Bob as my captain, and at that stage I wasn't sure about Rassie, as he didn't fit into my criteria for a big loose forward. Rassie had played well in that year's Super 12, but when we went into the international season, he started struggling, and he seemed almost incapable of getting across the gain line. That was why I opted for Joe van Niekerk. Rassie and André were very close, and that was why my relationship with André broke down."

Markgraaff confirmed that the decision to appoint Skinstad and drop Erasmus was the final straw and the reason why he approached Viljoen after the PE Test to inform him that he no longer wanted to be involved.

"I was never a fan of Vos. I didn't think he was good enough for Springbok rugby and [I did not think he was] a captain. Nick Mallett had chosen him, but as far as I was concerned, he was not up to standard," Markgraaff says. "Harry is a nice guy, and [because of] that he couldn't always face up to a player and be honest to his face. He booked Rassie a ticket to Bloemfontein but no ticket from there to Cape Town, where the next game was to be played. That was how Rassie learnt that he was not going to be involved in the next Test. He was given a one-way ticket home. I thought Harry trusted me with the forwards, but I could see that if Bob was the captain and Rassie was another strong guy there, there would be problems."

A contributing factor to Markgraaff's decision to part ways with Viljoen was his discomfort with the increasingly prominent role Mark Keohane was playing in the management team.

"He was acting as the director of the business unit, and I got the feeling [that] Mark was calling the shots and playing a big role in selection meetings.

That [hadn't been] the initial plan. I walked out of my own free will. I went to Harry and said, 'Let's not fight.' We parted on good terms."

Viljoen replaced Erasmus with Van Niekerk, who was then an under-21 player who had yet to play senior provincial rugby. Also called up at around that time was Marius Joubert. According to Keohane, both players were called up without Viljoen having seen them play – he had taken the word of people whose opinion he valued.

But the way Viljoen then treated Van Niekerk remains a bit of a mystery, for while he spoke highly of the Lions No. 8, he used him only sparingly during the rest of that year. Perhaps the penny dropped only after Van Niekerk had been selected that he wasn't really a No. 7 and, in fact, played in the same position as Skinstad, who was duly appointed to replace Vos as captain.

The Boks beat Italy 60-14 at the old Boet Erasmus Stadium at the end of that turbulent week, but Italy was a weak team and the Bok victory didn't mean much. Instead, the big story after the match was Markgraaff's decision to make a voluntary exit. The Afrikaans media really ran with it, and it was bigger than anything that had happened in the game.

Only later did the massive disagreements that had taken place on the field emerge, when Keohane wrote about it in *Springbok Rugby Uncovered*. Markgraaff had wanted Johan Ackermann to stay on the field and Mark Andrews to be brought off, while Viljoen and the other assistant, Tim Lane, wanted Andrews to stay on and Ackermann to come off. When he didn't get his way, Markgraaff went into a sulk.

After the Italy Test, the Boks had to play the first game in the Tri-Nations, a wet-weather game in Cape Town that better suited New Zealand. However, the Springboks could well have won the match had it not been for Percy Montgomery's poor goal-kicking performance. The Boks had much of the play and were still very much in the game when Butch James took over the kicking duties from Montgomery 10 minutes from the end ... and also missed.

At the post-match cocktail party, I bumped into SARFU executive committee member Keith Parkinson. "Where the hell is Braam van Straaten, why wasn't he playing?" he bellowed at me.

Keith hadn't seen the team before the kick-off – he must have been out of the country on business or something that week – and was shocked to learn that the Western Province sharp-shooter had been sitting in the stands watching the game rather than participating in it. James had been selected ahead of Van Straaten on the basis that he was a better all-round player.

And sure enough, the youthful James was dropped after that 3-12 defeat – as was Montgomery. Into the side came Van Straaten and Conrad Jantjes, and that was the end of any pretence on Viljoen's part that he still wanted to play the style of rugby he had set out to establish when he started.

The following week the Boks won against Australia at Loftus, ironically playing the type of rugby that would probably have pleased Markgraaff had he still been part of the management group. But even Markgraaff would not have appreciated the path the Boks took from there, for they just became steadily more conservative as the year went on.

"That game was the turning point," agrees Viljoen. "If we'd won that New Zealand Test, which we should have done, we would have won the Tri-Nations, remembering that we went on to beat Australia in Pretoria and then draw [against them] in Perth. That would have been enough to win the Tri-Nations, as Australia beat the All Blacks. Had [we won the New Zealand Test], who knows how my career might have turned out.

"That was when the pressure was really coming on, and we were being attacked for not fielding better goal-kickers. Percy was just starting his relationship [with Tamsin, who would later become his wife] at the time, and he wasn't working as hard as he should have. I told him that we were having problems with goal-kicking and he needed to work hard at that aspect of his game, but he just wasn't as focused as he should have been. It was different after he came back from overseas in 2004, but that didn't help me much.

"I was very disappointed with that New Zealand game, and that is when I made the change to our approach. I regret it now; I should have just continued down the path we were on. Braam van Straaten might percentage-wise have had a better kicking game, but Butch James was a better flyhalf for the Springbok game. He was also very young at the time and everyone was making an issue about his dangerous tackles."

After the draw against the Wallabies in Perth, the Boks were well beaten by the All Blacks in Auckland in what became a Tri-Nations decider, and then it was time for the end-of-year tour, this time to France, Italy and England. By then everything had regressed dramatically from where the Boks had started out under Viljoen 12 months earlier. Louis Koen had come in as flyhalf, and by the final Test of the tour, against England, Van Straaten had moved to inside centre.

Viljoen had become indecisive about selection, and in his book Mark Keohane writes how he had confused the two De Kocks, Deon of the Falcons and Neil of Western Province, when he announced his squad for that November tour. Viljoen had said that he was going to pick Neil and then suddenly picked Deon, giving rise to the rumour that he had changed the teams as the players' names were being released to the media.

Defeat to France in the tour opener in Paris increased the pressure and forced Viljoen to coach for survival. By then I could see what was happening and was a lot more supportive in my reports than I had been earlier, but some writers back home were laying it on thick. The big match of the tour was against England at Twickenham, but the Boks were never in the game, only managing to keep the score down by employing spoiling tactics. However, the Bok defence, under Les Kiss, was excellent throughout, and the Boks might have lost by more than 9-29 had it been any less.

As it turned out, losing against England hastened the end for Viljoen, who on his previous visit to Twickenham in 2000 had already started doubting that his men could beat an England team that had been building for some time under Clive Woodward.

A 54-26 win over Italy in Genoa was the only Europe-based Test-match success of that tour, which ended with a workmanlike victory over the United States in Houston.

While the pressure of the job was cited as the reason for his resignation in January 2002, Viljoen says that it was the realisation that his team was not capable of winning the World Cup that really decided it for him.

"I had pressures on me, for sure, but if I had a team like England had at that time, I would have been prepared to take the shit I was getting, as at least we would have had a chance of winning the World Cup and proving everyone wrong," he says now. "One of the problems was that while I knew we had had talent in the past, rugby goes through cycles, and I had come to the realisation that South African rugby at that time was at the bottom of a cycle.

"I wanted to play a certain type of game, but when the pressure came on, we seemed incapable of sticking to the plan. And the flyhalves that were available just weren't suited to the style I wanted. Apart from that, we were also at a stage when the black players just weren't good enough, and I needed three on the field and two on the bench. It meant we were starting matches with players who weren't necessarily the best in their positions. Conrad Jantjes was still very young then.

"I always had pressure on me to play black players, and yet there weren't enough of them playing in the Super 12, so there wasn't much of a pool to choose from. I had clashes with the sports minister earlier in the year and we had a big meeting in Cape Town before the match against the All Blacks."

Sports minister Ngconde Balfour called the meeting, as Viljoen had failed to meet the unofficial quota for black players, an issue the minister wanted to address. Balfour wanted five players in the match 22, and it wasn't happening.

At the meeting, Viljoen explained that three of the six black players competing in the Super 12 had been selected for the Boks. Balfour responded by pushing the cases of individual players, such as Deon Kayser. Viljoen was a bit vague about the details when I met with him, but Keohane had also attended the meeting, and he confirmed that Viljoen told Balfour that Marius Joubert, who won his first cap in that Newlands Test, was just better than Kayser. He also pointed out that he had given Etienne Fynn a chance at prop and he hadn't measured up.

There wasn't much Balfour could do about it and he eventually ran out of counter-arguments. The parties were all smiles at the press conference after the meeting, even though nothing had changed. But the experience had worn out Viljoen's patience. It drove him in the direction he took in the summer of 2001/02. He decided he'd had enough.

"Apart from the pressure I was under from politicians, I also struggled with the other South African coaches, who just didn't buy into what I was trying to do," says Viljoen. "The top players needed to be exposed to my kind of rugby more regularly so that they could become comfortable with it.

"We just never seemed to have any backs, and I looked ahead and realised that while I had two years to go to the World Cup, the amount of time I would actually have with the squad would amount to only about two months. I realised it just wasn't enough time to [impart] what I needed to, and there were all those other obstacles I've referred to.

"I started to think to myself that I must be a sucker to take all that flak. I had fights with [radio personality] Darren Scott, who wanted James Dalton back, whereas I was pushing for John Smit. I just felt that after the 2001 tour, people were coming at me from all angles. It felt like I was taking on the world, and there comes a time when the criticism gets very ugly.

"I started to weigh it all up and, as I say, it was becoming apparent that I was probably taking all the flak for nothing, as we had little chance of winning the World Cup with the talent we had."

But a meeting he had with SARFU chief executive Rian Oberholzer and president Silas Nkanunu was the final nail in the coffin.

"They said I wasn't allowed to play Mark Andrews and Ollie le Roux any more. It wasn't so much Rian as Silas who was pushing the point. He was determined that I would drop Mark," recalls Viljoen. "So I thought to myself, 'Shit, now I am not even going to be allowed to pick my own team?' I valued Andrews' input and Ollie was a senior player, but it seemed [as if Rian and Silas] had had enough of that pair. I decided I couldn't put up with it. I left the meeting fuming, and that was when I made my decision that I wanted out of the job. By then I'd just had too many fights, and they had taken up so much of my energy."

Viljoen's sudden departure in January 2002 took most rugby people by surprise just as they were enjoying their summer holidays, and it left the members of his management team feeling very vulnerable. How quickly it all happened also didn't benefit the man who was to replace him.

Not one bit.

18

A sense of duty

After a week of inclement weather that smashed into the sea-facing windows at the Swansea Marriott with a scarcely contained fury, Guy Fawkes night brought clear skies and a welcoming calm to the beachfront of the Welsh city. It was 1994, and the Springboks had just hammered Swansea at the St Helen's ground. The many expatriate South Africans in town for the game had reason to be joyous.

But the skyrockets that trailed into the darkening night sky were not the only fireworks I would see that night. Some friends from Durban who were working in London came back to my room with the intention of spending the night. The thought that we could be bust for bilking didn't cross my mind until the early hours of the morning, when the hotel's fire alarm came to life with jarring urgency.

My friends thought it was just a drill, so they were happy to stay in the room while I set off for the foyer, but when I opened the door, the situation suddenly seemed more serious. Heavy smoke was wafting down the corridor. My consternation was only eased when I saw big Springbok No. 8 Rudolf Straeuli and his mate Uli Schmidt huddled together, ignoring the alarm, preparing to send the next rocket down the passage.

Rugby players have always been pranksters, but when the same Straeuli became the Springbok coach less than a decade later, it was hard to tell that story and expect the listener to believe it. A Rudolf Straeuli with a sense of humour was hard to equate with the serious disciplinarian whose name would become synonymous with the infamous Kamp Staaldraad, a debacle that seriously embarrassed the South African game.

But Straeuli, the player, was a good guy. He was also a funny man, and as a rugby writer from Durban and later Cape Town, I found his friendliness rare for a player from the Transvaal; most of them seemed quite arrogant, but not Straeuli.

Indeed, a few weeks before the 1995 Rugby World Cup, while I was attending a coaching clinic the Springboks were conducting in a township outside Cape Town, Straeuli shocked me when he made his way through a throng of people to warmly shake my hand. I hadn't seen him since the 1994 end-of-year tour, but he wanted to thank me for a positive article I had written about him the previous November.

"Have you met Rudi Visagie?" I stammered to a fellow journalist who was with me at the time. I'm not sure if Rudolf picked up on the mistake, but if he did, he doesn't remember it. When I interviewed him for this book, however, he reluctantly admitted that his personality had changed when he became the Bok coach.

As he recalls: "Discipline was always important to me, as it would be if you consider that I learnt my rugby at Northern Transvaal, where the big influence on the culture there had been Brigadier Buurman van Zyl. Being disciplined didn't mean you couldn't have fun, and I have a lot more stories other than those skyrockets in Swansea from [my days as] a player. But it was innocent fun, and when you're a coach, you have so many extra responsibilities. You have to set an example. You have to ensure that what has to be done is carried out properly.

"Yes, I think my personality did change a bit, and my coaching style subsequent to being with the Springboks has changed considerably. Discipline is still a core part of it, but not as much as it was back then."

If you think Straeuli sounds like the other Bok coaches who, many years later, have learnt from their mistakes, you would be correct. In his current role as commercial manager at the Natal Sharks, Straeuli has regained at least some of his sense of humour, and he is once again the personable giant he was when he was a player and his father Hans used to catch a lift with the media bus when we were on tour.

So what happened? Well, to fully understand the Straeuli story, you have to start early in 2002, when he was first identified as the man who could replace Harry Viljoen as Springbok coach.

SA Rugby had not been ready for Viljoen's sudden resignation, and if the player depth was at an all-time low, so was the depth of available coaches. Nick Mallett had moved overseas, Kitch Christie had passed on in 1998, Ian McIntosh had retired from top-level coaching in 1999, and Jake White would only emerge later in 2002, when his South African under-21 team won the Junior World Cup.

The cupboard was pretty bare when it came to experience, but the most successful South African coaches at the time were Straeuli and Gert Smal. Both had cut their senior-level coaching teeth in South Africa with Border, although Smal had, of course, been part of the Springbok management team in 1997. Straeuli had left South Africa in 1996 in the fallout of the World Cup contracting saga, becoming the player/coach and then coach at Bedford.

By 2002, he had spent a relatively successful 18 months at the Sharks after taking over from Hugh Reece-Edwards halfway through 2000. Under his guidance, the franchise was competitive again, with the Sharks making the 2001 Super 12 final, where they lost to the Brumbies in Canberra.

However, although the Sharks had made two successive Currie Cup finals, they'd lost both to Smal's Western Province. In fact, Straeuli would be the first to admit that he was way too new to the coaching game to be considered for the Springbok position. And although he reminded me that hindsight is a perfect science (as did most of the coaches I interviewed for this book), in his case he'd actually known his limitations at the time.

"I remember having a meeting with Rudolf during the Sharks tour before he got the job," recalls Durban rugby writer Mike Greenaway. "He [wanted to know whether I would consider becoming his] media liaison, and I distinctly remember him saying that he felt he wasn't ready for the Bok job. He was only considering it out of a sense of duty because there was no one else available."

Greenaway wasn't interested in the liaison job, and besides that, Mark Keohane, who had been Viljoen's media advisor, was still contracted to SARFU. Rian Oberholzer wanted Straeuli for the Bok coaching job and not Smal, probably because the WP coach and former Springbok flank had taken SARFU to arbitration four years earlier. Smal, having heard that Straeuli was the preferred candidate, pulled out of the race, a move Straeuli did not welcome.

"I was hoping they would interview Gert for the job, and I phoned him and asked him to please make himself available," says Straeuli. Although the Springbok job was advertised, SARFU had asked Straeuli to apply for the position.

With Smal not available, Allister Coetzee joined Straeuli on the shortlist, as did Rudi Joubert and Jake White. By all accounts, Joubert came tops in the technical tests and the interviewing process, but the long and the short of it was that Straeuli was being headhunted, and he set aside his reluctance when he was offered the job.

"I should have coached for six or seven years at Super Rugby level and taken charge of many more campaigns before considering the Springbok job. I thought I was tactically up to it then, but I still had to learn a lot of life's lessons that are crucial for a coach. I had only been coaching for a few years. In retrospect, I was just way too young," Straeuli says.

Straeuli's public standing wasn't very high when he took up the job, as the Sharks had had a poor start to their 2002 Super 12 campaign. His appointment as Bok coach was cemented when Mark Keohane visited him in the small northern New South Wales town of Woollongong, where the Sharks were based ahead of their game against the Brumbies. By then, the Sharks had lost five out of five in a season that had started with an unexpected Kings Park defeat to a depleted Stormers team ... coached by Smal.

That the Sharks were in Woollongong at all should have sounded a warning. A working-class town that is difficult to find on any map, Woollongong appealed to Straeuli because it was far away from the bright lights and the players would not be distracted.

Taking players away from the "bright lights" was to be a recurring theme during Straeuli's reign, as was his penchant for devising military-style methods to fuse the players into a tight unit. Straeuli had completed an officer's course during his two years of military service, and conscripts from that period will recognise his methods, particularly the punishment sessions he deployed after a defeat. These were similar to the *opfok* sessions the army used to get the troops to work together.

On the Super 12 tour of 2002, the Sharks players were made to run around the field early on the Sunday after a defeat. According to Greenaway, who was on that tour, Straeuli's default mechanism was to revert to military-style punishment whenever the pressure was on, and not much would change once he was the Bok coach.

But if Straeuli's methods seem over the top, consider this – in the build-up to the 1995 World Cup, Kitch Christie had run the Boks until they were close to vomiting. Some of Christie's training sessions at the Silvermine camp were similar to those Straeuli directed in 2002, and which he would unleash on the Boks, too. Christie had been very focused on discipline, and in many ways Straeuli was a chip off the old block. If there was one major difference between the two coaches, it was probably that Christie had worked with experienced players and strong leaders, whereas Straeuli's men were not nearly in the same league.

"Kitch was a big influence on my coaching career, as I had worked closely with him when I was a player," Straeuli admits freely. "It was Kitch who lured me back to South Africa to play for Transvaal when I was playing in Italy in the early 1990s, and because I played No. 8, which was a key position, I was quite heavily involved in plotting strategy. In 1993, when François Pienaar was away on Springbok duty, I also captained Transvaal. Kitch and I worked closely together, and I appreciated a lot of his methods. Discipline and fitness were central to his success, and I tried to replicate that."

Not that Christie was the only influence.

"I played under a lot of coaches, including Doc Craven when I was at Stellenbosch and Ian McIntosh when I was at the Boks, and they all had an influence [on me]," he said.

From the outset, Straeuli had a very different approach from his predecessor, Harry Viljoen. Viljoen, like Nick Mallett, had kicked off the international season at a training camp in Plettenberg Bay, accommodating the Springbok squad at the luxurious Beacon Island Hotel. Straeuli, however, called a camp in Pretoria, where the players were billeted in police barracks. The general perception at the time was that the Boks needed discipline after Viljoen's tenure, which was right up Straeuli's alley.

"When I was a player, we only had two black players among us, Chester Williams and Tinus Linee, and most of us were from the same background. Except for a few English-speaking guys, we were mostly Afrikaans and, of course, white," he explains. "The [intention of the] first training camp at the police [grounds] was to bring the different cultures together. That was when the cultural issues should all have been dealt with, and I should have selected my squad and moved on with the youngsters I was identifying to take us forward. But unfortunately at that time I was sold on the idea of giving everyone a chance."

In Straeuli's view, "giving everyone a chance" also meant that he had to give all the candidates for the captaincy a shot at the job. So he had three captains to start with: Bob Skinstad, Corné Krige and John Smit.

"Skinstad was contracted to be captain, which SARFU made clear to me when I took over. But he had personal issues that I had to manage the whole time. Even Corné had personal issues that needed managing. John was the guy I wanted [for the] long term, but I knew that it would take a bit of time, because he needed to establish himself first.

"John was definitely my future captain, but I needed to buy time. I could have gone for Mark Andrews, who had been my captain at the Sharks, but his body was finished by that stage."

Today, Straeuli admits that the three-captain policy had been a mistake, as it made it impossible for the players to unite behind one strong, respected leader.

"Maybe you've got to be a more skilful manager than I was if you want to be a Springbok coach," Straeuli says.

But compromise was the name of the game for him, at least in the early days. Having effectively responded to an SOS call from the SARFU administration, he ended up working with a management team that had basically been appointed by his predecessor.

"When I look back at the compromises I made in the negotiation process, I realise that I should have said no to the job," Straeuli says now. "And the first compromise [I made] was on how I believed a management team should look. I had to deal with guys Harry had contracted, and a lot of the players were already on contract too. I was willing to give everyone a year, and [that] was the first compromise. [So] the whole process was wrong. Even the [tests] the coaching candidates [took] were questionable. For instance, if I tested badly on backline play, something should have been done to address that, but it wasn't."

During our interview, Straeuli told me how divisive the contracting process had been, from the moment he'd agreed to do the job until the contract was finally signed. "You end up in a situation where you've got your set of lawyers working against their [SARFU's] set of lawyers, so that almost from the beginning it feels like it is a case of you against them."

Tim Lane continued as the Bok assistant coach in the first year of Straeuli's reign, and while Mark Keohane stayed on as media advisor, his relationship with Straeuli differed vastly from the one he'd had with Viljoen. Keohane, and the media in general, would often question whether there was any trust between him and the coach.

"I never felt like Mark was working for me; it felt as if he was working for Rian [Oberholzer]. It was the same with the others, such as Adriaan Heijns [the security advisor who would become such a big player in the Staaldraad controversy]. It seemed like there were always guys doing things for Rian."

But Staaldraad was still a long way in the future when Straeuli started preparing for his first season in charge. He didn't have much time, as he'd only been appointed in April, but he managed to squeeze in a trial game, which didn't sit well with the players. For them, it was an unnecessary addition to a season that had already featured too many fixtures. However, it was of some value, as it showcased the skills of some exciting players who might otherwise have been overlooked.

Brent Russell was the surprise selection to the squad for Straeuli's first series, against Wales. Russell was totally unlike the stereotype one would have expected from Straeuli, who had been accused of playing antiquated rugby at the Sharks and put great store in the size of his players.

Indeed, in the early part of his reign, contrary to expectations, Straeuli appeared to encourage flair, and attacking players such as André Pretorius and Russell did well under him.

"My philosophy was all-out attacking rugby. Tim Lane and I did not differ on much; we both appreciated the same style of rugby, but I just felt we needed to play attacking rugby with [bigger] players," said Straeuli. Lane, as an Australian, seemed less preoccupied with size than Straeuli – and, for that matter, most other South African coaches.

After the Boks' good opening win over Wales in Bloemfontein, I was on my way to the post-match cocktail party when Straeuli approached me to say thank you for being positive about his selection choices. I had written that his selections thus far had not shown him to be a "Durban dinosaur", to quote another Cape-based rugby writer.

Straeuli's Boks followed up their strong performance in Bloemfontein with another in Cape Town, and then they also saw off Samoa in Pretoria and Argentina in Springs with minimal fuss. At least the new coach had the comfort of going into his first Tri-Nations season unbeaten after four games, and he had also spread his net wide in the selection process, with several newcomers being blooded.

"People said that I selected too many Springboks in my time, and maybe that is true, but I like to think that [by doing that], I helped the coach who [succeeded] me. The critics had a go at me when I moved Jaque Fourie from fullback to outside centre, but that was where he ended up playing for Jake White."

After trying different captains in the build-up to the Tri-Nations, Straeuli summoned Krige and asked him whether he would be his captain. According to Krige's autobiography, *The Right Place at the Wrong Time*, from that day forward Straeuli wanted them to have a relationship based on mutual trust.

Straeuli also told Krige that SARFU had not wanted him as captain, and Krige said that he appreciated Straeuli's honesty.

Krige said he quickly came to understand something about Straeuli, and that most of the Springbok players of that time would agree with him: the coach was honest in what he tried to achieve. According to Krige, the mistakes he made – and he did make plenty – were at least "genuine" mistakes.

Straeuli was drawn into his first controversy in his first Tri-Nations match, against New Zealand. The Boks started strongly against the All Blacks and the scrumming was solid. Lawrence Sephaka was playing his first Test and looked the part, only for Straeuli to surprise everyone by taking him off scarcely half an hour into the game.

The Boks went on to lose by 20 points, although they had been more competitive in the match than anyone had anticipated. But Straeuli was pilloried back home for bringing Sephaka off so early and was lambasted for not being flexible enough with his substitutions.

At home, the Boks were even more competitive and, like Viljoen before him, Straeuli has been left to lament the narrow margins that prevented him from winning the Tri-Nations. And Straeuli is right to feel aggrieved. Dave McHugh's refereeing in the Durban Test against the All Blacks was simply abysmal, so much so that a crazy fan, Piet van Zyl, felt impelled to run onto the field to confront him.

There was no justification for Van Zyl's behaviour, but McHugh had made several highly debatable calls that went against the Springboks in a tightly contested game. In fact, the Boks had even had the upper-hand for long periods of time. The All Blacks won it late, with their composure coming through in the final quarter, but McHugh had made it more difficult than it should have been for the hosts.

"That was one of three games that I now see as turning points in my coaching stint," Straeuli says. "We should have won that game. Apart from the refereeing, we didn't use all our opportunities and, had we done so, we would have won the Tri-Nations. That might have had an impact on how my career [continued] from there."

The Boks played some good rugby in that Tri-Nations series. In fact, they were outstanding against Australia at Ellis Park the following week. Brent Russell had been called into the side as a last-minute replacement for André Pretorius, who was injured on the eve of the game. The Wallabies weren't expecting the unpredictable Russell at flyhalf, which helped the Bok cause, but even so, they still impressed with the way they pierced holes in the Wallaby defence.

One try, featuring Bob Skinstad and Joe van Niekerk dove-tailing together as they struck from long range, was particularly sublime. The Boks were well up before a series of events conspired against them to allow the Wallabies back into the game. It looked ominous for a while when the Australians took the lead late in the game, but a brilliant try and conversion from Werner Greeff won it at the death.

The overseas media were mightily impressed with the flair and innovation displayed by the backline players, whom some scribes nicknamed the "Bok pygmies", and Russell became known as the "Pocket Rocket". And so the Tri-Nations ended on a positive note.

But it was to be the last positive smidgen the Boks would derive from Straeuli's first year in charge. The unmitigated disaster that was the end-of-year tour started with several top players not being available for selection because of injury or because they needed rest, and continued with the horrible knee-ligament injury the young debutant, Jean de Villiers, suffered in the first Test of the tour, against France in Marseille, forcing him off the field within eight minutes of the start of the game and out of rugby for eight months.

De Villiers was just 21 at the time and still an age-group player who had played in only one or two friendly games for the WP senior team. So who said Straeuli couldn't be bold in his selections? He certainly tried. Bakkies Botha joined Victor Matfield for the first time in the second row in that French Test.

Recalls Straeuli: "I was convinced that some of the older guys were coming to the end [of their rugby careers] and I needed to bring in youth. It didn't work out for me, but I like to think it worked for the coach who came after me, and may have played some part in us winning the [2007] World Cup."

Unfortunately, that tour would do nothing for the present-day Boks in the build-up to the following year's World Cup, to be played in Australia. The Boks stayed on a golf estate on the French Riviera the week before the French game, and all seemed calm. Perhaps too calm, for nothing could have prepared them for the cacophony that greeted them at the Stade de Velodrome. There is good reason why visiting teams fear the Marseille venue, and that night the Boks were outplayed from the first whistle to the last.

By all accounts, the mood in the camp in Bandol, where the Boks were staying, was very glum after the Boks' defeat, and the after-effects did nothing to unite the squad.

Matters didn't improve when what was effectively a second-string team were well beaten by Scotland on a wet day at Murrayfield, and England were still lying in wait ... This was a team that had been building for years and was bristling with confidence. Although the Boks started as rank underdogs, no one would have bet any money on the hosts winning as comfortably as they did.

"I really never thought I would see the day," *Daily Express* scribe Steve Bale said, shaking his head and looking very earnest as he pressed past me and disappeared into the Twickenham darkness towards the post-match press conference.

I never thought I would either – not in my wildest imagination. The final score – 3-53 – will forever be a blot on the Bok pride (as will the 0-49 defeat Jake White's team would suffer against Australia a few years later). Of course there were mitigating circumstances, as there always are with that type of score line ... The Boks had started confidently enough, but then lock Jannes Labuschagne was red-carded for a cynical late charge on Jonny Wilkinson – or, as Nick Mallett called it in his column in the next day's *Sunday Telegraph*, a "clumsy late charge".

But in truth, the Boks never had a hope in hell. There were just too many inexperienced players in the mix against a quality team, and when reduced to 14 men, the new players just weren't able to cope.

"I could see in the eyes of some of my fellow players that they just didn't want to be there," Corné Krige admitted afterwards.

The situation led Krige to do something for which he still apologises to this day – it was the equivalent of what an outgunned military regiment does when the realisation dawns that defeat, and probably death, is imminent. In other words, just take out as many of the other guys as you can. And that is exactly what the Boks did. Butch James and Robbie Fleck joined their skipper in the war, but unfortunately in his zeal, Krige also managed to take out one of his own players.

Of course, denial is sometimes the best form of defence, and at the post-match press conference, Krige reacted with incredulity when he was accused of dirty play. "Do you think we would take out our own player?" he asked, visibly shocked.

He was referring to the broken jaw André Pretorius had suffered during play. To his eternal embarrassment, though, Krige later discovered that the cameras had picked up a haymaker he had aimed at an Englishman and it had landed flush on his teammate's sweet spot. It was just one of several incidents that SARFU CEO Rian Oberholzer had to defend when both the media and the IRB started studying the Sky footage.

After the game I had a chat with English journalist Peter Jackson, and I mentioned the fact that several first-rate players were missing from the team and that that might make a difference when the Boks arrived in Perth for their World Cup pool game against England the following September. Of course, when they heard me saying that, some of Jackson's colleagues enjoyed a good laugh at my expense.

Up until then, Straeuli had been viewing the tour defeats as part of a learning curve, but he admits that after Twickenham, everything changed. It was probably after that defeat that he embarked on the downhill path that would lead to Staaldraad, among other infamous events in the year that followed.

"That was the second of the three turning points in my coaching stint," Straeuli remembers. "The defeat at Twickenham was hugely embarrassing, and it did start introducing a lot of doubts. When you start doubting yourself as a coach, [you have a big problem]."

The disastrous tour left the Springbok squad divided, and although uniting it once more would be the major focus of the turbulent year that followed, the coach and his players would only become increasingly isolated from one another.

19

Out of control

Mark Andrews wasn't selected to play under Rudolf Straeuli when he became the Bok coach, so he wasn't at Kamp Staaldraad, the infamous military-style camp that made a joke of South African rugby in 2003, a World Cup year. But when I interviewed him in 2013, he could shed some light on what Straeuli's intentions might have been with the camp, as he himself had attended something similar when he played for Straeuli at the Sharks.

"From what I understand, [the camp] was handled very differently in 2003, but when Rudolf first [started] at the Sharks, he sent us [away] on a bush camp. I [wasn't] crazy about [the idea] when I first heard about it, but it turned out to be of huge benefit to us. It was all done extremely well, and I think I learnt more about myself in that three-day *opfok* than I did over the whole of the rest of my career. It definitely brought the team together. I think the other guys will agree with me on that."

While the Springboks were suffering the ordeal of Staaldraad, England were on an exercise with the Royal Marines on the Devon coast, carrying logs across mud flats to help the players bond as a team. So the actual idea behind Staaldraad – to unite the squad – was not so off the wall. It was the way in which the camp unfolded and its repercussions that stunned the nation. Details of the camp, accompanied by graphic pictures, were leaked to the media in the weeks following the World Cup, and it soon became clear that this had not been a normal team-building camp; it went way beyond that. Most of the players who experienced Staaldraad and spoke about it subsequently said it was an ordeal they would not want to endure again.

Images of naked players huddled together in a pit and clinging to each other for warmth in an ice-cold lake were augmented by stories of shots being fired over players' heads, of them being forced to fight one another and having to manoeuvre their way through the sort of survival course one would expect to be set for members of the special forces in preparation for war.

When Straeuli and I met for this book, he didn't want to talk too much about Staaldraad. Understandably, he wants his coaching stint with the Boks to be judged on other criteria: the selections he had made, the success or failure of his game plan, and whether he had identified players who could make a contribution to his successors.

Unfortunately, life doesn't work like that, and Straeuli is acutely aware that Staaldraad has been his legacy. He says he has never specifically apologised for the camp, as it could have served a useful purpose if it had been better executed, but he has apologised to several of the players for what they had endured.

"I didn't approve of a lot of aspects of Staaldraad," Straeuli admits. "It was signed off by Rian Oberholzer and the idea came from Adriaan Heijns. Rian was close to [Heijns]. At times [during the camp] I intervened and stopped things. It did get a bit out of control. But the way [in which] it was published and the way SA Rugby later sold it to the media was wrong. It was a bit like a *Carte Blanche* programme where you get interviewed for five hours and then they cut a few things out and [the end result doesn't] quite reflect the full story or what was [actually] said.

"Heijns's company, Pro-Tect International, put forward a proposal to Rian, and SA Rugby bought into it. Their brief [was to focus on] security, which had become a big [issue] after the incident with the referee at Kings Park. Then they said they could do a nice camp for us that would bring the players closer together. It seemed a good idea to bond the players, but I didn't know how it was going to turn out.

"The whole thing was poorly [handled]. SA Rugby, the security company that arranged the camp and me ... we all handled it badly. Somebody on the inside sold the photos [to the media], and that [turned] the press against me. I take the criticism on the chin, but the full story hasn't been told."

Straeuli was quite vague when he talked to me about Staaldraad, but he did invite me to take a look at some paperwork that he said revealed the full story. Straeuli, who qualified as a lawyer in 1995, describes himself as a "paperwork-and-files type of person".

"Rather than just give you my opinion," he said, "I would rather you read through all the detail as it is in the files and on paper and [you can then] make up your own mind. Then you can tell the story in sequence."

Straeuli wants to write his own book one day, and I hope he does, as this book is too broad in scope, and the space dedicated to each coach too limited, to do his story full justice.

I never got to see the documents Straeuli mentioned. In the end, he decided that their contents were too sensitive, and he wants to hold onto them until his work in rugby is done. It's a pity, as the documents might mitigate the way he is perceived.

Hopefully, if there is information that will throw new light on Staaldraad, it will emerge in time. And it's important to remember that Straeuli was not sacked by SARFU – he stepped down. He was also financially rewarded for signing a confidentiality clause. Who is being protected by that confidentiality clause? What is the true story behind Staaldraad? Who should really be held responsible for the whole debacle?

All one can do at the moment is speculate. Straeuli's intention had been to recreate a camp similar to the one Mark Andrews had experienced with the Sharks, but instead things had got out of control. And, it seems, Straeuli may not have been the driving force behind the camp at all.

In his book, Corné Krige confirmed that the coach had been no more than an observer. More importantly, the players were told that Heijns and his men would have total control over them. Rudi would have no influence whatsoever; he would simply be an onlooker.

Twickenham 2002 had caused Straeuli to doubt not only himself, but also his players. Staaldraad, therefore, had been another in a long line of attempts to find the X-factor that was so clearly missing from the team. Straeuli admits that, because of the pressure, he did start doubting himself in 2003. Even Krige acknowledged that the extreme pressure would have negatively affected the coach's decision-making abilities.

As he explains in his book: "Everyone believes they can do better than the incumbent coach … We demand the impossible. Microscopic attention to everything he does translates into fearsome pressure on the coach."

For the Boks to win the World Cup that year was expecting the impossible, and even Krige later acknowledged that if someone other than Straeuli had been the coach, the results would not have been much different. The Boks simply lacked the talent.

Straeuli, however, may not have helped his cause by dropping experienced players during the course of the year. The season also kicked off with a significant change to the management team – Tim Lane and Les Kiss's contracts, which they'd signed with Viljoen, had expired and were not renewed.

"They worked out the year they had left on their contracts when I took over," Straeuli explains. "I wanted to bring a South African flavour to [the management team]. Maybe in retrospect Tim did give me a good running style of rugby. But if I [had to do] the job again, I would not compromise [as much]. You have to have your own management members in place from the outset. I had a management forced on me.

"Mark Keohane was good at what he did. He was essentially a spin doctor, but I felt he created divisions [within the group]. That was not good for the team at the time, as there were many different cultures within the group. And Brian van Rooyen was working behind the scenes at the time to become [the SARU] president, so there was a lot of politics.

"[But it] wasn't all bad, and we had some good times on tour. But when I dropped Tim, I think Keo felt he would be next."

Keohane spoke to the public and the media on Straeuli's behalf, and he put a certain spin on everything that happened in the camp, which did not help the coach's cause.

"[For someone else] to talk on your behalf is wrong. We're all intelligent enough to know what is sensitive, and we should know how to get advice. I was definitely not myself at the time, and maybe it would have been better if I had dealt more directly with the media. I think I got on okay with the guys on a personal level and [I never had] problems [with the press] before becoming Bok coach.

"So if I did it again, I would rather do the media stuff myself. You can get your PA to answer the phone and take down a number if you're not available. I felt I just wasn't myself during that period, and even the last statement I signed was a confidentiality clause."

There was far too much emphasis on trying to control the media at that time – something Keohane discusses in detail in his book, *Springbok Rugby Uncovered*. For instance, SARU even tried to wrest control of an opinion forum, which was quite bizarre. It was one of those idiotic and rather shallow player-rating pieces that newspapers seem to love so much. According to Keohane, during the Straeuli era the ratings that were published in *Rapport* were supplied by the coach and not the newspaper's rugby writers. The manipulation was extensive enough to conjure up images of George Orwell's book *1984*: Big Brother is watching you ...

201

Straeuli is right when he says that this interference did not help his cause with members of the Fourth Estate. As a rugby writer, you were expected to see only the positive side of the Springboks, but we would have been hard-pressed to find anything good to say about the first half of the Test against Scotland, which was the Boks' first Test of the year. In those 40 minutes, the Boks took the concept of turgid rugby to a whole new level. Virtually nothing appeared to happen for what seemed an endless period of time.

Nevertheless the Springboks, led by Joost van der Westhuizen and including combinations that seemed to signify the coach's intention to move away from the all-embracing rugby the Boks had tried to play the previous year, eventually scraped home 29-25. And then, the following week, a late flurry of scoring enabled them to win the second Test against the Scots 28-19.

By now Gert Smal and Rudi Joubert had replaced the Australians as assistant coaches, and while watching them take charge of the Springbok warm-up that preceded the Test against Argentina in Port Elizabeth, I wondered what new angles they might bring.

But what a dog's bollocks of a game that turned out to be. The Boks played well in patches, but mostly they were discordant and just plain horrible, with no continuity or pattern to their game and a blight of unforced errors. A last-gasp Louis Koen penalty from the touchline won it at the death (26-25), saving the team from the ignominy of being the first Bok team to lose to the Pumas.

By that stage, Koen was more or less the established Bok flyhalf. Even though he was the star of a Bulls team that had shown some improvement from previous efforts in the Super 12, they were still only playing 10-man rugby. It was clear to me that with Koen's selection, Straeuli was moving away from the running game his team had played when André Pretorius and Brent Russell had been the flyhalves. Under pressure, the coach was reverting to his Blue Bull roots.

There was so much chopping and changing in the team selections over those first three Test matches that one could only hope that Straeuli's "master plan" was unfolding. I said as much when I bumped into some fellow journalists having supper on the patio of a restaurant on Port Elizabeth's boardwalk. They guffawed with laughter, but their levity didn't stop me from filing a column for Supersport.com with the headline "Rudolf is a man with a plan".

I'm not sure what possessed me to think as much, but Stephen Nell of *Die Burger* (in those days, he was with the *Cape Times*) still rips me off every now and then with the words, "Rudolf is a man with a plan".

And he did keep telling us he had a plan; he kept telling us to "wait until the World Cup". Several of the senior players had been left out of the squad, and I naively believed that Straeuli would bring them back in later in the season. But Robbie Fleck, for example, who was one of my favourite players for an attacking game, was given only one opportunity in a friendly featuring an SA B team in Namibia, and A.J. Venter and Rob Kempson were either shunned or they quit. Skinstad was injured.

In his book, Krige relates how Venter infuriated Straeuli by telling him that he ruled by fear. And Fleck apparently called Straeuli a liar for making selection promises he didn't keep. Straeuli did not like to be challenged. Just like Nick Mallett in the 1999 World Cup, he became more and more withdrawn, and not even the captain could talk any sense into him.

According to Krige, it didn't take a genius to see that Straeuli was beginning to suffer under the pressure. In this, he was no different from any other Springbok coach who had succumbed to the pressure at some stage. It was almost certain as night following day that it would happen. As Krige puts it: "There are millions of people in the country who would swear on their mother's life that they know far more about rugby than the national coach ..."

Krige also said that Straeuli had his own ideas on team selection and, although it was obvious he was concerned, he didn't let on very much or discuss many aspects of it with his captain. In Krige's opinion, he should have. "If a coach doesn't communicate his feelings and thoughts to his captain, it makes it much more difficult for him out on the field during a match."

It had been a similar story with Gary Teichmann and Mallett in 1999, but fortunately John Smit and Jake White would set the benchmark for the coach–captain relationship in 2007. White and Smit were almost joined at the hip in the build-up to the Springboks' World Cup triumph, and the current Bok coach, Heyneke Meyer, has emphasised how important it is for him to have a captain who can be an extension of himself on the field.

Significantly, both Mallett and Straeuli contracted Mad Coaches Disease in a World Cup year. The success of François Pienaar's team, and the nation-building legend that sprung from it, has perhaps allowed the tournament to transcend sport for South Africans, and perhaps as a result we attach too much importance to it.

When I interviewed Straeuli in 2013, it became apparent that he had assumed additional responsibilities in his head when he took on the job, perhaps concerning himself with matters that were best left to others. As he explains: "There was unacceptable social behaviour, which was different from my playing days. A lot of [my so-called] paranoia were actually ploys designed to protect the players. I wanted to try to keep the team together. There are a lot of things the players won't want to talk about. Yes, I wanted to take them out of the limelight, and yes, that can be construed as a laager mentality. But in 1993, when I played for Transvaal, we would fly to the venue of our away game on the morning of the match in Louis Luyt's plane, go straight to the field, have a captain's run, then go to the hotel for a pre-match meal. Day rooms would be booked for us, and then it would be back to the pitch for the game, and we would fly back to Johannesburg afterwards.

"Our wives or girlfriends would pick us up at the airport, we would go to Luyt's house for maybe a braai and a few drinks, and then we would go home again. It was a protected, family environment."

Overprotective is probably the right word to describe Streauli, but according to Krige, he just didn't trust the players enough and wasn't prepared to treat them like adults.

After the narrow squeak against Argentina in Port Elizabeth, the wobbly Bok ship steadied with a great win over the Wallabies in Cape Town, although one couldn't really ascribe the victory to any planning on Straeuli's part. Instead, an injury early on in the game brought Brent Russell onto the field at fullback. The Pocket Rocket ended up making the difference between the teams in the second successive Bok/Wallaby Tri-Nations match on South African soil.

A combination of the heavy rain that fell for much of the week leading up to the Newlands Test, as well as Straeuli wanting to get away from the microscopic and all-pervasive attention of the Cape rugby media, impelled the Bok management to make a hasty change to their schedule. Instead of staying in Cape Town in the build-up to the Pretoria Test against the All Blacks, as had been intended, they opted to go to Durban instead.

I was booked to fly to Pretoria on the following Friday, but the Boks were leaving town and it was my brief to write about them, so I quickly had to change my plans, which wasn't very convenient. But there is nothing like embarking on a long drive through the Karoo to get rid of a bad mood. Heading for Durban early on that Sunday morning, with the clear skies and wide-open spaces surrounding me, I quickly forgave Straeuli his sudden change of mind. But the Springbok players, who were made to endure a torrid week, were not quite as forgiving.

For one, Straeuli had insisted upon a trial match for the Bok reserves. The match was played at Durban Varsity, and although the media were not informed of it, we knew it was happening. And then there was his decision to secretly change the accommodation arrangements in Pretoria ... The players had not been told that they would be staying at a hotel an hour or so outside Pretoria on the night before the game, with the result that their wives, girl-friends and friends pitched up at their usual team hotel to collect tickets for the game and wish the men well and found none of them there. It was an unmitigated disaster for the players. Krige was stating the obvious when he wrote: "Players like routine before a big game, and when it is disrupted, they get tense."

And that tension can lead to disaster on the field. The All Blacks, coached by John Mitchell, smashed the Boks 52-16 in the third of the three matches Straeuli sees as turning points in his tenure.

"It was a massive game for us, as it was Madiba's birthday and there was a lot of focus on that, so it was embarrassing to lose so heavily. Along with the Durban game against the All Blacks, when we should have won the Tri-Nations, and the 3-53 defeat at Twickenham, that was a turning point for me," says Straeuli.

The mind boggles as to why, if it was such a big game, Straeuli would have wanted to mess the players around so much on the eve of it.

"Maybe in retrospect I was wrong to do it, but at the time I wanted to take them out of their comfort zones. I believed in doing that."

The heavy defeat to the All Blacks, as well as the inept way in which the players had been managed in the build-up to the game, caused big problems within the group on the away leg of the Tri-Nations. Both Keohane and Krige wrote about the crisis meetings that were held throughout the tour and the elaborate attempts to keep prying eyes away from the Springbok camp.

Straeuli has an explanation for his actions, though. "Spying does happen," he says, "and it would be naive to think that opposition teams don't resort to underhand tactics to give them an edge. Perhaps my problem was that I had been exposed to it when I was playing for Luyt."

When I asked him to elaborate, he just smiled enigmatically and declined to say any more on the subject.

The Boks lost both Tests in Australasia, although they put up a competitive showing at a wet Dunedin pitch on a night best remembered for prop Richard Bands's brilliant solo try. At least it brought a flicker of hope for the eternally optimistic ... And then it was time to start the final preparations for the World Cup.

The extent to which Straeuli dropped and capped players can be gleaned from the fact that 21 of the 30 players who went on the 2002 end-of-year tour didn't make it to the 2003 World Cup. The result was that an unsettled squad became even more fragmented when an unseemly race controversy broke out at the training camp that preceded the World Cup squad announcement.

Again, Straeuli was trying to overcome what he perceived as cultural differences, but some players objected to being forced to interact with one another. When Bulls lock Geo Cronjé allegedly refused to share a room with Quinton Davids of Western Province, the details were leaked to Dale Granger of the *Argus* via Davids's connections in the Province team.

When Straeuli discovered that the two players had swapped rooms, he ordered an *opfok* session for the two men. Krige, who could not participate in the contact session with the rest of the squad, joined Cronjé and Davids. It was all very militaristic, and the irony was that it happened at the police training camp where Straeuli had elected to stay while in Pretoria.

The upshot of the *Argus* story was that Rian Oberholzer flew to Pretoria – as he had to Cardiff a few years earlier – to read the culprits the riot act, although this time only the management was on the receiving end and not the players. Straeuli was instructed not to pick Cronjé, but the coach was reluctant to leave him out.

The incident highlighted a marked division in the way the media approached the controversy – the English press attacked Straeuli, but on the Sunday after the squad announcement, when unbeknown to everyone outside the camp the Boks were *kakking off* at Staaldraad, *Rapport* appeared more concerned about who had leaked the story than anything else.

There was widespread booing when the Springbok squad was announced on the Saturday afternoon. Both Davids and Cronjé had been left out. The mood was ugly, and not for the first time a race issue was proving to be a divisive factor. To top it all, Mark Keohane had resigned his position because he couldn't "countenance racism any longer", and he was quite vocal about what had transpired.

Straeuli's take on events is interesting. As he explains: "The camps were good but not transparent, and I think the media attacked me because I didn't expose the guys so that [the media] could get [their] stories. They had to deal with Keo, and he would only [talk to] three guys and give *them* all the stories. Both he and Adriaan Heijns worked for Rian Oberholzer, and they would cover certain things up. I soon became aware of how much people in Rian's camp wanted to please him. But the stories never get told of what the real demands are on the coach, what requests are made on a daily basis that don't get into the papers and which SARFU are never upfront about. In my view, it is quite flipping important that the chief executive, the coach and the president are aligned, as they have to work closely together. They need to all have an intimate understanding of what the blueprint is.

"We never quite [got] that right. I always thought about what the rainbow should look like, but there was a lot of haggling over the team and its make-up, and behind the scenes there were hassles between me and the president and the chief executive about [which players] we were going to leave out.

"I ended up compromising, as I wanted to go to the World Cup so badly. I knew we were up against it, but I thought to myself that maybe we would steal it against England in the pool game and then, who knows? I felt I gave everything possible to guys like Corné to make them successful, but they often put me in a difficult spot.

"I wouldn't agree that I became unapproachable at that time, but I did become very sensitive and protective. In retrospect, I think I should have been more transparent; I should have avoided the temptation to put a spin on everything and just been honest in the press conferences and said it like it was."

Straeuli wouldn't be the first or, for that matter, the last Springbok coach to run into problems with unofficial race quotas, and the Sports Ministry at the time didn't help with their lack of clarity on the issue.

In the end SARFU appointed a commission of inquiry to investigate the allegations of racism within the Bok camp after their lawyers had already conducted their own inquiry. Surprise, surprise, neither inquiry came up with anything, probably because they lacked the will to uncover anything that might further have embarrassed SA Rugby.

With all the fun and games off the field, the Boks never stood a chance at the World Cup. Not that they'd had one anyway. Late injuries showed up the lack of depth in the squad, and the Boks lost the crucial pool game against England in Perth 6-25. Although they were competitive for much of the way,

Louis Koen missed some kicks and England scored a charge-down try just before half-time.

Hope was briefly rekindled back home when the Boks smashed Samoa 60-10 later in the pool phase, mostly because England had only just snuck in against the Samoans. But it was to prove false hope, as the Boks were never in their quarter-final match against New Zealand.

Of course, Straeuli didn't survive the World Cup. Nor did Rian Oberholzer. The latter made a heartfelt speech at a press conference I attended in Cape Town, telling us "what a wonderful ride" he had had and how he had enjoyed every minute of it. Straeuli snuck out the back door and didn't face the media.

Until now he hasn't spoken about his experience, and this is only half the story. Hopefully in time we will get to hear all of it, not only so that we can decide for ourselves who the real Rudolf Straeuli is, but perhaps also to lay the matter to rest once and for all.

20

Restoring some pride

SA Rugby was getting everything wrong at the start of what would become the Jake White era. The former Springbok technical analyst and successful national age-group coach wasn't even on the shortlist the new administration had drawn up. They had been appointed in the wake of the resignation of SARU chief executive Rian Oberholzer after the 2003 World Cup and Kamp Staaldraad debacles, and the departure of president Silas Nkanunu, who was not re-elected.

Brian van Rooyen came in as the new executive president, restoring the power that the provincial presidents had lost when Oberholzer and the professional, full-time administrators were holding sway. Some welcomed it as a good thing, but it would turn out not to be. The statesmanlike Morné du Plessis' tenure as an independent director on the SA Rugby board was short-lived, as he quickly resigned because of the way in which "all decisions are made on the basis of me being able to give you a bit of this in return for you giving me a bit of that", to quote the man himself.

In other words, too much bartering was going on between amateur office-bearers who had day jobs in addition to their rugby functions and who tended to make important decisions over bottles of wine. Lobbying was usually done over dinner the night before a scheduled meeting.

According to White, it was thanks to Du Plessis that his name finally made it onto a shortlist that had initially included coaches who weren't even involved at the top level on a full-time basis. André Markgraaff once again materialised as a potential role-player, probably because of the support he had given Van Rooyen during the electioneering phase. But he didn't want the job.

"Van Rooyen offered me the job as Springbok head coach; I had the job if I wanted it," says Markgraaff. "But I wasn't interested. I hadn't had any interest in being the Springbok head coach since I resigned in 1996. I had also been out of the loop for a while as a coach, so it would have been a crazy idea to accept."

Chester Williams was the Springbok Sevens coach at the time, and if you just considered his stature in rugby after a celebrated playing career, he was a likely candidate. But he had little experience and no track record coaching a 15-man team. Heyneke Meyer, the Bulls coach, was one of the four initial candidates, but after calling Markgraaff to confirm that he had been offered the job, he withdrew himself from the race, as he felt he had only been included to make up the numbers. (It is an interesting aside that Markgraaff says Meyer would probably have been appointed if he'd stayed in the running, and Markgraaff should know – he headed the committee that chose the coach.) The other member of the initial four was Border Bulldogs coach Dumisani Mani.

Du Plessis, at that point still one of the independent directors, asked why White wasn't an automatic inclusion on the shortlist, given that he was the under-21 coach. So his name was added, and with the preferred coach having withdrawn from the race, the playing field was level when the candidates, who were joined by Peter de Villiers and a few others to swell the number to nine, went through the interview and selection process.

"That was the only time during my long involvement with SA Rugby that the coaching appointment was done in the proper fashion, [as] it should be done for such an important position," says Markgraaff. "I was the head of the technical committee, and the process we conducted was thorough and exhaustive. Every other time it was done, even subsequent to that in 2008 and again in 2012, with Peter de Villiers and Heyneke Meyer respectively, it was a shambles. In 2004 we ensured that we appointed the best man for the job; there were no other considerations."

By all accounts, White "nailed" the presentation, although De Villiers was later to claim in his autobiography, *Politically Incorrect*, that SA Rugby had overlooked the fact that, in his position as a full-time employee of the organisation, White had been involved in formulating and setting the actual tests.

But there could have been no debate over White's coaching credentials. A schoolteacher before he became a full-time coach, White had risen through the ranks and progressed through all the necessary levels. He had already experienced Springbok rugby first hand as a member of Nick Mallett's management team, as well as Harry Viljoen's, had coached the successful 1999 SA under-21 team, along with Eric Sauls, and had then won what was effectively the junior world championship in 2002.

White had a hunger for improving his coaching education, and he was well known within the international rugby community. He was personal friends with, among others, England World Cup–winning coach Clive Woodward and Eddie Jones, the man who had coached the 2003 losing finalists, Australia.

White's appointment was announced at a joint press conference with Brian van Rooyen at the plush Santé Winelands Hotel and Wellness Centre near Paarl on a hot day in mid-February. It was a Friday, and the South African national cricket team was busy beating New Zealand in an ODI international in New Zealand. That series didn't turn out so well for the Proteas, but they were doing just fine when White addressed the media.

"I was watching the cricket team in action before coming into this press conference, and I was thinking that it was funny that they seem to have a habit of winning that we can't manage with our rugby team," said White. "There is no excuse for that. The Proteas are expected to beat smaller opposition when they play them and winning is an expectation and not just a hope. There is so much talent in this country. We need to be near the top of world rugby, if not at the top, and that is what I intend doing – we need to re-establish the pride in the Springbok jersey and make it admired again around the world."

Having worked with both Mallett and Viljoen, White had a very clear idea of what was best for the Boks. In 1997, he had been appointed as Mallett's technical advisor at Markgraaff's behest. Markgraaff had a high regard for White's rugby brain after his years working in the school system. White was the technical advisor at the Golden Lions at the time he first joined the Bok management team.

White was impressed with Mallett's coaching methods. For instance, Mallett brought in a businessman, Tim Southey, who imprinted on the players the importance of a team ethos and playing for the badge. White was also impressed when Mallett declined to go onto the field and join the players after they had won the Tri-Nations tournament at Ellis Park in 1998. He always put the players first and didn't want to steal their thunder.

When White was dropped from Mallett's management team in 1999 because of differences with assistant coach Alan Solomons, he became Eric Sauls's assistant coach at the 1999 SANZAR/UAR championship in Argentina. The Baby Boks had endured a nightmare 1998, but with White adding his expertise, they won the tournament in 1999. White was always superb at identifying talent, and players such as John Smit, De Wet Barry and Jaco van der Westhuyzen were destined to play important roles during his stint as Springbok coach.

Then followed a disastrous period as assistant coach to Hugh Reece-Edwards at the Sharks in 2000, and then another brief spell with the Boks, this time under Viljoen, before he took up the position of head coach with the SA under-21 team.

White's gift for identifying talent really came to the fore with the Baby Boks. Accompanied by Prof. Derik Coetzee, White flew around the country testing players and building up a database that catalogued the youngsters' strengths and weaknesses. The result was that he and his team lifted the inaugural Under-21 World Cup, which South Africa hosted in 2002.

"Victory put to rest some doubts about my credentials. I had never doubted myself, but a World Cup win, at any age group, was an important addition to my CV," White said.

Many of the young players who won the World Cup with White were senior players by the time he took over as Bok coach in 2004, so he was well primed on the talent he had available. He had identified a lot of the players who had come through, and he was a walking encyclopaedia on the background, strengths and weaknesses of each player.

With White already clear on which of the players he would use when he took up the job, one of his first tasks was to remove the stain Kamp Staaldraad, as well as the race controversy that had preceded the 2003 World Cup squad announcement, had left on the Springbok name.

White was only in the job a few weeks when he initiated the first controversy of his tenure by appointing John Smit as his long-term captain. Not that people thought he had made the wrong choice – they just didn't understand the rush. But White knew how important the captaincy was in the South African context – with all the disparate race, cultural and language groups that make up a Springbok team, he needed a leader whom all the players would follow and respect. White wanted one player to be in charge, preferably a leader who could be an extension of himself on the field.

The first camp under White convened in Bloemfontein a week before the Stormers, who provided seven Boks, played their Super 12 semi-final against the Crusaders in Christchurch. There were 22 players in the first squad and, in retrospect, White felt it was too few. He said Markgraaff, who was the national selection convener, had suggested the number.

Van Rooyen's reign as president had got off to a chequered start, and there was more than enough off-field controversy to undermine the public confidence in the Bok team. There was, once again, uncertainty over player contracts, and Van Rooyen's stance on the issue didn't endear him to the players. Later in the season, the players would wear white armbands in protest against the way they were being treated.

There were also injuries, with several players unable to complete the training camp in the build-up to White's first series, against Ireland.

But White remembers that the players were receptive to his ideas, which he found to be very positive. While the media was generally being quite negative, and some of White's selections were considered contentious (particularly those that pushed the transformation agenda), he was certain about his actions and his confidence was infectious.

I remember having a chat with him in the build-up to the first Test against Ireland – I think it was after the team announcement. He asked me for my thoughts on the match, and I said Ireland would be tough. I expected him to respond the same way most modern coaches do, which is to talk up the opposition. It was an off-the-record conversation, but White still surprised me with his confidence. He had no doubt that his team would win, and he made the point that South Africa should always expect to beat Ireland in South Africa.

And he had obviously inspired *me* with his confidence, because the night before the Test, after a function on the outskirts of Bloemfontein, I had a chat with Joel Stransky, who, like a lot of people, wasn't too convinced about the Boks' chances. But I tried to convince Joel otherwise, as White's positive outlook had persuaded me that his players would do well.

"There's something about that guy, as if he knows something we don't and knows how he is going to win," I said.

The next day, White started the practice of phoning stakeholders to inform them of the strategy the Boks would be adopting and what the aim of it was. His outreach initiative had the desired impact and gained him even more converts, as Straeuli had been of the opposite inclination, keeping everything top secret.

White was still a disciplinarian, but he was more relaxed than Straeuli, and it rubbed off on the players. He didn't want to rule by intimidation. Indeed, his first speech to the players was about fear and the need to control it. Rugby isn't life or death, he told them, so enjoy just the game and don't have any fear.

The Springbok forwards got stuck into Ireland from the outset, after which they maintained the momentum. Ireland had won the Triple Crown that year, so the fairly comfortable Bok win (31-17) was a good omen, particularly as so many of White's critics had thought they might lose.

But the Boks were not quite as emphatically superior in Cape Town the following week, where they won 26-17 on a damp field. However, considering the events at the close of 2003 and where they were placed on the IRB ranking list, they had every reason to be pleased when they completed the incoming-tour phase of the season with a big 53-18 win over Wales in Pretoria.

The Boks played a Pacific Islands team in Gosford, Australia, before the start of the Tri-Nations, and the 33-0 win over a strong composite team built confidence at a time when South Africans weren't winning overseas much. It was a good thing they played so well too, for that was the game in which they wore the white armbands in protest against Van Rooyen's refusal to offer national contracts. White had his first experience of being on the wrong side of a SARU president when Van Rooyen gave him and manager Arthob Petersen the third degree afterwards. White claimed that neither he nor Petersen had been in the change room when the players pulled on the armbands.

A slightly smaller controversy erupted when Victor Matfield flew home early from the tour, and the media speculated that there had been a falling-out between Matfield and White. It is true that the two men were never the best of buddies, but in that instance White felt that the reports were mischievous. The simple explanation was that Matfield had a knee problem which needed to be sorted out.

The Boks lost their first Tri-Nations Test – against New Zealand – under White in the cruellest possible way, conceding the lead only late in the game. But they scored three great first-half tries and led 21-12 before eventually going down 23-21 to a last-gasp try.

"The fact [that] we didn't win the match came down to a lack of self-belief," White told the team afterwards, but he had seen enough to be convinced that he could turn that around. After all, the game was played on Kiwi soil, where the Boks don't often win.

Although devastated by the loss, he was very careful about how he addressed the team. He emphasised that the Boks had the talent, the skills and the structures – it was just time to change the mindset.

But then White's former SA under-21 captain, Clyde Rathbone, who had emigrated from South Africa and taken up Australian citizenship, killed the Boks in the next game, in Perth, scoring a late try in a game where the lead changed seven times. However, the two bonus points they picked up overseas put the Boks in with a sniff of winning the Tri-Nations, provided they won their two matches at home.

The spirited way in which the Boks were playing had by now shown that White was on the right track and that the Boks were on an upward graph under his coaching. It had been a while since they had been competitive in the Tri-Nations matches in Australasia. Now they just needed to learn to win ...

And learn they did, most emphatically, in the first home Tri-Nations game, against the All Blacks. In the build-up to the match, White had his first real taste of political pressure being exerted on the selection process. He was forced to choose an extra black player, so he dropped Fourie du Preez for Bolla Conradie, and I am not sure Du Preez ever fully forgave White for that.

In fact, White had already decided on the team for the match and had even announced it to the players, but when Brian van Rooyen saw the names, he insisted that White start with Conradie. Fortunately Victor Matfield was back in the team, and the Boks won 40-26, one of their biggest ever wins against the All Blacks. Centre Marius Joubert scored a hat-trick of tries, joining Ray Mordt in the rare achievement.

The final game, in Durban, was the Tri-Nations decider, and the build-up was as entertaining as the game itself. White and his old mate, Eddie Jones, the Australian coach, were waging a bit of psychological warfare against each other.

White said a "hate the Wallabies" campaign should be launched, and called Jones hypocritical for defending his lock, Justin Harrison, on eye-gouging claims. Jones responded by saying White was orchestrating a "smear campaign" and that he was guilty of a "cheap and personal" attack. Many of us suspected they were just having some fun, which they probably were.

There was lot riding on the match, though, as the Springboks had won the Tri-Nations only once before, and that was six years previously under the captaincy of Gary Teichmann. The Boks always looked like they had the game in hand, and they led 23-7 when Percy Montgomery and Breyton Paulse were both yellow-carded towards the end of the game and the Wallabies came back to force them to hang on for the win. Despite the close shave, pride had at last been restored in the Bok jersey.

A four-Test tour to the United Kingdom was next, and it presented a chance to achieve a Grand Slam. This inspired much hype in the media leading up to the Tests. However, White saw it differently. He wrote in his autobiography, published three years later, that he saw the tour as an opportunity for new and fringe players to gain experience ahead of the 2007 World Cup.

His tour selection was much criticised. Eleven black players, including Jongi Nokwe, the lightning-fast wing, formed part of the squad. The issue of black players and transformation agendas was thrown into the spotlight after the Test against Wales in Cardiff. The Boks were leading comfortably when White, thinking the clock had nearly run down, emptied the bench, with several black players, including Tim Dlulane, coming on.

As it turned out, however, there was significantly more time left than White had thought, and the Welsh came storming back to make it a close game. Afterwards, at the press conference, White explained that he had got the time wrong, which was why he had made the mistake of sending so many replacements onto the field and why the game had ended up being so close.

The question many of us then asked was why he was selecting those players if they weren't good enough, which he seemed to be implying by his comments.

The next match, against Ireland, will be remembered for the ludicrous mistake made by New Zealand referee Paul Honiss. Honiss had instructed John Smit to talk to his teammates after an infringement, and several of the Boks had their backs turned to the Irish when their opponents took the tap and scored what turned out to be the winning try.

The build-up to the game had not been without controversy either. White had made public pronouncements that said a lot about his confidence and ability to think outside the box. An example of the latter was his intention to play Jean de Villiers, who up till then had played most of his international rugby on the wing, at flyhalf. The actual flyhalf, Jaco van der Westhuyzen, was struggling with an injury, but he recovered in time and was able to play. However, White had fully intended to play De Villiers in the No. 10 jersey if Van der Westhuyzen did not make it.

And White's confidence was evident when he was asked which players in the Ireland team would make his Springbok team. His answer was that there were only one or two Irish players he considered good enough for the Springboks. It was a case of answering a straight question with a straight answer, something White almost got right to a fault for much of his stint as Bok coach. But boy, did the Irish let him have it in the media that week; Dublin was certainly a fun place to be for South Africans.

White might have won the Tri-Nations earlier in the year, but if he thought that would exempt him from pressure, he was quickly convinced otherwise. Back home, the defeat against Ireland was regarded as a major setback. And worse was to come the following weekend when they lost 16-32 against England on a dark, wet London afternoon.

That match was played at the end of a week in which White got embroiled in a major political selection storm. He had selected Jaque Fourie to cover England's big wing, Ben Cohen, but that left him with an all-white team, and while many in the media supported his decision, I did not. White should have been savvier about rugby politics and known that he wouldn't get away with it. When I arrived at a training session at a Richmond club ground and saw Breyton Paulse, the man dropped for Fourie, training among the reserves, I immediately knew White was going to get into trouble.

I approached manager Arthob Petersen, who was standing on the side of the field, and asked him if he was happy with the team. He said he wasn't. And it didn't surprise me when the team was later changed. Paulse, with so many Test matches behind him, should never have been made to feel like a quota player.

As it turned out, there was a long-term solution to any threat of the Boks becoming too lily-white during White's tenure. It was provided by Bryan Habana when he came off the bench at Twickenham for his first cap and scored the only try for the well-beaten South Africans.

White's biggest concern after the game was the physical beating his team had been given. Addressing a press conference in a room under one of the Twickenham stands that doubled as a gym, he pronounced that it had been like "men playing against boys".

White was absorbing a few lessons himself about the realities of playing rugby in the northern hemisphere. I picked that up from skipper John Smit when I interviewed him for a magazine feature during the last week of the tour. Smit told me that the Twickenham experience had been a wake-up call for everyone, including the coach.

In his book, White says that he started to get irritated with André Markgraaff before the final Test of the UK section of the tour, against Scotland in Edinburgh. The former Bok coach was interfering with team selections and had also been sending White messages via assistant coaches Gert Smal and Allister Coetzee on when to make substitutions.

With Jaco van der Westhuyzen producing one of his better games and kicking well out of hand, the Boks easily dispensed with Scotland, winning 45-10. Not only did the Boks impress, but White also advanced the transformation cause by selecting Solly Tyibilika, Gcobani Bobo and Gurthrö Steenkamp. The team for the last game of 2004, against the Pumas in Argentina, had a similar multiracial look to it.

The Boks beat the Pumas 39-6 to complete a year in which great strides had been made. White seemed untouchable at that point, as the Boks had improved significantly from the end of the Straeuli era. For his achievement in turning the team around, White was named the IRB Coach of the Year, the Boks were named Team of the Year, and Schalk Burger Player of the Year at the end of his first full international season.

When the Boks arrived home, the rugby public was in a much better mood than it had been 12 months previously, when the team had exited the World Cup in the quarter-finals.

One wondered what great things lay in store for the coach and his team the next year ...

21

A stay of execution

During his first season in charge, Jake White's results were good enough for his contract to be extended by two years, up until the World Cup in 2007. But while he had enjoyed a more successful first season than most of his post-isolation predecessors, it would be wrong to assume that the pressure that leads to Mad Coaches Disease wasn't already bearing down on him.

SARU had appointed Ian McIntosh to mentor White, and McIntosh saw at first hand what effects the pressures of the job had on White in his first year.

"The issue of pressure and what it does to you is very pertinent to any story about the Springbok coaches," says McIntosh. "The pressures are huge, and I am not sure that people who haven't experienced it can relate. Even Kitch Christie struggled with it, and he won every game. Kitch had never been matey with me, but in January 1995 he asked me out to lunch in Durban. What he really wanted to know from me was how I'd dealt with the pressure.

"I saw Jake go through it. Many people helped Jake during his four years, and I was one of them. When he came back from his first trip with the Boks, he called me to say that he was struggling to cope. He asked me to come to Cape Town. When I got there, he was as white as a sheet. He said 'Everyone is criticising me. What can I do?'

"I told him that even though he had lost some games, there had been a hell of a big improvement on the previous year, and that he should ignore the criticism because he was doing a good job. You could almost see the colour coming back into his face as I spoke."

Winning the 2004 Tri-Nations did not exempt White from the pressures McIntosh mentioned. On the contrary, they intensified in 2005, and when

White would not succumb to what was nothing less than political bullying, it nearly cost him his job before the Tri-Nations even started.

It happened in Port Elizabeth, in the build-up to the second Test against France. The teams had drawn the first Test in Durban, so the match at Boet Erasmus was a series decider, and yet manager Arthob Petersen, also a member of the SARU executive, wanted White to rest Schalk Burger, one of the best players in the team, so that Solly Tyibilika could bolster the black representation.

Dan Qeqe, a legend of black rugby in the Eastern Cape, had died the week before, and White, assistant coach Allister Coetzee and skipper John Smit attended the funeral. Tyibilika was part of the squad, and White was going to introduce him when he was ready, but Petersen wanted Tyibilika to start out of respect for Qeqe.

White told Petersen there was no room for sentiment. Up till then he had exceeded the transformation requirements laid down by SARU, and he was frustrated that he was now being told whom to select.

"Suddenly it wasn't about transformation, but about picking the black players they wanted when they wanted them. I had to put my foot down," he wrote in his book, *In Black and White*.

After the press conference during which the team was announced, White was informed that the board of SA Rugby would be holding an emergency meeting to discuss his refusal to toe the line. White stood his ground, and Petersen then called a management meeting and informed White's assistants that he had resigned. Petersen asked them where they stood on the matter. They made it clear that if White was out, they would follow him.

But White expected the worst. Although his contract was loaded with key performance indicators, all of which had been exceeded, his bosses were shifting the goalposts. The behind-the-scenes drama had been published in the Independent Group's Saturday newspapers, with Dale Granger, as usual, the first to break the story.

If ever a coach needed the team to play well to save him, it was White on that day at Boet Erasmus Stadium. And the Boks rose to the occasion, turning in a powerful performance and winning 27-13. Afterwards, White was reminded of something that has remained true throughout the post-isolation era – win the Test and whatever crimes you were accused of beforehand are quickly forgotten. At the post-match cocktail party, it was congratulations and back-slapping all round.

But unbeknown to some of us on the press beat, Brian van Rooyen had vowed that he would get a black coach to replace White. Early the next morning, I bumped into White outside the breakfast room at the Kings Beach Garden Court, and I said how delighted I was that Peter de Villiers's SA under-21 team had just won the junior world championships in Argentina the night before. In retrospect, I now know why he shot me such a dark look – he would have known that De Villiers's success threatened not only his standing with the administrators, but his very job.

But White retained control over the team, and nothing further was said to him about his personal revolt in Port Elizabeth. The team then travelled to Australia, where they lost the Mandela Plate game in what was to be the last match that some of the stalwarts, such as De Wet Barry, were to play as first-choice players.

Although they didn't manage to retain their Tri-Nations title, the Boks continued on their upward trajectory in 2005, the highlight being a great win over the All Blacks at Newlands. The Kiwis had just whitewashed the British & Irish Lions and were rated as a freakishly brilliant team, so the Bok victory was one that resounded around the rugby world.

And the Boks had actually improved on their Tri-Nations performance of 2004, winning as many games as New Zealand but losing out on bonus points. With three victories in four starts, the results were superior to the previous season's two out of four, when they'd won the trophy.

With two games already scheduled against Australia in the Tri-Nations, adding two Mandela Plate matches to the schedule seemed crazy. For the return Plate game in Johannesburg, White chose nine black players in his match 22, six of whom were starting, and the SARU administrators actually reproached him for not taking the game seriously enough. They even accused him of "dishonouring Mandela", which was deeply ironic coming from the same people who shortly before had pressured him into choosing players of colour.

But White's contention was that his team could beat Australia at home no matter whom they fielded, and that was how it turned out. With Tyibilika doing well on the flank and Jean de Villiers and Jaque Fourie excelling in their first outing together as a midfield combination, the Boks raced into a 20-3 lead, and at one stage led 33-8 before eventually cruising home 33-20. De Villiers had played mostly as a wing before then, but after that game, the No. 12 jersey was his.

It was a great advert for the depth that was available to White, a confidence-booster for the Tri-Nations and a good indicator of the way forward.

The big off-the-field news at the start of the Tri-Nations was the battle that was raging between Brian van Rooyen and André Markgraaff. Markgraaff, as head of the technical committee, was supposed to be in charge of rugby matters. White, however, resented his interference, and claimed that Markgraaff became irritated when he did not consult with him.

Matters came to a head on the eve of the Tri-Nations, when White told Van Rooyen that he was tired of Markgraaff dictating to him on issues such as selection and tactics. White pointed out that his contract said nothing about him having to report to Markgraaff, who was then also the deputy president of SARU.

As White told Markgraaff: "My contract's quite simple – I don't deal with you, André. You're the deputy president. If you want to change the contract, that's up to you, but I deal with the managing director of the company."

According to White, Markgraaff was fuming by the time the squad arrived in Pretoria for the opening Tri-Nations game. However, Markgraaff says his anger with White had nothing to do with rugby, but with the way that White was meddling in rugby politics.

"I had a lot of fights with Jake, and we really hated each other at one stage, but none of those fights were about rugby," says Markgraaff. "The Springbok coaching stuff was secondary. Jake was meddling in the politics and getting involved with Van Rooyen, who I knew was conducting bad corporate management."

Markgraaff subsequently took leave of SA Rugby in protest against Van Rooyen. This was after White had sent a letter to Van Rooyen via his agent Craig Livingstone, in which he complained about Markgraaff's interference, his attitude towards selections and his "constant badgering" about the tactics White employed. This letter was leaked to Dale Granger, or so Markgraaff believed, and it was splashed all over the newspapers.

"To this day Markgraaff thinks I sold him down the river with that letter," White wrote in 2008. "I wasn't happy with his constant interfering, but I would never knowingly have stooped to stitching him up." Markgraaff, however, remains convinced that White had leaked the letter. "How else would it have ended up in *The Argus?*" he asks.

The Wallabies led at the break in Pretoria, but the Boks came back strongly in the second half to win a tight Test match 22-16. That was followed by the great win over the All Blacks in Cape Town by the same score. Then two breakaway tries by Bryan Habana set the Boks on the road to a rare away Tri-Nations victory, in Perth, which set up a Tri-Nations decider in Dunedin the following week.

Not only the Tri-Nations but also the world No. 1 ranking was up for grabs. There was also the satisfaction of winning three consecutive games against the All Blacks. But the South Africans were again denied off the last move of the game, as they had been the previous year, and lost 27-31.

Missing out on the No. 1 ranking by the narrowest of margins only served as extra motivation for White as he started to look into the future and focus on the 2007 World Cup. He was convinced that if he could keep the players together, they would be serious contenders. Because of that, he saw the Tri-Nations as a success, even though his team didn't win it.

The big end-of-year tour game would take place in Paris, and for White it was an important juncture in the build-up to the World Cup, as the tournament would be held in France.

However, before travelling to Europe, the Boks first played in Argentina. They won the Test in Buenos Aires 34-23, a game I will always remember for the adulation shown soccer star Diego Maradona, who sat in a suite not far from the press box, and the incident where Jean de Villiers unwittingly pushed wing Lucas Borges into a 10-foot moat running around the perimeter of the playing area.

It was also a game in which flyhalf André Pretorius was badly injured, and White, addressing a few media people early the next morning, said he would back rookie Meyer Bosman to start the next Test, in Cardiff. It was a hugely controversial decision, as Bosman had hardly played flyhalf for the Cheetahs. But the pivots who had been left at home did not fit into White's game plan.

At that early-morning press conference, he joked that at least he would never be the first Springbok coach to lose against Argentina, as the Boks would not be playing the Pumas again while he was the coach. Of course I reminded him of his words when his team ended up playing the Pumas in the 2007 World Cup semi-final.

The Boks then travelled to Wales, and won 33-16 in Cardiff. However, the media was divided in their opinion of Bosman's performance. It was a similar story when the Boks lost to France on a bitterly cold night at Stade de France. It snowed in Paris on the morning of the match, and the Boks looked pretty frozen too, as they trailed 0-15 after as many minutes before making a comeback and eventually losing by just six points (26-20).

Little did White know it then, but that defeat was the start of a long period of heartache that would end, and only partially so, when his team beat England at Twickenham exactly 12 months later.

And what a 12 months it was for both White and Springbok rugby, for to say that 2006 was a rough year would be an understatement.

It was always going to be taxing on the playing side, not only because of the wear and tear the players had been subjected to in the first two seasons, but also because SANZAR had decided to extend the Tri-Nations schedule from four matches to six.

White already knew how important it was to give key players some time out before the World Cup year, so he would not have been happy when one of his best players, Schalk Burger, was ruled out with a long-term neck injury in the second Test of the year, against Scotland in Port Elizabeth.

White had also started the year seeking clarity on his request for an extension of his contract. The issue was complicated when the RFU approached White, asking him to make himself available for a director-of-rugby position after 2007. Those two factors, along with the loss of Burger, added to an already highly stressful week before a match against France at Newlands.

The SA Rugby board had promised they would respond to White's request for a contract extension before the Bok camp in May, but by mid-June he still hadn't heard anything. He says he just wanted a yes or a no so that he could start making other plans for after the World Cup. Of course, he was still hoping that his contract would be extended.

An agency had headhunted White for the RFU job, and he was just asked to apply; he was not being offered anything. If he did get the job, it would only commence after the following year's World Cup.

"It came back to bite me," White said in his book. "The story that ended up in the media was that I'd been offered the RFU job, and was going to walk away as Bok coach unless SARU upped my contract. Someone had leaked that idea to the media. I was disappointed but not surprised, because it suited the board to ensure that I looked like the bad guy."

As a result of the media fallout, White and SARU's manager of national teams, Andy Marinos, answered some pointed questions that had little to do with rugby at a press conference on the eve of the French Test. It fuelled the speculation and drove the controversy as the Boks suffered what was to be their first home defeat under White.

The team for that Newlands game had been poorly selected, with regular No. 8, Joe van Niekerk, playing on the open-side flank in Burger's place. Other injuries just added to the shambles. It wasn't a huge surprise when the Boks lost 26-36, and White knew he was now in a weaker bargaining position, as Bok coaches always are following a defeat.

Suddenly, the Boks were stagnating after the growth of the previous two seasons. The defeat against France had been preceded by underwhelming 36-16 and 29-15 home wins over Scotland and a sloppy performance against a weak scratch World XV.

White admits now that the pressure of the job was getting to him, and as he wrote in his autobiography, he was probably coaching for his survival rather than trying to take the Boks forward.

And then, of course, there was the Luke Watson issue. The son of the controversial Eastern Cape activist Cheeky Watson was captaining the Stormers and Western Province at the time, and judged purely on his rugby ability, the critics were right to slam White when he did not call up Watson when Burger was out injured.

White justified his decision by saying that he was not a fan of the specialist open-side "fetcher" role for a flanker, and came up with what would become a famous quote when he said that the only fetchers he knew were his sons, whom he dispatched to the fridge to fetch him beers.

But Watson was a better all-round rugby player than most specialist fetchers, and while admittedly not tall enough to be a line-out option, he has subsequently gone on to play effectively in all three back-row positions. It is hard to imagine, again from a purely playing point of view, that Watson would not have been a better option at No. 6 than Van Niekerk, or, for that matter, Solly Tyibilika or Pierre Spies, who succeeded Van Niekerk in the role of open-side flanker towards the end of that Tri-Nations season.

However, while there were valid reasons to include the in-form Watson, assembling a rugby team requires sensitivity to issues that go beyond individual players. And when Watson fired off some unflattering salvoes against White in an interview with *SA Sports Illustrated* magazine, he was as guilty as the coach of creating a situation that helped neither of them.

White's back row was horribly out of balance for the first 2006 Tri-Nations match, against the Wallabies in Brisbane. I wasn't on that tour, but listened to the game on the radio as I was driving back from a holiday in the Transkei. Nicky van den Berg was covering it on the Afrikaans channel, and it was almost like listening to a song as the score just kept mounting… "Australia gabble gabble Springboks NIL… Australia gabble gabble Springboks NIL." It ended with Australia 49, Springboks … nil. It was a day to rival the massacre at Twickenham a few years earlier, when England won 53-3.

Injuries and poor selection had played a part in the debacle, but White claimed that issues off the field had not helped matters. For a start, there was no team manager on that trip, as Arthob Petersen had run into contract problems. Naas Botha was White's team manager at the Baby Boks in 2002, and White wanted him back, but SARU wouldn't allow it because Botha worked for SuperSport. White was also told that he had to have Vusi Kama as his media liaison, which was a crazy decision, as Kama would replace Rayaan Adriaanse, possibly the most efficient media man the Boks had employed in 22 years.

As White later recounted: "I didn't have a team manager, I was told to take a back seat with the media, and then I was given an inexperienced media manager. Their reasoning was that [Kama's] skills needed to be developed by getting him out of the office and touring with the team. I've got no problem with that, but in one breath they were saying my interaction with the media was a problem, and in the other they were giving me a media man who, by their own admission, needed to be developed."

The identity of the media liaison was a minor problem in comparison to the demand for greater progress in transformation. White had selected Breyton Paulse, Ashwin Willemse, Lawrence Sephaka, Tonderai Chavhanga, Gurthrö Steenkamp, Ricky Januarie, Bolla Conradie, Hanyani Shimange, Solly Tyibilika, Tim Dlulane, Quinton Davids and Jongi Nokwe over the two and a bit years building up to 2006, but suddenly there was a new demand for "ethnic black players" to be included. The Ndungane twins, Odwa and Akona, were the only ethnic black players playing regular Super Rugby.

The press and the ethnic-black issue would conflate during the Australasian leg of that year's Tri-Nations and spark a major controversy in the build-up to the Test against New Zealand. White selected Solly Tyibilika for the game against the Kiwis, and although he was a specialist fetcher, he was nowhere near the league of Luke Watson. And then Dale Granger got White hopping mad when he wrote that White had been forced to select Tyibilika to satisfy a racial quota.

As Granger later told me, the whole situation became quite silly after that. White took up the issue with Granger's employers, the Independent Group, back in Cape Town, and he went straight to the top. He was extremely irritated that Granger had reported that Tyiblika was being selected because he was a black player.

"That was incorrect and insulting to Solly and the story did some damage. SA Rugby were annoyed that I'd been quoted in the media when they had told me to stay out of it. It was an official press conference, which I had to attend. And besides, what I said and how it was interpreted were quite different ...

"I was annoyed, too, because board members were staying in the same hotel while this was going on. They never came to a media conference, never came downstairs and said to the media: 'Hang on chaps, let's understand this. Thank God we've got a coach who understands transformation, who's bought into transformation, who's been genuine about transformation and who's prepared to give players opportunities.'"

But in his autobiography, Jake's explanation of the whole saga suggests that Dale was right – his motivation for selecting Tyibilika was to give the board members what they wanted – an ethnic black player in the team. It seems as if White was blaming the messenger when the real issue was the administrative hurdles he had to jump.

The Boks got points on the board early on in the Wellington Test when Fourie du Preez scored a charge-down try, but after that it was mostly the Kiwis. And the pressure on White intensified. The ugly side of South Africans' passion for rugby surfaced back home, with White's son Clinton actually being verbally abused because of the Bok defeat.

There were flickering hopes of redemption when the Boks concluded the away leg with a far more competitive performance against the Wallabies in Sydney, with just a late Mat Rogers try four minutes from the end preventing them from winning the game (they lost 18-20). But any hopes of complete redemption were dashed when the All Blacks beat the Boks 34-18 at Loftus.

That was when the grey beards of SARU stepped in and, with no clue of what else to do, arranged the meeting between White and the former Bok coaches. White's head was on the block, and with the next match against the All Blacks looming, at the Royal Bafokeng Stadium in Rustenburg, it seemed there were many who hoped he would be axed.

At this point, White suspected that there were sections of the media who wanted him out. This was confirmed to me by the reaction of one of the

Afrikaans scribes when I suggested that the win over the All Blacks was important. The All Blacks' fate was sealed by a late André Pretorius penalty, which was perhaps not the most convincing way to win. "Does this mean that everything is okay now?" the journalist asked me with a sneer as I hurried into the post-match press conference.

Five losses on the trot was one defeat away from equalling the Boks' worst ever run of defeats, whereas the All Blacks had won 15 games consecutively heading into the Rustenburg game. So regardless of where the All Black heads may have been after a week of enjoying the pleasures of Sun City's Valley of the Waves, it *had* been a good win.

My own attitude to White had softened on the eve of the Test when I bumped into him after the taking of the team photograph at KwaMaritane. White owned up to his mistakes, and maybe the meeting with the former Bok coaches had steadied him a bit and staved off a heavy dose of Mad Coaches Disease. He seemed more humble than he was at a press conference in Umhlanga Rocks just the week before.

Although he and I differed over the inclusion of Luke Watson, at least White was able to explain why he had left the player out. The reasons were simple: he didn't rate Watson as a player, but he also couldn't fathom how he would fit into the team environment when he had been so public and personal in his criticisms of the coach and the Springbok symbols.

Instead White had chosen Pierre Spies, who had not played since a nightmare debut at No. 8 in Brisbane a month earlier, at open-side flank for the Rustenburg game, and while it was a left-field selection, the Blue Bulls loose forward played out of his skin. A.J. Venter and Pedrie Wannenburg were also brought back, with White opting for traditional Bok physicality. And it worked, just as it did at Ellis Park against the Wallabies the following week.

Fortunately the Australians turn into a group of bumbling pscyho cases whenever they go near Ellis Park, so that win was hardly unexpected, but the two victories at the end of the Tri-Nations season at least bought White a stay of execution.

22

Vindicated

Jake White's face looked tense as we approached him in the crowded bar area of the Burlington Hotel in Dublin. I was with Mark Keohane, who was embroiled in a war with White via his website and other media forums, so I braced myself as the pair approached each other. They shook hands rather tersely, with Keohane seemingly the friendlier of the two.

"Good luck tomorrow," he said.

White responded by pointing around the room, at the general heaving throng of Springbok supporters who had converged on the team hotel on the eve of the match against Ireland.

"It's amazing how many people I know here. I've bumped into a whole lot of guys from Jeppe, guys who support me through thick and thin. Real tough buggers who don't take shit," White said.

Later on I asked Keohane if he thought that White, in a veiled way, was threatening him. He hadn't thought of it, but said that it was possible. Dale Granger had told us that during the Australian tour White had mentioned the name of some guy who might "sort him [Granger] out". Granger felt he had been threatened.

Whether that was the case or not, I personally witnessed the interesting but complex relationship between White and Keohane over the next year. In November 2006 they couldn't stand each other, but 12 months later Keohane and I were sharing a flat in Paris and he was taking regular early-morning calls from the soon-to-be World Cup–winning Springbok coach, who was asking for his advice.

It progressed to the point where Jake was confiding in Mark to such an extent that he and I infuriated the other journalists because we could write the news of the day without having to travel out to the Paris suburb where the Springboks conducted their training sessions.

I mention all of this because it illustrates how vulnerable White was at critical times of his tenure, and also in some ways how human he was. He was intensely hurt whenever Mark criticised him – it was as if he was being attacked by a friend, and he reacted like most ordinary people probably would in such a situation. And then, when the pressure was on, he sought Mark's advice and saw him as a shoulder he could lean on outside of the camp.

In *The Springboks and the Holy Grail*, Dan Retief mentions how White enjoyed having the odd drink during the World Cup, often with Keohane. It is true – I was present at some of those sessions.

As Keohane was not on the 2006 end-of-year tour, it's not clear who White's drinking buddy was then, but he would have needed one. It will be remembered as the tour during which White was called home to justify his selections to the SARU President's Council. I will never forget how I first heard that he had been called back. I was in a nightclub near the Liverpool Street Underground in London when Doug Anderson, then the sports editor of the *Weekend Argus*, reached me on my cellphone.

"We've just heard that Jake has been called home by the SARU bigwigs to defend his tour selections," said Anderson.

When I asked him why he was calling me in the middle of the night, he pointed out that it was already 10 a.m. back home. I checked my watch, and he was right. It was 8 a.m. London time, and it would be light outside. Whatever had happened for that night to disappear so quickly will forever be a mystery to me, but less mysterious than the forces that conspired to order White home to explain tour selections he had been perfectly upfront about from the outset.

Professor Tim Noakes of the Sports Science Institute in Cape Town claimed that Nick Mallett had erred during his tenure by overplaying some of his key players, and White was determined not to repeat the same mistake the year before the World Cup. It was the centenary of the first Paul Roos–led Springbok tour of the United Kingdom, and the Boks were desperate for some success after their failures earlier that year. However, White was in the difficult position of having to juggle the desire to win against the necessity of resting players for 2007.

He secured a small victory when he managed to negotiate a rest period for the Boks during the Currie Cup, and the SARU board also acquiesced to his request that some players be rested instead of going on the end-of-year tour. John Smit had to be there as the captain, but otherwise most of the other top players would stay behind.

"For once, everyone [among the administrators] seemed to be pulling in the same direction," White said.

But nothing creates pressure as much as defeat does, and, after the Test against Ireland, it was enough to make the administrators forget their agreement with White and to start hopping around like they themselves had Mad Coaches Disease. White had chosen Jaco Pretorius on the wing and Bryan Habana at centre for the match against Ireland, which was so insane that I wrote a column in which I wondered whether he had had enough of the pressure and was trying to get himself sacked.

It turned out not to be the case, but White had reason enough to feel down in the dumps. Prior to the start of the tour, he had asked for Morné du Plessis or Naas Botha to replace Arthob Petersen as team manager, but he was told that he had to have "an ethnic black guy" in that position.

Enter Zola Yeye, who had actually been appointed eight months earlier without White's knowledge. White was only told of Yeye's appointment when the team had already gathered in Johannesburg. White was supposed to go to the airport to meet Yeye, who was flying in from Port Elizabeth, but he refused on the grounds that he hadn't been consulted about the appointment.

As a result, White was summoned to a President's Council meeting at O.R. Tambo International Airport on the eve of the Springboks' departure. Needless to say, it was an acrimonious meeting. White asked, quite fairly, why Naas Botha had been ruled out because of his SuperSport connections when Yeye, an SABC employee, was considered acceptable.

"SARU vice-president Mike Stofile implied I was a racist," White said in his book. "The council members were annoyed that I didn't agree with them often enough, and that I didn't follow their instructions. They even accused me of being a 'Brian van Rooyen man', saying I'd campaigned for him in the presidential elections earlier in the year. It was rubbish and when I denied it, they accused me of lying."

Before White left on the tour, the board made it clear to him that they found it hard to support him, and, as it turned out, it would become increasingly hard for anyone to support him after the Lansdowne Road Test.

Jaque Fourie was supposed to have been on tour, but he had broken his hand, so Habana was moved to centre, where he had to mark Gordon D'Arcy and Brian O'Driscoll, who were in top form. Much of the rest of the team was also out of sync, particularly the back row, which made for a disastrous match on a chilly and windswept evening. Ireland were always in control and won 32-15.

"It was all experimental. We made our priority beating England, as we would be drawn with them in the World Cup the following year," explained White.

The plotters and schemers in South African rugby politics began to circle White. While the coach could understand the outcry in the media, he couldn't fathom the reaction of the administrators.

"The team had been signed off not only by the president, but also by the two vice-presidents, as well as the chairman of the board. That was a clear indication to me that they understood what the intentions and objectives of the tour were."

White made six changes for the first Test against England, the most significant being the return of Butch James at flyhalf. Jaco van der Westhuyzen had been jettisoned earlier in the year, and André Pretorius had started against Ireland. James ended up playing a blinder against England, and it was no coincidence that the side was well ahead when he went off with a season-ending injury and then ended up losing the match in the last quarter.

White was slammed for the substitution, but it later emerged that James was injured, and he played no part the following week. The defeat gave all the Jake-haters the ammunition they were looking for and it provoked the President's Council into ordering White home. But I was actually encouraged by the Boks' performance in that game and was one of the few rugby reporters who refrained from criticising the team and the coach.

Perhaps because I had been present at all the other Twickenham defeats in the preceding years, I had good reason to believe that the team would break their long drought at the stadium the following week. And with the pack and Pretorius playing a blinder, that is exactly what they did. The result was a lifesaver for White, as South African rugby was way too cowardly to replace the coach when his team had just beaten England.

"But it was a close-run thing," says the man in the know, André Markgraaff. "I know for a fact that Jake was effectively sacked and it was only really the intervention of Johann Rupert that saved him."

Indeed, *Rapport* had even run a story under the headline "Koebaai Jake" on the Sunday after the *first* England Test. That Jake was fired was written as fact, and the story was based on the crisis meeting Oregan Hoskins, Mpume-lelo Tshume, and vice-presidents Koos Basson and Mike Stofile had held on the Friday night before the first Test. There they had apparently decided to inform the President's Council that they had lost faith in the coach and the selectors.

Hoskins and Tshume met with White the following week to deny that any of it was true, but by then they had been overtaken by events back home.

I was at the Holiday Inn in Woodstock the following Wednesday when a sheepish-looking White arrived for his dressing-down by the SARU President's Council. He had been in the air all night, in business class admittedly, but he looked like a naughty schoolboy waiting outside the headmaster's office as he exchanged nervous banter with the journalists.

"Of course the win over England helped, and hugely so," White said later. "I'll probably never really know how much the sponsors and Johann Rupert's interventions were responsible for helping me keep my job, as a lot of it happened behind the scenes. But I suspect they weren't insignificant."

When White was finally called into the room where the meeting was being held, it was clear to him that the board had already cast their votes. He was later told that five of the 14 unions had voted against him.

"I was grilled for two hours. Some questions were good, others rather ridiculous, but I was ready. It soon became clear that most of the presidents were basing their questions on what they had read in the papers ..."

White left with "a tentative backing until the World Cup", which was a huge relief for him, and he returned to England just in time to see a mix-and-match Bok selection, led by Chiliboy Ralepelle, the first black Bok captain, win against a scratch World XV to conclude a nightmare year.

The next year didn't start much better than the previous one had ended. White was finalising a 44-man squad that selection convener Peter Jooste would present to Hoskins when he started to hear rumours that moves were afoot to get Luke Watson into the team.

White was accused of being opposed to Cheeky Watson's political stance, which he denied, saying that he didn't even know Cheeky until he started criticising him.

"I never rated Luke Watson as a Test-quality flank. It was as simple as that," White said emphatically.

White also didn't view Watson, who was educated at Grey College in Port Elizabeth, as a previously disadvantaged player in the way some politicians appeared to do. But he desperately wanted the Watson issue to go away permanently in the World Cup year, and for that reason had been considering an offer made to him on behalf of Cheeky Watson by lawyer Brian Bierbuyck.

White met with Bierbuyck, and the latter pulled out a document consisting of nine points, the gist of which was that Watson would be picked for the Springboks and would go to the World Cup.

Recalls White: "They were listed like a set of demands stating that, in return for my co-operation, the Watsons could ensure that I would work in South African rugby beyond the World Cup. It went on in that fashion, until we got to point nine, which warned that if I did not agree to these 'terms', I would not coach the team to the World Cup."

White considered it only because it would get the media and politicians off his back, and one "approved" player might be worth the sacrifice if he could have another 29 players he actually wanted. But the Watsons called off the deal, which left White feeling a little relieved, as it had made him uncomfortable, but at the same time he was also peeved that the Watson issue would not go away.

When White was called to a President's Council meeting on the Tuesday before the first squad announcement of 2007 for the purpose of "clarifying his thinking", he feared that the Watson issue would again rear its ugly head.

As he relates in his book, the Council first quizzed him over Odwa Ndungane. Zola Yeye tried to push Odwa Ndungane's case by saying that the family had told him that the player had been "almost suicidal" after being left out of the squad for a previous tour.

White argued that Ndungane was too slow to play for the Boks, and in White's defence, the wing had not always been the first choice at the Sharks that season either. The President's Council didn't want Bob Skinstad, Ashwin Willemse or Tonderai Chavhanga in the group, and, as White had suspected would happen, he was then told that the Council would like Luke Watson to be considered.

Flying back to Cape Town, White and selection convener Peter Jooste discussed what had transpired. After arriving home and giving it some thought, Jooste phoned White to say that while "politically it's the right thing to include Odwa, politically it's wrong to include Watson".

So Jooste went back to the presidency and said that they would include Ndungane.

Later in the week, Hoskins, who was under a great deal of political pressure, called White and asked if he couldn't just include Watson in the squad. White blew Hoskins off and, perhaps naively, thought the matter would rest there.

But it all went pear-shaped on the Saturday afternoon in the build-up to the team announcement at Kings Park, where the Sharks were playing in one of the Super 14 semi-finals. White had stayed in Cape Town to let Peter Jooste and Hoskins handle the announcement.

"At 16h30 I received a text message from Jooste, saying, 'You won't believe it. They've announced the team on a pre-recording, and Watson's name was read out.' They had handwritten his name at the bottom of the pre-typed 45-man squad."

As White correctly remembers it, this interference would backfire badly on SARU, as the media soon found out that Watson's name had been added after the fact, and most rugby commentators and scribes came at them with both barrels firing.

White's lawyers drafted a letter to SARU expressing his unhappiness with what had happened in Durban, but they never got an answer. Watson himself, after undergoing "tremendous personal growth" during his stint with English club Bath, later said that his selection had been "wrong" and that he should never have gone through with it. He said he'd felt like a pawn in a political game, which was how most of us saw it at the time. For White's part, he was right to treat Watson the same way he treated every other player.

All the political back-stabbing unfortunately deflected attention from the high point of what was South Africa's first ever Super Rugby final, featuring the Sharks and the Bulls, which was both sad and infuriating for all concerned.

There were so many sideshows at the time. I remember interviewing John Smit and asking him how he felt about SARU deputy president Mike Stofile, who wanted Schalk Brits to be selected ahead of him. It wouldn't be the last time that the people appointed to administer the game in South Africa were running it into the ground. And the coaches and players, as usual, were caught in the middle.

Eventually a deal was brokered between White and the board chairman, Mpumelelo Tshume, allowing for Watson to play against Samoa in an early-season game, but it was little more than a farce. And it was all going down in an all-important World Cup year.

In the end the rugby fates conspired in favour of White. The Bulls won the Super Rugby final and were so gracious in victory that the 46-man

Springbok squad was immediately harmonious. An under-strength England team was easily dispatched in two Tests, and the Samoan match, overshadowed by Watson's controversial debut, was a no-brainer.

White planned to rest his key players for the away leg of the Tri-Nations, but he fielded a full-strength team for the first match against the Wallabies, in Cape Town. That was the game in which John Smit was injured early on and the Boks lost their shape and structure before Frans Steyn saved the day with two drop goals.

The second home game, against New Zealand, was a big one. Kiwi rugby was thought to be on the back foot after their failed Super 14 campaign, in which two South African teams had contested the final. However, key players in the Bok team were injured, with Bob Skinstad playing at No. 8 in a team that was without, among others, Fourie du Preez, Juan Smith and Jaque Fourie. The Boks were also tired after playing non-stop for so many weeks, whereas the All Blacks had been able to rest during the week of the Super 14 final. This may explain why the visitors managed to finish so much stronger than the Springboks in the Durban Test, winning 26-21.

For White, the result confirmed that it was the right decision not to send the entire squad to Australasia. The Boks lost the away games, but White saw enough to know which guys he wanted for the 10 World Cup positions that were still up for grabs.

The 19 players who did not travel to Australasia gathered in Cape Town for a training camp supervised by technical advisor Rassie Erasmus. Erasmus would later resign from the Bok camp when he was offered a job with the Stormers and Western Province, thus allowing for Eddie Jones's appointment. The former Wallaby coach had initially been called in as a consultant and was expected to be present at just a few sessions, but in the short time he was with the Boks, White recognised the value he could add. Jones was a man adept at taking existing ideas and putting a different spin on them, which appealed to both White and the players.

So White approached SA Rugby via national teams manager Andy Marinos and acting chief executive Jonathan Stones to obtain board approval for Jones's appointment as his assistant, and although there was some resistance, he eventually got the go-ahead. Jones had coached a team to a World Cup final, and his experience would help White maintain his equilibrium both as the World Cup drew nearer and during the entire Springbok campaign.

The Boks built up to the event without much fanfare, and fortunately there was none of the negativity that had accompanied Rudolf Straeuli's team to Australia four years earlier. In the World Cup itself, White's consistency in selection paid off, and little went wrong for the Boks apart from Jean de Villiers's injury in the opening game. That brought Frans Steyn into the mix, and Schalk Burger's four-week suspension for dangerous play offered an opportunity to Wikus van Heerden.

With Fourie du Preez and Juan Smith playing out of their skins, the Boks smashed current champions England 36-0 in the big pool game to book themselves the high road to the final. Fiji and Argentina were the play-off opponents en route to a return match against England in the final.

However, there were a few hiccups along the way. Mark Keohane and I were on the TGV from Montpellier, where the Boks had played a pool game against the USA, to Marseille when White phoned Keohane to tell him that C.J. van der Linde had just gone down injured. Van der Linde recovered and played in the final, but B.J. Botha had been injured in the previous match and had to fly home, so there was a mini prop crisis for a while, and Jannie du Plessis was then flown to France as cover.

New Zealand and Australia had been knocked out of the tournament in the space of a few hours, prompting me to get uncharacteristically excited and run through the streets of Marseille shouting, "Four more years, guys, four more years," to anyone who looked remotely like a Kiwi. The World Cup was there for the Springboks' taking.

The emotion of seeing them win the World Cup aside, I vividly recall the behind-the-scenes drama that was unfolding due to SARU's poor handling of the succession plan. White had been quite disingenuous too, as he had already made up his mind months before the tournament that it would be his last hurrah. In retrospect, I fail to understand why he then made such a big issue of the fact that his employers were looking for a new coach.

SARU advertised White's position before the quarter-final match against Fiji, which was an unnecessary distraction. At a meeting between White and Stones, the coach was told that he had waived his rights regarding negotiations when he had made it public before the tournament had even started that he would not be coaching beyond the World Cup.

"I assumed that my performance would be reviewed after the World Cup and I would be able to make a decision then," argued White, not without justification.

The coach was nervous in the build-up to the final, and understandably so, and it was evident when he had a drink with some of us at the team hotel in St Émilion a few days before the match. He kept on asking us what we thought, seeming to need some reassurance.

It was during this period that Eddie Jones was worth his weight in gold as a calming influence. He told Jake that there was nothing else that could be done, that the players had been prepared as well as they could be. That calmness may be one of Australian rugby's big strengths, as I recalled something I was once told by Tiaan Strauss, who played for both South Africa and Australia.

"With the Boks, we were psyching ourselves up the night before the game and still doing last-minute things; with the Wallabies, it was a case of switching off after the last practice and then just switching on again before the game," said Strauss.

The Boks did not have a special game plan for the final. They just needed to be clinical and efficient and deny England the field position they needed in order to smother them, and that is how it turned out in the game.

It was an emotional moment when the team lined up to receive their medals and White let Eddie Jones go in front. Then it was on to the party at the team hotel, which lasted into the early hours of the morning. White probably hadn't slept much, and neither had I, to be honest, when he pitched up for the press conference the next day, and it was there that he said that he would like to carry on if he could, as there was still a lot to achieve with the team.

SARU should have stepped in then and asked him if he was available to continue. He had just won the World Cup, for goodness sake. It might have spared us the speculation that followed, and White having to call a press conference after he got home where he said: "For the record, I didn't feel like I should need to reapply for the job because I had just won the World Cup. But I'd had enough anyway."

And he had.

"Without the support of your leaders, you're ultimately going to fail" should probably be remembered as White's most telling parting shot, for it sums up so much of what has gone wrong in Springbok rugby over the past 22 years.

23

An insult from the boss

When Jake White and his team paraded the William Webb Ellis trophy around the country after their 2007 World Cup triumph, the multicultural support that rained down on them from all sides said one thing – South Africans will put their racial identities and cultural consciousness aside if the national team wins and brings pride to the nation.

But politicians aren't necessarily sports supporters and their agendas are often quite different from what the people they serve really want or need. And by the end of 2007, there were enough politicians both on the periphery of and within the South African Rugby Union who felt that it was time for the sport to take the next big step: to appoint a black Springbok coach.

To achieve that end, the more scientific and performance-orientated approach André Markgraaff's technical committee had brought to the process, and which had led to Jake White's appointment in 2004, was abandoned.

Instead, the technical committee now consisted mainly of administrators, many of whom had a political agenda. As a result, one of the committee members, Sharks chief executive Brian van Zyl, abstained from voting. According to him, Heyneke Meyer had nailed all the tests that had been set and was clearly the best candidate for the job.

Meyer was the public favourite after becoming the first South African coach to win the Super 14, with the Bulls, the previous year. Yet the other eight members of the committee wanted Peter de Villiers, and it was on that basis that De Villiers was called from his home in Paarl early one January morning to attend his first press conference as the new Springbok coach.

The eccentric De Villiers opted to wear a Bulls blazer to the media event to convey a message to the nation. He wanted everyone to know that although he lived in the Western Cape, his selections would be all-inclusive and he would be representing the whole country.

It was the job he had always coveted, but De Villiers did not have a good first day at the office. When he arrived at the SARU offices, acting chief executive Johan Prinsloo met him at the entrance and informed him that he may not be the new Bok coach after all.

It turned out that the provincial presidents had objected to the technical committee's decision, and the President's Council was now voting on the matter. So De Villiers spent an agonising few hours awaiting his fate, wondering who would ever believe that for a short while he had, in fact, been the Bok coach. He had been instructed the previous night to keep it under his hat, and he had.

But eventually the decision went in De Villiers's favour, by one solitary vote (11-10), and he found himself facing the media. What could possibly go wrong now? Well, as it turned out, quite a lot. De Villiers could hardly believe his ears when he heard SARU president Regan Hoskins announce him as the new coach and almost in the same breath proclaim that he had not been appointed "for rugby reasons alone". Essentially, what Hoskins was saying was that De Villiers was an affirmative action appointment.

In his autobiography, *Politically Incorrect*, published a few months after he had left the Bok job, De Villiers claimed that Hoskins's words set the tone for his tenure, and that the media and the public saw everything in terms of that statement.

"I had really wanted the day of the announcement to be the last day I was referred to as a 'black' coach. Although I did see myself as breaking the mould and offering hope to the black kids in the townships, to be seen always as the 'black' coach would also put unfair pressure on me. And I was already putting enough pressure on myself.

"Focusing on the colour of my skin made me feel tainted, as if everyone was judging me as a black man who was a coach, instead of just as a coach who happened to be a black man. I didn't want to look for an easy way out if I made a mistake; I wanted to be judged on my coaching abilities alone.

"The upshot of Regan's words was that everyone perceived me to be a political appointment. I had to decide how I was going to live with that. I was no different from, say, the traffic cop who becomes the chief of traffic because of the colour of his skin when everyone knows he's not the best traffic cop in the department."

I was away on holiday in the Drakensberg on the day of De Villiers's appointment, so could not personally judge the mood at the press conference. But Cape Talk presenter Mike Wills asked me what I thought of the appointment, and I said that De Villiers had won trophies with both the national under-19 and under-21 sides, similar to his predecessor, Jake White.

Wills reminded me on air that at least White had also been a part of the Bok management for a long time, first under Nick Mallett and then under Harry Viljoen. I took note of his point, and mentioned it in a feature I wrote for the following Saturday's *Weekend Argus*. I adopted the same approach I had 11 years earlier, when Carel du Plessis was appointed: only time would tell whether De Villiers was the right choice or not.

But I also took on board a quote attributed to De Villiers in an internet article I read: "The perception that I am the first black coach must end now."

I decided that I would adhere to De Villiers's request – I would not treat him as a *black* Springbok coach, but as just another Springbok coach. But it got me into a lot of trouble with De Villiers's supporters over the next 12 months. For it quickly became apparent that this particular coach, despite wanting to be assessed just like any other Bok coach, could not be criticised in the quite same way one criticised others.

"I agree with you, but do you realise that this is very sensitive? You are writing about the first *black* Bok coach," a colleague of mine commented after reading one of my articles.

That sort of logic made no sense to me, nor did the double standards applied by some of the people who disagreed with me. One internet blogger based in New York in the same breath said that my views were racist but that De Villiers was an affirmative action appointment, and why couldn't I see that? Even a member of the Springbok management said that.

"I can't understand your line. You know he's an affirmative action appointment, so why are you being so hard on the guy?" he asked.

It astounded me.

I didn't see De Villiers as black, and I refused to see him as an affirmative action appointment, so when he started talking about trying out a new, unstructured game plan with the Boks, much like the one Carel du Plessis had tried, I criticised him for it. After all, the Boks were the world champions at the time and had won the World Cup playing their own style of rugby.

I was starting to feel increasingly isolated because of my views, but then I received a huge compliment that put everything in perspective for me. I was the ghostwriter of Brendan Venter's column in the *Cape Times*, so I used to speak to him regularly, and he shared a lot of my views. But he warned me that I had a problem that wasn't really permissible in the South African context – I was colour-blind. Three years later, De Villiers would echo Venter's assertion when he asked me to write his book. According to him, even though I had been his biggest critic, my criticism had always revolved around rugby issues.

I'm not sure whether Peter was being completely honest when he said that, because at times my various employers took me to task for what I was writing, as they were on the receiving end of complaints from Div. I believe in writing it like I see it, and what's the point of having an opinion if you can't express it openly?

It annoys me intensely when rugby commentators are asked which team they think is going to win a match and they respond by saying that they're proudly South African and are backing the Springboks on that basis. Does that answer the question? I think not. Years ago, when the same Venter was on tour with the Boks in New Zealand as a player, he tackled me about something I had written and accused me of being unpatriotic. I told him I was a reporter and not a supporter. Although it's hard not to get emotional – my colleagues reproached me for having tears in my eyes when John Smit lifted the World Cup in 2007 – that should be every sportswriter's goal.

In early 2008, I received an email from Chris Hewitt, who was the Bok media liaison at the time. He told me that De Villiers objected strongly to an article I had written during the first training camp of his tenure. In the article I had said that, because he was new to international coaching, he would have to rely heavily on the experience of his captain, John Smit.

But I had also been the first to applaud his decision to bring Smit back from France, a move that some of De Villiers's main backers at the time, such as Cheeky Watson and Mike Stofile, vehemently opposed.

At the first Bok training session under De Villiers, which took place in Stellenbosch, I took a seat next to Venter, who was watching from the stands. He was delighted to see that far from rolling out an "unstructured" game plan, De Villiers was focusing entirely on structure. I was just as delighted. The only problem was that it was a carbon copy of the Stormers' structures. This would infuriate Rassie Erasmus, the Stormers coach, who obviously wasn't happy to see his ideas exported, and it led to a temporary rift between him and Gary Gold, who was assistant coach both at the Stormers and at the Boks.

But once the season got going, the adherence to structure was no longer so absolute. The Boks comfortably won De Villiers's first Test in charge, against Wales in Bloemfontein, playing a very structured game. But then the next week at Loftus, in the second Test against Wales, they nearly ran aground when they played quick-tempo rugby. Someone close to the assistant Bok coach, Dick Muir, observed that he could see the "Dickie influence" at work. The uncertainty over what style they would play continued for a few months and tripped the Boks up on occasion.

If anyone was done an injustice during the De Villiers era, it was Muir. The former Springbok centre had agreed to become De Villiers's assistant on the basis of the style of rugby he wanted to play. However, Muir soon found himself fighting a losing battle. As the pressure for good results escalated and the realisation dawned on De Villiers that he would have to rely heavily on his senior players, he started veering from his intended path. Muir's reputation took a battering while he was their assistant coach, as many critics quite bizarrely blamed him whenever the Boks struggled.

And yet a year before he became the Bok assistant coach he had been within a few minutes of becoming the first South African coach to win the Super 12. Only a freak late try by Bryan Habana prevented Muir from touching the coveted trophy, and this in a game that was played in Durban, because the Sharks topped the log, and that had been dominated by the Sharks. If Muir had won the Super 12, would he have been a candidate for the top coaching job? It was something I thought about a lot when Heyneke Meyer was appointed in 2012 essentially because he had been the first South African coach to win the competition.

The early part of De Villiers's tenure as Bok coach was not an easy ride. He and his family were racially abused at that first Test in Bloemfontein, and when the media turned on him with uncontained fury after the Boks lost their first Tri-Nations Test, against the All Blacks in Wellington, he even considered giving up the job.

While there was nothing unusual about the defeat – the Boks had not won in New Zealand since Gary Teichmann's team had tasted victory at Athletic Park in 1998 – there had been massive expectations back home. The All Blacks were under-strength, and it was the first clash between the traditional giants of the game since the Boks had become World Cup champions in France six months earlier.

But the Boks seemed to be playing two different styles of rugby in that game, neither of which they executed to perfection, and they lost 8-19. I strongly criticised De Villiers after the defeat, and perhaps in retrospect I was a bit over the top. It was just one game, after all. But I was informed from within the camp of the clash between the two different rugby philosophies preached by Muir and De Villiers on the one hand, which espoused heads-up, off-the-cuff rugby, while on the other Gold and the senior players wanted to stick to the structures they knew.

Still, that may not have been reason enough for the strong criticism I directed at De Villiers. In *Politically Incorrect*, he said that he felt he just couldn't win – half the country wanted him to fail because he was black, and the other half wanted him to fail because he had selected white players.

And he certainly wasn't popular with his backers when he decided to recall Smit and Victor Matfield, who would play dominant roles within the squad. I had been unaware of it at the time, but in the week leading up to the Wellington game, a political faction was applying tremendous pressure on the new coach. And this group would bug him constantly over the first two years of his tenure.

Cheeky Watson, political activist and father of Luke, was one of De Villiers's big backers in his quest for the Bok job. Watson pitched up in Wellington and demanded to meet with De Villiers at his hotel. There, Watson informed the coach that he was the emissary of the sports minister, Makhenkesi Stofile, and had been sent to tell Div that he had better put Luke Watson in the starting team.

De Villiers later confronted Stofile about the incident, and asked him why he would support the aspirations of a white player when there were so many deserving black players in the country. The sports minister denied that he had ever spoken to Watson.

But the message was abundantly clear to De Villiers – the advisory group he had assembled to help him with his decision-making had backed him only for their own ends. And one of their aims was for De Villiers to select Luke Watson. The other factor that united them was their enmity towards the Springbok emblem.

A year earlier, De Villiers had been quoted saying that Luke Watson would make a good captain (he had coached him at age-group level), which wasn't the same as saying he wanted him to lead the Boks. No promises had ever been made. And as far as the Bok emblem was concerned, De Villiers was emphatic:

if the emblem was banned, he would take SARU to court, as his contract specifically stated that he had been employed to coach the "Springboks".

De Villiers's support group had been assembled after Mike Stofile, who had been a big De Villiers supporter when he was vice-president of SARU, left the organisation. In his absence, De Villiers felt alone, as he knew he didn't enjoy much support within SARU. And the statement Hoskins had made at the press conference still rankled ...

Although he had been successful at age-group level and had coached the Baby Boks to tournament victory in the 2005 IRB championship, De Villiers had never been popular with his bosses. The main reason for this was his belief that he would be appointed to a position only if he was good enough to fill it, and he therefore felt that he didn't owe anything to anybody. In his eyes, he was where he was only because he was the best man for the job.

De Villiers had served as an assistant Bok coach under Mallett in 1997, and was also an assistant coach with the Bulls. But these were short-lived and mostly controversial stints, as he objected once he started suspecting that he was there mainly for window dressing – which he abhorred.

Knowing that his support group had deserted him, and with the backlash from home to his team's first defeat hurting him to the core, De Villiers wondered if he should call it a day in the build-up to the next match against the All Blacks, in Dunedin.

"By then I had started to think I wouldn't be coaching the team after the tour. I reckoned that I would be relieved of my position when we got home. Everyone just seemed so divided over me as the coach."

To crown it all, De Villiers, in his inimitable, eccentric way, confided in the press that he had no control over whether his team won or lost a game, which of course did not exactly enhance his reputation as a coach. For De Villiers was right when he later came to the realisation that everyone wanted the Boks to win every game they played, regardless of how pretty they were while doing it.

The coach made some key changes for Dunedin, most notably Percy Montgomery returning at fullback. In the match, the Boks made a return to their more structured approach, which they'd displayed to perfection at the 2007 World Cup, and hung on just long enough for a moment of inspired individual brilliance from Ricky Januarie, who scored the winning try.

It was a big moment in De Villiers's career: it was the first Bok win over the All Blacks in Dunedin, and also their first victory on New Zealand soil since 1998. It ensured that, like the Lions series victory and Tri-Nations triumph the following year, De Villiers's tenure would not be remembered as a reign devoid of major achievement.

Unfortunately the Boks then lost the next game, in Perth, when De Villiers made a few changes counter-intuitive to the structured approach that had won the game in Dunedin. After that 9-16 defeat, the pressure was on when they got back to South Africa. Awaiting the Boks was a return match against the All Blacks in Cape Town.

Percy Montgomery would celebrate his landmark 100th game in the green and gold, and afterwards De Villiers blamed the "sideshows" for deflecting the focus of the players that week. But De Villiers was also being subjected to massive political pressure. He read in the newspapers that members of his supposed "support group", such as Cedric Frolick, had criticised him for recalling Fourie du Preez, who was returning from injury, ahead of Januarie.

De Villiers had always considered Du Preez to be his No. 1 scrumhalf, and had told him as much when he'd met with the Bulls player in Stellenbosch earlier in the year. But Du Preez had been out with a shoulder injury, and in his absence Januarie had won the game for the Boks against New Zealand. De Villiers would brook no debate, however – Du Preez was a world-class player.

Although he may himself have become the Bok coach to satisfy a transformation agenda, De Villiers's own attitude towards transformation differed markedly from those of the politicians and rugby administrators.

"Transformation is a bit of a swear word for me. I'm more concerned about a change of attitude than a change of skin colour," he said.

To some extent, De Villiers had been naive about his backers' motives, although it is hard to believe that he could have been completely oblivious to them. Be that as it may, the matter was to become particularly ugly after the humiliating 0-19 defeat to the All Blacks at Newlands. This loss elicited further criticism of De Villiers's game plan, but much, much worse was to come.

After the game, media liaison man Chris Hewitt approached De Villiers and informed him that Cheeky Watson and Cedric Frolick had in their possession a video tape of De Villiers in a compromising position with an unnamed woman. The alleged incident had occurred in an East London car park, and Watson and Frolick had asked Hewitt to inform De Villiers of the existence of the tape. De Villiers immediately called in Hoskins, who made Hewitt repeat the allegations.

Whether Hewitt just had an overactive imagination or there really was a sex tape we will probably never know, for he was tragically killed in a light-aircraft accident later that same year. But it didn't take long for the sex-tape controversy to hit the headlines. The story broke after the completion of the Tri-Nations in a move De Villiers believes was orchestrated by Watson and Frolick. Far from being the support group De Villiers so badly needed, they were now actively working to have him removed from the position.

"I would rather have a white coach who listens to me than a black coach who doesn't," was one quote that De Villiers attributed to Frolick in *Politically Incorrect*. There were vague threats of taking legal action after the book was published, but nothing ever came of it.

For once, though, I would like to see a rugby book that has not been written with incidents involving the Watsons as a selling point, so let's move right along – to that second game of the home leg of the Tri-Nations, where the Springboks lost 13-27 and De Villiers was booed by the Kings Park crowd afterwards.

In the week prior to the match, a crisis meeting between management and players was called. One faction implored De Villiers to go back to the World Cup style of rugby, and the players in general demanded that the senior players be allowed more input. De Villiers had always based his management style on player participation anyway, and the Boks did start to return to a more direct approach in the game that followed.

But not all was well. Someone within the camp told me after the game that the Boks had been given conflicting messages at half-time. One coach had preached one thing, and then Victor Matfield was told to ignore what he had just heard. I never wrote about this myself, but I did tell my colleagues about it and the story made the newspapers. Of course it resulted in a witch-hunt in the camp to establish who had leaked it.

When I interviewed De Villiers for *Politically Incorrect*, he did not deny the confusion that had reigned at the time.

"It was rooted in the different philosophies of the assistant coaches. I had chosen them because of their divergent philosophies, but when we got down to the nitty-gritty, it amazed me just how much their philosophies differed. Gary was conservative in outlook and had a rigidly structured approach, whereas Dick was more like me – he wanted to play the situation."

After that loss, with the Boks at the bottom of the Tri-Nations log and being lambasted from all angles, De Villiers contemplated jettisoning several of his senior players.

"We were at a crossroads, and I realised that the players either weren't getting the message or they weren't understanding it," he said. "I considered changing the team and risking short-term knocks for the long-term objective of building a new team. I called the players in and told them that I would rather lose with a bunch of no-names than continue with a team of big-name players who were not prepared to take the team to the next level. When the guys realised their careers were on the line, my job suddenly became a lot easier."

The Boks went on to thrash the Wallabies 53-8 at Ellis Park to complete a first home-season sequence for De Villiers that was uncannily similar to that of Carel du Plessis, who was axed after a 61-22 "dead-rubber" victory over Australia at Loftus in 1997.

Halfbacks Butch James and Fourie du Preez kept the ball in front of the forwards and it all just fell into place, with Jongi Nokwe scoring four tries.

"Some people said we won that game because we were more direct, which was true, but for me it was more about the guys just all being on the same page at last and they made the right decisions," said De Villiers.

There was further game correction on the end-of-year tour, where the Boks beat Wales and Scotland playing really conservative rugby before they ran up a record 42-6 victory over England at Twickenham. It ended De Villiers's troubled first year in charge on an emphatically positive note.

"There was a lot of debate about my coaching philosophy in my first season as Bok coach, and in particular those early days building up to the series against Wales. Unfortunately, this was one of the many instances where what I was trying to say probably got lost in translation. I had no plans to radically change the Springbok game – it would have been a stupid thing to do," De Villiers explained in his book. "While I came from a running background, which was the style of play of most of the teams I played for, you just had to look at my track record at national age-group level to know that it wasn't as if I believed only in Barbarians-style rugby. I had never coached a team to just run the ball willy-nilly from all over the field."

For De Villiers, the common denominator with all the poor performances that year was plain and simply an inability to get through the phases, and in his view the root cause of that was uncertainty about the division between cleaners and carriers.

"We didn't get the balance quite right, which was the way it stayed for much of that season," said De Villiers.

That Christmas, the coach should have felt vindicated on several fronts, as several of his plans had come off. For instance, he had been severely criticised for bringing Adi Jacobs back from obscurity, but in the absence of the injured Jaque Fourie, Jacobs did well for him and was one of the best Bok players in the win at Twickenham.

By the end of that year, the players had also assumed greater control in driving the team forward.

"Up until the end of that Tri-Nations season, I had relied a lot on my assistant coaches, much in the same way that I had relied on my support group before that. But later that year I got the impression that Gary and Dick saw my desire to adopt an inclusive approach as a sign of weakness. It was as if they, too, had started to believe what Hoskins had said and had become too eager to hold my hand."

He said that Smit and Victor Matfield were the two guys he could trust the most and he called a meeting with them, where he discussed the situation at length.

"We agreed that we would need each other's support going forward, and that we had to trust one another. This is probably where the story originated that the players had taken over the team. In truth, the players' committee had been there from the first day. But I had become aware that the technical component in rugby becomes less relevant the higher you get up the food chain."

That may be correct, but De Villiers was afforded this luxury because he had an experienced and decorated team at his command. He said that he recognised that different situations require different solutions. In the second half of that first year, he also realised that winning was as all-important to South African fans as it was to the local media, and that he had to play the game the players were capable of playing. Of course, none of that is really rocket science and it may even explain the frustration he evoked in so many people.

24

Controversy, even in triumph

It says something about the nature of Peter de Villiers that even in the year of his greatest triumphs, a period of almost unprecedented success for the Springboks, controversy still dogged him. The series win over the British & Irish Lions at the start of the year was overshadowed by his public utterances that had the visiting media alternatively in stitches of laughter or fits of outrage, and impelled the SARU administration to give him a severe dressing down.

At the start of 2009, De Villiers was the subject of a controversy involving the ANC, who announced that he had backed them for the general election that was to be held that year. De Villiers had done no such thing – he had been invited to a party hosted by the ANC's Cape leader Chris Nissen, but had had no idea that he was going to be interviewed on television and seen to endorse the party.

Politicians would bug De Villiers throughout his four years. He was later even subjected to an outrageous reprimand from SARU president Oregan Hoskins after the Springbok coach's daughter had been spotted outside a DA election office and his father had complained to an ANC canvasser about service delivery in his suburb of Paarl. When the politicians complained to Hoskins, he called De Villiers and gave him an unwarranted telling off.

Then there was the slap on the wrist he received for making "negative" comments about the FIFA World Cup. De Villiers had merely said at the start of the 2010 international season that his players had to take their minds off the soccer and focus on rugby instead. At least that was what he'd meant to say, but it either came out wrong or was misinterpreted.

It is true that a lot of what De Villiers said was lost in translation, and when I interviewed him for *Politically Incorrect*, one of the biggest challenges was to try to understand what I called "Div-speak". But confusing though his conversation may be, the bottom line is that De Villiers refuses to be anything other than his own man – and that is what I ended up liking about him.

Of course De Villiers didn't help his cause by refusing to be helped, or to be coached on media-speak. Instead, he felt that people were trying to turn him into a "white" person, and he felt he owed it to *his* people to remain true to his culture. So he refused to bow to the expectations of political correctness, hence the title of his autobiography.

On the rugby front, some of his better selections of 2009 happened by accident rather than design. For instance, it was only the injury to Schalk Burger that brought Heinrich Brüssow into the mix at the start of the series against the British & Irish Lions, and then he came onto the field after an injury to Danie Rossouw to play a pivotal part in the Boks' series-clinching victory in the second Test, at Loftus.

The Boks staged a late rally in that match, and one of the best tries in their comeback was scored by Jaque Fourie, who had come on as a replacement for Adrian Jacobs. Fourie had, up till that point, looked set to play second fiddle to De Villiers's favourite player, but in 2009 Jacobs had lost the form he was in during the previous season. And Ruan Pienaar had been De Villiers's preferred flyhalf, so much so that before the Lions series, the Bulls' match-winner, Morné Steyn, never even got a look-in for the initial squad selections. But then the Sharks utility back lost confidence after he missed a few goal-kicking opportunities in the second Test, and Steyn, who came on in that game as his replacement, played in most of the matches that followed.

From a selection viewpoint, one of the big talking points of the year was when De Villiers played John Smit as a tighthead prop. Even though the Boks were winning their matches, the press kept on hassling De Villiers about problems they perceived in the scrum. And they were proven right on the end-of-year tour, when the Bok scrum *was* shown up, resulting in some losses in the northern hemisphere. That was when De Villiers saw the light and shifted Smit back to hooker.

That move would create its own problems, though, and in my opinion cost the Boks the 2011 World Cup. But there weren't any issues between Smit and Bismarck du Plessis when they packed down together in the front row that destroyed the Lions in the first half of the first Test. Beast Mtawarira spear-headed a scrum effort that will cause his direct opponent, Phil Vickery, to forever remember Kings Park in the same way some people remember a type of alcoholic beverage after a particularly bad night on the town.

Pienaar was playing out of his shoes to give the Boks a great start, but then De Villiers made a series of substitutions in the second half that left everyone, including some of the Bok management, confounded. The disruption this caused allowed the Lions back into the game, and the Boks had to put everything into it to win 26-21. The next day, the substitutions hogged the headlines.

And then, on the Monday, De Villiers was questioned about his decision to bring Ricky Januarie, who looked palpably overweight, onto the field in Durban, which set him off on a tangent about race and, of all things, mechanics.

"I am not concerned about Ricky's form," De Villiers said. "If you go to a black mechanic and he doesn't fix your car, you don't go back there. But if you go to a white mechanic and he doesn't fix your car, you go back and make sure he fixes the problem. What I am saying is, give Ricky a chance."

De Villiers's foot-in-mouth disease continued into the second Test, when flank Schalk Burger was yellow-carded in the opening minute of the game for an alleged eye-gouging incident. The British press was outraged, and were lying in wait for De Villiers at the press conference after the match. De Villiers, flush with joy after seeing Morné Steyn kick the last-minute penalty from the Loftus halfway line to secure the series win, was asked if he condoned the incident. And he said "yes".

In *Politically Incorrect*, De Villiers explained that he had confused "condone" with "condemn". Of course De Villiers's first language is Afrikaans and not English, so perhaps his gaffe could be blamed on that, but he should have explained himself at the time.

And he only made it worse when, at a follow-up press conference on the Monday after the game, he tried to explain himself in an anecdote about ballet and tutus, and then came out with the memorable quote that when South Africans want to "eye-gouge lions, they got into the bush to do it".

De Villiers was like a deer caught in the headlights, and he just wasn't equipped to deal with the aggressive questioning dished out by the British press corps. He later said that he'd expected some help from the South African media, whom he accused of sitting there like dummies and letting the British hacks run the press conferences, but in truth he was just indefensible.

I heard that the players were also unhappy, as De Villiers's off-field antics were diminishing their massive achievement in beating the Lions and thus avenging the 1997 series loss under Carel du Plessis.

If Du Plessis had made mistakes on the pitch in that series, De Villiers made them mostly away from the rugby field in 2009. He just couldn't keep his foot out of his mouth, and any temptation to feel sympathetic towards him was eroded by the knowledge that the SARU communications personnel had offered him assistance and he had refused it.

De Villiers was showing the stress when he read out the team for the last Test of the series – it included 10 changes to the side that had won at Loftus. The changes weakened the side considerably, and not everyone in the camp was happy that they had been made. The Ellis Park Test may have been a "dead rubber", but the South Africans nevertheless desperately wanted to make a proper job of avenging 1997 by taking the series 3-0.

As it was, the team was starting without their big second-row enforcer, Bakkies Botha, who had been cited for quite legitimately cleaning out a Lions player at Loftus. In fact, it was a textbook clean-out, and the Boks were understandably incensed at the suspension that had been slapped on him. Perhaps their reaction was a bit over the top, though. The team ran onto the field in Johannesburg wearing armbands with the words "Justice 4 Bakkies" written on them, and it would land them in hot water.

In fact, it was one of the reasons they were nearly denied the IRB Team of the Year award at the end of the season. Also, it just added to the many fires SARU had to put out in the four-week break between the end of the Lions series and the start of the Tri-Nations.

The Boks were hammered (9-28) in the final Test, making it the complete reverse of 1997, when the Boks had lost the first two games and won well in the last. After the match, the Lions behaved as if *they* had won the series. "I speak to you tonight as a winner," their skipper, Paul O'Connell, declared in his post-match speech. Coach Ian McGeechan was just as smug. It was as if they were in complete denial that they had lost the series, so I suppose Nick Cain would not have understood what I was on about if I had chided him by saying, "We did you!", as he had said to me 12 years previously. I resisted the temptation to try to rub it in, even while giving him a lift to the end-of-tour function. For the truth is it didn't really feel like we'd "done" them. The controversies and last Test had marred the series victory.

Soon after the Boks reconvened for the start of the build-up to the Tri-Nations, assistant coach Gary Gold phoned me to say that there was "big shit" going on. And by all accounts, there was. De Villiers and Regan Hoskins were accusing Gold of leaking information to me from inside the camp based on the stories I was writing. Although Gary had spoken to me from time to time, so had other people linked to the camp. But that wasn't all. De Villiers later told me that SARU was even putting pressure on him to stop making biblical references when he spoke to the press. It was never a dull moment with De Villiers around ...

Whatever his critics may have said after the third Lions Test, De Villiers's decision to field an under-strength team in that match may, in retrospect, have been a masterstroke. Giving the players maximum time out between the two series was another. These decisions allowed the Boks to start the Tri-Nations invigorated, and after winning fairly comfortably against the All Blacks in Bloemfontein (28-19), they beat them by an even bigger margin in Durban. The final score of 31-19 actually flattered the Kiwis, as the Boks had completely suffocated them. Morné Steyn scored all the points.

Despite the resounding victories, the Australian media criticised the Boks for being too conservative. And it was true that the central tenet of the Bok game plan, which had reverted completely to the pre–De Villiers era, was based on constricting and suffocating the opposition, which is seldom pretty.

So the Springboks were expected to kick every ball against Australia in their first away game in that Tri-Nations, and when they instead unleashed stunning running rugby, the Australians were taken completely by surprise. The Boks scored four tries and won comfortably. I had been tipped off by Gary Gold that at some stage this would happen, that the opposition were being set up to think the Boks would never run the ball. It was great to see a plan coming together so perfectly. But perhaps they got too complacent, as the roles were reversed in Brisbane the following week. And it was a bit ironic that they were beaten by an Australian team that was playing "their" type of game.

Nevertheless, the Boks were able to wrap up the Tri-Nations title by beating New Zealand in Hamilton in the last Test of the tournament. The Boks reverted to the type of structured rugby they had played in South Africa, and Frans Steyn destroyed the All Black morale with some massive long-range penalty kicks. Although the New Zealanders staged a late rally, the Boks were always dominant in this series decider – the hosts actually needed to win by a big score to win the Tri-Nations, and that always looked unlikely. In the end, the Boks won 32-29, and if that seems close, you need to take into account that Richie McCaw scored a try two minutes from full time.

Five wins in six starts in that year's Tri-Nations was an emphatic triumph, and the Boks were entitled to feel that they were on top of the world. They had won most of their games comfortably, and had beaten the All Blacks in three consecutive matches. The World Cup was still two years away, but they were being written up as favourites and would have been justified in feeling that they were.

But rugby never stands still, and neither does time. It is my opinion that the Springboks lost the World Cup when John Smit made the decision to continue playing for the next two years. He was of an age where another World Cup appearance might have been a bridge too far (Victor Matfield retained his athleticism to the end), and with a World Cup title and a Lions series win under his belt, I believe that was when Smit should have said goodbye.

In that winning year, Smit had proved his point; the value he had added to the team was immeasurable. I said it often enough in my columns, often to the chagrin of the coach, who probably felt he wasn't getting enough credit for his part in the team's success. And maybe De Villiers was right. Whatever you might say about him, he did create the right environment for success, and he deserves credit for recognising that the Boks had to play the game that best suited their talents.

The players might have been unhappy with De Villiers's off-the-field blunders during the Lions series, but they now fully supported the coach and it was a happy camp. Perhaps his support for Schalk Burger and Bakkies Botha after their disciplinary infractions against the Lions had won him the loyalty of the playing staff.

But then the end-of-year tour sounded a false note that was to prove the onset of De Villiers's "annus horribilus". The Boks lost two of the three Test matches, starting in Toulouse against France. Perhaps the Ras Dumisane rendition of the national anthem, which belonged in a beach bar and not on a rugby pitch before such an important Test, set the tone for the match. They suffered their second defeat in the last match of the year, against Ireland in Dublin, where former Bok assistant Gert Smal, who had become the Ireland forwards coach, played a big role in neutralising the South African line-outs.

The midweek team played two games on that tour too, and they lost both, prompting serious questions about De Villiers's selections. The scrumming was shown up both in the Test team and in the midweek side.

The tour defeats meant that while the Boks were named the IRB Team of the Year for beating the Lions and winning the Tri-Nations, De Villiers missed out on Coach of the Year. The award went to Ireland's Declan Kidney.

The next year, which turned into a disastrous series of events for De Villiers, started with a major controversy over comments he had made in a media session. One of the journalists had understood De Villiers to be saying that he wanted to get rid of an assistant coach, assumed to be Gary Gold, and reported on it. It resulted in a crisis meeting between Gold and De Villiers in Paarl. De Villiers assured Gold that he had been misquoted, which only partially placated the assistant coach, and even skipper John Smit climbed into De Villiers, telling him that he was providing fodder for future opponents to use against the Boks.

Despite the internal problems, the South Africans started the international season in a confident mood, as the Bulls and Stormers had contested the Super 14 final. However, De Villiers later reflected that this may have been more of a hindrance than a help, as the sense of complacency that had already set in after the previous year's domination was only compounded by the Super 14 success.

The Springboks kicked off the international season with a good away win against Wales, and that with an understrength team, and enjoyed two regulation home wins over a weak Italy. They also thrashed France at Newlands. So the consensus before the first Tri-Nations Tests against the All Blacks was that the Boks would start the tournament as favourites.

De Villiers later admitted that he made some selection blunders that unbalanced the team. He'd never effectively replaced Heinrich Brüssow when he was injured before the 2010 international season had even started, and Bakkies Botha, who could partly make up for the lack of Brüssow's ball-scavenging abilities with his forceful cleaning at the rucks, would be out for much of the southern hemisphere season too.

Defence was also a major problem, and so was discipline. Botha set the trend when he was carded in the opening match in Auckland, which the Boks lost by 20 points.

"After that," said De Villiers, "we found ourselves in a downward spiral from which it was difficult to extricate ourselves. As the tour progressed, the aspects of our game requiring work started to accumulate, and we soon got to a point where we couldn't cover everything in one session."

Indeed, as good as the Boks had been in 2009, so poor were they in 2010. The media were quick to pick up that the veterans John Smit and Victor Matfield seemed some way off the pace. It was also obvious that the overseas teams had adjusted their games, and the Boks seemed unable to counter their ability to use the width of the field.

For the first time I didn't feel alone in questioning the coach's ability, and by the time the Boks reached the last Test of the Tri-Nations, against Australia in Bloemfontein, it became quite ugly. The patently out-of-form Bryan Habana was booed on the field, and De Villiers was jeered off it as he made his way through the spectators at half-time, when the Boks were trailing 13-31.

Although the Boks fought back, a late Kurtley Beale penalty sealed their fate, thus condemning the team to the humiliation of being the first Springbok team to lose to the Wallabies on the Highveld in more than 40 years. However, Gary Gold told me a story that sums up the fickleness of the South African rugby public.

According to him, a group of South African fans had kept banging aggressively on the window of the coaches' box every time the Australians scored or exposed a Bok defensive error in the first half, but when the Boks started fighting back in the third quarter, the same guys were giving the coaches the thumbs-up, enthusiastically indicating their approval.

"I didn't mind that so much," De Villiers said of the fans. "[They] have a right to be angry when we don't play well. It was the racial abuse I received in Bloemfontein in my first season that I couldn't handle."

A Tri-Nations record that reflected five defeats in six starts, the exact reverse of the previous year, was compounded by a series of off-field events that very nearly cost De Villiers his job.

It started when the Bok coach was cited for bringing rugby into disrepute for something he had said on *The Rugby Club* television programme in Australia. De Villiers was responding to a question about the dodgy refereeing the Boks appeared to be encountering. "I've got my own observations about the last two Tests and I can't say it in public. But we do have a World Cup in New Zealand next year, and maybe it was the right thing for them to win the games so that they can attract more people to the games next year."

Everyone knew, or thought they knew, what Div was trying to say, including Simon Jelowitz, a Wellington-based lawyer working as a citing commissioner.

"Was I saying that there was a conspiracy and that the referees were cheating? I suppose you can interpret my words that way if you are shown only the part of the interview that was broadcast," De Villiers explained afterwards. "But my words in their entirety were a different story. They were misinterpreted. I was accused of saying that the IRB was allowing cheating in order to fill seats at the 2011 World Cup. I acted quickly to refute the interpretations by issuing a statement in which I stressed that in no manner did I suggest that the All Blacks were being favoured ..."

But the SANZAR hearing went ahead at Jelowitz's behest, although Div never had to say anything in his own defence. The other people in the tele-conference took Jelowitz on once they had watched the full video recording of the television programme. Jelowitz even admitted that he had not seen the entire interview but had based his citing on what he had read in the papers and seen on *The Rugby Club*, but wanted to press on with the hearing anyway.

There was another incident where a full recording had to be heard in order to bail the Bok coach out. It occurred at the tail-end of the Tri-Nations campaign, when De Villiers publicly supported Bees Roux, a Bulls prop who had killed a Pretoria Metro policeman while allegedly in a drunken rage.

De Villiers felt that SARU should have released a statement on the morning of the Test in Pretoria, as that was when the Roux incident appeared in the papers and he thought the media would ask him about it. But they didn't ask him about it there. It was only in the build-up to the final Tri-Nations Test, in Bloemfontein, that De Villiers made the comments that were perceived as support for the accused rugby player.

Mike Greenaway called me at the Beverly Hills Hotel, where I was wait-ing to interview one of the Wallaby players, to tell me that De Villiers hadn't even been asked about Roux – he had volunteered the quotes, which were widely publicised in the media the next day.

Hoskins summoned De Villiers to a meeting in Johannesburg the follow-ing week, and the SARU chief arrived in a mood that suggested he was on a mission. He had told at least one reporter that De Villiers was very close to losing his job, but I will let De Villiers relate the story:

Regan told me he was fed up with how I kept embarrassing South African rugby. He took me on again for quoting the Bible. And this thing about Bees Roux, he said ... Hell, he was in my face ... Up to that point a lot of people, including Butana Komphela, had spoken a lot of shit about what I had said about the Bees Roux issue, but no one phoned me to ask me. I reminded Regan he had the wherewithal to be sure of his facts, and his facts were wrong.

Fortunately, as I was leaving Paarl that morning, I had called Anthony MacKaiser [Bok media liaison] to ask him for the USB flash drive on which he had saved the recording of the Bees Roux interview. I played the board members the recording, but Mark Alexander and Oregan Hoskins said they couldn't understand what I had said as neither of them was proficient in Afrikaans. So I asked James Stofberg and Johan Prinsloo to explain, as they were both Afrikaans ...

So James started, "What he said might have been interpreted ..."

"Hey, don't tell them what I might have said and how it might have been interpreted," I interrupted, "tell them *exactly* what I said."

James concurred with me that what I had said in the interview did not correspond with what I was being accused of. Oregan was extremely upset. He knew he was caught short and was severely embarrassed.

Then, according to De Villiers, the attack shifted to his assistants, as well as Neels Liebel, the fitness trainer. The board had identified replacements for each one. After a short break the meeting resumed, and now Dick Muir and Gary Gold were the clear scapegoats for the Tri-Nations failure. De Villiers felt he had betrayed his assistants with the concessions he made to the board.

"It would be easy to say that I am only human and so justify the thoughts that went through my head – how much I was enjoying my job and that I did not want to give it up to save someone else. But I am not going to look for excuses or justify my actions. I let myself down. There is no other way to put it. As a proud, principled guy, I betrayed my principles when I was faced with the hardest choices. As a leader, I let my followers down.

"I was told to go and look for coaches who would be prepared to work with me. It was a difficult situation, as I knew the right thing to do would be to call Gary and Dick and tell them what was going down. And of course I didn't really want to start working with a new coaching team at such a late stage."

Allister Coetzee was apparently available. Frans Ludeke was too, but the administrators didn't want him. De Villiers was made aware of a visit that Hoskins had undertaken to Ireland to speak to Gert Smal, which was a renewed sign to De Villiers that they wanted to get rid of him, too.

To say that the assistants were incensed at what had transpired would be an understatement. I spoke to Gold a lot during that period, and he told me that Muir, who always strongly supported De Villiers, was now as angry as he was with the coach.

The result was a showdown in Durban between Hoskins and the three coaches. I have been told that it would damage South African rugby irreparably if the details of what was said there were ever divulged. But that a rift had been caused was obvious for all to see during the end-of-year tour that followed.

25

Denied by a freak show

There were many people who wondered how I went from being Peter de Villiers's biggest critic to being the co-author of his autobiography and, in truth, it wasn't an easy decision to make. He approached me near the start of the international season leading up to the World Cup, and my biggest concern was that he would expect me to adjust my viewpoint to suit him.

I made it emphatically clear I would not do that, and he equally forcefully let me know that he would not expect me to.

"I'm not expecting you to become my praise-singer; I'm just expecting you to write a bloody book," he said.

So I wrote the "bloody book", and there was an occasion during the World Cup in New Zealand where he proved true to his word. On the afternoon after the team announcement had been made for the quarter-final against Australia, he and I met to talk about the book, and he immediately detected that I wasn't happy.

"What's the matter with you? You look so damn angry," he said when he saw my face.

"It's you!" I said. "How the hell can you leave out Bismarck [du Plessis] for this game? It's going to cost you the World Cup. I've taken you on big time in everything I've written today."

De Villiers said that he understood how I felt. Everyone, he admitted, knew that Du Plessis was a much better player than Smit at that point. But he had made a commitment to Smit two years previously and intended to honour it.

That "commitment", as De Villiers called it, was a mistake. In their one really good pre–World Cup performance of 2011, against New Zealand in Port Elizabeth, the Boks had shown that they could win with Victor Matfield as captain and Du Plessis as the starting hooker. Du Plessis was outstanding in that game and could hardly be blamed for showing his anger when he was, bizarrely, replaced by Smit in the last 20 minutes.

I was always one of Smit's biggest supporters, and I attributed the Boks' 2009 successes largely to his input and leadership, but there were times when his judgement was questionable. I said it in private to people after the World Cup and I will say it again here – in my view, Smit, more than referee Bryce Lawrence or the coach, may have lost the Boks the 2011 World Cup.

By the time South Africa beat New Zealand in PE, John Plumtree of the Sharks had already decided that Du Plessis was his first-choice hooker, and instead of arguing with him about it, Smit should have been big enough to accept it as a fact. Maybe he had a place at the World Cup as a squad captain, but he should have let Du Plessis play in the big games.

Even De Villiers's management team was trying to convince him to drop Smit, but if it was the one big mistake the coach made in 2011, at least it was rare. This was the season in which a seismic shift took place in De Villiers's management style.

And that was the reason why I felt far more comfortable with the man in 2011. He had changed, and changed for the better. A big reason for this was his decision to recruit Rassie Erasmus as his technical advisor.

In the first three years of De Villiers's tenure, the Bok squad had lacked a strategy heavyweight in the group, which left a major gap. I always argued that the player-driven system would only be able to take the Boks so far but no further. In my view, it was the reason for their disastrous 2010 Tri-Nations campaign. While the Australian and New Zealand coaches spent their down-time devising a way to beat the Boks, the chief strategists for the Springboks were playing Super 14 rugby. It was therefore no surprise when the international season started and it became clear that the Australasian coaches had stolen a march on us.

But with Erasmus's arrival, the gap was filled, and the intellectual capital in the Bok squad was further enhanced by the addition of Stormers defence coach Jacques Nienaber. Few other people in the game are as bright as Erasmus and Nienaber, and once they were part of the mix, I had fewer reservations about the Boks' ability to win the World Cup.

When De Villiers and his team arrived in New Zealand for the Tri-Nations, he denied that his first-choice players, who had been left behind in South Africa, were busy at a training camp in Rustenburg. I couldn't understand the fuss some of my colleagues made about it. After all, Jake White had done the same thing, and his team had won the World Cup! Okay, perhaps De Villiers shouldn't have denied it, but then he was genuinely blindsided by the question.

But otherwise De Villiers hardly did anything wrong in 2011, and his relationship with the media improved too. Those of us who were following the Boks appreciated the "new" De Villiers, but unfortunately some of my colleagues were unable to accept that he was capable of changing and continued to criticise him for past mistakes.

The Boks regained some winning momentum after the previous year's Tri-Nations misfire when Victor Matfield led a depleted team to the UK and Ireland, and while the results leading up to the World Cup weren't great, it has to be remembered that De Villiers was mostly fielding a second-string team. Jake White had done the same in 2007, and that team didn't win on the away leg of the Tri-Nations before the World Cup either.

But De Villiers nearly didn't go to the World Cup at all, for he says he again considered quitting the job during the summer of 2010/11.

"The debacle with SARU over the assistant coaches and the sordid way it was portrayed in the media soured everything for me. Although we had enjoyed relative success on the end-of-year tour, my relationship with my assistant coaches had been irrevocably damaged. I could hardly blame Dick Muir and Gary Gold if they didn't trust me. That's how I would have felt had the roles been reversed."

In his search for an X-factor that would lift the team for the World Cup, De Villiers approached Morné du Plessis – the umpteenth coach since Kitch Christie to do so – and asked him to be his ceremonial manager, but after some consideration Du Plessis turned down the offer.

It was De Villiers's search for what he called the "wow factor" that made him decide on the Royal Bafokeng Sports Campus near Rustenburg as the Boks' training camp during the Tri-Nations, and in addition to recruiting Erasmus and Nienaber, Dr Derik Coetzee, who had worked with Jake White, was called in to crack the whip as the fitness sergeant major.

"With Rassie working on technical details and adding his excellent organisational touches to everything, I was freed to be more of a manager. For the first time I didn't feel like I was looking over my shoulder all the time," De Villiers said in *Politically Incorrect*. "I could delegate with confidence. It even had an impact on how I dealt with the media. Whereas before I was often criticised for my 'tetchy' attitude to the press, this was no longer the case in the run-in to the World Cup."

The second-stringers didn't do well in Australia and New Zealand, losing both games badly, and it brought a lot of pressure to bear on the Boks, although they did start playing better once they were back home. Morné Steyn was one of the few supposed first-choice players who travelled to the antipodes for the Tri-Nations, a sure sign that De Villiers was considering dropping him, but after Butch James missed a sitter against Australia in Durban, De Villiers became convinced that he had to have Steyn for his goal-kicking. In my opinion, James would have brought more to the Boks' all-round game, although admittedly he did spend way too many of the training sessions at the 2011 World Cup being nursed on the sidelines.

Of course, the whole of South Africa still wonders what might have transpired had it not been for Bryce Lawrence's lamentably poor performance with the whistle at Wellington's "Cake Tin", where the Springbok quest for glory came to an end in the quarter-finals.

The New Zealand referee appeared to make a glaring mistake when he awarded the Wallabies an early try after they had illegally obtained the ball at the breakdown, and it then seemed as if he just froze with fear. As De Villiers related in *Politically Incorrect*, Lawrence was normally a cocky referee, bordering on the arrogant, but in that game he kept on apologising to both sides. It was a freak show; there's no other way one can put it.

The Boks weren't blameless – their playing style on the day was out of character, and it benefited an Australian team that was injury ravaged and had looked exhausted even before the match. Playing a spoiling game, the Wallabies were fortunate that they had a ref who wouldn't penalise negative play.

The match brought the curtain down on De Villiers's stint with the Boks. I felt quite emotional when I listened to him talk at his final press conference, as it was impossible not to reflect on how much his work had improved during his four-year tenure. De Villiers was the one Springbok coach who was definitely much better equipped at the end of his reign than he was at its start.

He cut a disconsolate figure, and why not, after having been denied in such a cruel way? Nevertheless, he departed the World Cup arena in a dignified manner.

De Villiers's popularity across all sections of the South African population was amply demonstrated when he and his team received a hero's welcome at O.R. Tambo International Airport on their return to South Africa. De Villiers had expected to be jeered, but instead he was warmly embraced and given a rousing welcome by cheering fans when he walked into the airport arrivals hall.

"It was an experience I felt very fortunate to be part of, and I made the most of the moment," De Villiers says in his book. "It was such a far cry from the negativity that had surrounded me and forced me, even at an early stage, to reconsider my future as Springbok coach. And it was light years away from being booed by the Durban crowd later in that 2008 season, an incident that coincidentally also followed a loss to Australia. We may not have won the World Cup, but the two vastly different reactions three years apart to defeats by the same nation suggested that all I had gone through during my four years in charge had not been completely in vain. Perhaps my mission to make the Springboks the people's team had been successful.

"The passing of time will determine how history will judge the team and me as a Springbok coach, but on the day we got back from the World Cup, which signalled the actual end of my tenure, I knew that even the bad days can be very, very good indeed. And knowing that made me feel like a winner."

As is customary, it took a while for SARU to inform De Villiers of the fact that his contract would not be renewed, and it may even have given him false hope when they extended his contract until the end of January 2012. But the inevitable finally came to pass when he was told that he was no longer wanted just a few days before Heyneke Meyer was unveiled as the new coach.

So should De Villiers have been appointed the Bok coach? On pure rugby grounds I would say it's debatable, for when he first took over he wasn't equipped to take the Springboks to the next level. And that was something the coach should have been able to do, as most of the players were still young.

When you appoint a coach for an international team, you should be appointing him to win, first and foremost. But events after the World Cup have made me wonder whether, in a South African context, we do need at times to take factors such as the outreach of the game and the Springbok brand into account when making national coaching appointments.

Whether they were car guards in Port Elizabeth, Indian waiters in Umhlanga Rocks, businessmen from Joburg or vegetable hawkers in his home town of Paarl, people of all hues and backgrounds wanted speak to De Villiers and get a piece of him when we travelled the country on our book tour. It amazed me, and it impressed me. I have spent time with other Bok coaches, and the adulation was never as great, or as multicultural.

At one point we arrived at a factory where we were expected to make an appearance for some of our sponsors. The security guards, at first seeing only me in the car, demanded identification. Then, when they noticed Peter, their whole demeanour changed, and they waved us in saying, "Ah, it's the *coach!*" And this happened on more than one occasion.

I joked with Peter that perhaps we should take advantage of the situation, as almost every security guard in the country seemed happy to give us free access to whatever they were guarding. As I say, whether his popularity with the people justified his reign as coach is open to debate, but I think SARU are missing a vital opportunity to increase awareness of the game by not appointing De Villiers as an ambassador at large and actively using him in that role. He could, for example, travel to underprivileged areas and use his teaching skills to familiarise would-be supporters with the sport.

It may all sound like pie in the sky, but one thing I know for certain – if you take into account his popularity among the people of this land and how he managed to turn the Springboks into a team for all South Africans, on some levels De Villiers is going to be a very hard act to follow.

26

Surviving the first year

Heyneke Meyer wasn't SARU's preferred choice to replace Peter de Villiers. Former Springbok assistant coach Gert Smal was approached first, and the job would have been his had he been prepared to lower his asking price and had his family not had reservations about returning home. His children are happy at their schools in Dublin, where Smal is based in his capacity as Ireland's forwards coach.

Smal is very committed to transformation, so he can hardly be described as conservative, and it might not be fair to accuse Meyer of being conservative either. But nevertheless, a few conspiracy theorists were very suspicious of what SARU seemed to be looking for in the next coach. During Peter de Villiers's reign, concerns were expressed that he might be alienating what Rian Oberholzer once referred to as South African rugby's "guaranteed market". And some time in 2010, the media rumour mill alleged that a conservative bloc was pressurising Meyer to return to coaching so that he could become the next Bok coach.

As both Smal and Meyer are white and Afrikaans-speaking, am I being paranoid if I ask whether SARU took a conscious decision *not* to appoint another black coach?

Smal's qualifications for the job were based on his role as one of Jake White's assistants at the 2007 World Cup. But Allister Coetzee, a black coach, had also been an assistant coach to White, and in White's opinion, if SARU was looking for a black coach specifically, Coetzee, and not De Villiers, should have been their choice in 2008.

As far as the 2012 options are concerned, you could argue that after 2008, Smal had gained further experience as assistant coach of Ireland, but then Coetzee had gone on to coach the Stormers for three years, a period in which they lifted their game considerably. While Coetzee hasn't yet done what Meyer did by winning a Super Rugby trophy, three consecutive appearances in Super Rugby finals is excellent for a union that had previously struggled to make the play-offs.

It is odd to me that Coetzee's credentials were not considered more seriously in 2012 than they were. But whenever I mentioned him as a possible candidate for the job, a disturbingly large number of people told me, "We cannot go that route again." Their logic confounded me, as Coetzee and De Villiers are very different from each other as both coaches and people. Would you lump Jake White and Carel du Plessis together on the basis that they have the same skin colour? It's ridiculous.

If, however, you go back to 2008 and if SARU considered only what was best for Springbok rugby, Meyer should have been appointed then. He would have been disappointed and disillusioned when he lost out, and he immediately left for a coaching job at the English club Leicester Tigers. It turned out to be short stint for Meyer, and he left there for "personal" reasons.

One could also understand why, having been away from the coalface for three years, he thought twice about accepting the top job in South African rugby when it was offered to him in 2012. It was no secret that he had trouble making up his mind. The weekend before he finally accepted the job, I spoke to two journalists and a coach who are members of Meyer's inner circle, and he had asked them all for advice. He was deliberating long and hard over whether to take the job. And it was understandable.

In 2008, Meyer would have taken over a team brimming with players he had coached and nurtured, but it was a different story in 2012. Most of the legends of Bulls rugby who had won trophies under Meyer had either retired or gone overseas, and it was clear from as far back as 2010 that whoever replaced De Villiers would have to bleed in a new generation of players.

I have attended many press conferences over the years where the new Springbok coach is announced, and I don't think I have ever seen one look as nervous as Meyer. We were in the auditorium of the Sport Science Institute in Newlands in late January 2012, and Meyer was visibly shaking when he took a seat next to SARU chief executive Jurie Roux. Probably aware of the legacy his predecessor had left, he immediately started talking off the Peter de Villiers hymn sheet, announcing that he wanted to be the "people's" coach.

Of course that would be easier said than done, given his skin colour and Afrikaans background, not to mention his affiliation with the Bulls. An immediate assumption had been made that he would favour players from his former franchise.

And he certainly didn't dispel those suspicions in the early months of his tenure. Although it was understandable that he would select some of the players he had recruited during his time as the Bulls' director of rugby, he erred in selecting too many marginal Bulls players in his early squads. It didn't exactly endear him to rugby fans outside of Pretoria.

But more than that, he assembled a management team that consisted almost exclusively of Bulls people. André Markgraaff, for one, questioned Meyer's decision-making.

"I thought it was ridiculous that Heyneke surrounded himself with people in his management team who wouldn't challenge him. A good coach should be prepared to have his thoughts challenged," Markgraaff explained.

Markgraaff has earned the right to his opinion, as he was bold enough to include the opinionated Nick Mallett in his management team in 1996. But he wasn't the only person to criticise Meyer. At the time, I weighed in too, as I was confounded that the genius of Stormers defence coach Jacques Nienaber was being ignored when he had made it clear he was available for the Boks.

Meyer is an honest man with plenty of integrity, but perhaps that is not always a suitable attribute when you are the Springbok coach. Being honest can sometimes make you unpopular, and in those early days Meyer was guilty of sounding just like a former Bulls coach. Saying, for example, that he knew "only one kind of rugby, and that is winning rugby" did not go down well with fans and critics who feared he would be too conservative in his playing style.

Rugby fans and other experts generally thought the Bulls had been too rigid and dour under Meyer, though it's probably not a completely fair assessment. The Bulls often showed that they were anything but boring to watch once they had perfected Meyer's game plan, and the results spoke for themselves. Just ask Gert Smal, whose Stormers team was smashed 14-75 by Meyer's Bulls in his last match in charge.

And when we were alerted to the fact that Meyer had approached Victor Matfield to come out of retirement to lead the Boks, fans and rugby writers alike started wondering whether this new coach perhaps feared innovation. If so, how would he move the Boks forward?

At the time of writing, Meyer had just selected some exciting new players for the backline, and his team had played some good running rugby in the Incoming Tour Series featuring Samoa, Italy and Scotland. He has also consistently said that his team will become more attacking once it is properly settled. Unlike De Villiers, he did not inherit a team; he had to create a new one.

But although I am confident in my belief that he will be a successful Bok coach – Ian McIntosh has even suggested that he will be the national coach who finally formulates and introduces the South African rugby blueprint – it remains to be seen how bold he will be. Some of the selections he made in his first year were ultra-conservative, and at the beginning of 2013, the matches against second-tier opposition were exactly that – a top team playing inferior opponents.

However, it was also Meyer's first opportunity to experiment, for any Bok coach's first season is always going to be just about survival. Meyer's tenure kicked off with a series against England, and it wasn't the most opportune start. The first Test was played just five days after he managed to assemble the squad following bruising Super Rugby derbies. And Meyer had been involved in a protracted battle with the Blue Bulls Company to secure the release of his assistant coaches, who were contracted to Super Rugby right up to the start of the series against England.

He had also spent a great deal of his time orchestrating his own exit from the Bulls and negotiating his contract with SARU.

So Meyer was playing catch-up and chasing his tail from the moment he took the job. Keep in mind, too, that up until mid-December 2011, SARU were pretty certain that Smal was going to be their man, and he was really their only choice.

To start with, Meyer seemed oblivious to the political expectations of the job, and it was only at the start of his second season that he seemed to see the benefits of compiling his squad in a way that conveyed the right message about inclusivity.

The Cape fans and press pilloried him in his first year for omitting players like Gio Aplon, Siya Kolisi and Juan de Jongh. Meyer wants to opt for big players – and I concur with him that size does matter at international level. Also, at that point Kolisi had played in only one season of Super Rugby. Nevertheless, Meyer could have been more circumspect in his selections. For instance, Bulls flank Jacques Potgieter was selected to make his debut against England in Port Elizabeth, and, although it's a subjective opinion, one would be hard-pressed to see him as a superior player to Kolisi.

Meyer's schedule in his first year meant he was on a high-pressure tread-mill from the get-go, but in his second season he is at last able to experiment and, in his words, spread the net. It will perhaps allow us at last to start better assessing the outlook for Meyer and his team.

Not unlike Harry Viljoen, Meyer cares a great deal about what the media and public think of him. In 2012, he informed the media of his plans in a series of seminars conducted in various South African cities, which must have taken a tremendous amount of effort. It's the kind of guy he is. For example, he is the only Springbok coach who has ever phoned me to apologise for some-thing he did. At the start of the 2013 Incoming Tour Series, he had hinted that he would select Pat Lambie as his flyhalf in the second game (indeed, Lambie was told the same thing), but Meyer then stuck with Morné Steyn after his good performance against Italy.

The fact that he had misled me didn't really bother me, and while readers may have accused me of an inaccuracy, you can't be a rugby writer and worry about little things like that – whatever is an issue on Monday doesn't matter any more by Tuesday. Or it shouldn't. And that's what I told Meyer. But I appre-ciated his call and, frankly, it didn't surprise me, as I have known the guy for a long time and he has always been the same earnest, honest human being.

Way back in 1999, when he was assistant coach to Nick Mallett in the build-up to that year's World Cup, he sought me out to inform me that while he knew Mallett and Alan Solomons were not happy with me, he and I were fine. I actually met Meyer a few years before that, when he was coaching South Western Districts. I never turn down any excuse to head to the Wilderness on the Garden Route, so the *Argus* budget had to make allowances for several trips to the George union when Meyer was talking of turning the region into the "Bath of South African rugby".

But the fact that Meyer and I have a long relationship does not preclude me from criticising him, and I did so quite a lot during 2012, when he too often opted for the conservative option and wasn't bold enough in his approach. I reserved my judgement on his first year in charge until the last international of the season, against England at Twickenham. Victory there, narrow though it was, determined that he finished on the positive side of the balance sheet in terms of win percentage, and considering there were no easy games in 2012 and he was starting afresh, that was good enough for me. There had been many high-pressure points along the way, however, and there were times I wondered whether he would survive the year.

Considering that he had only five days with his team and that the team was essentially new, the Boks didn't perform too badly in the first Test of the year, against England at Kings Park. They then dominated the first half of the second Test in Johannesburg, with the big loose forwards thrusting across the gain line and the rest of the team thriving on the momentum. It was a quint-essential version of the Meyer game being perfected. England looked dead and buried at half-time, only for the Boks to nearly lose it in the second half before J.P. Pietersen scored a great try to clinch the match and the rubber.

The following week, in Port Elizabeth, with the series already decided, the Boks fielded a team that was drastically weakened by injury and were fortunate to escape with a draw. Criticism of some of his selections rained down on Meyer afterwards, and this was one game where his decision to leave out Heinrich Brüssow may have shown him up.

With Willem Alberts sidelined due to an injury, Meyer selected Jacques Potgieter on the flank, but he just wasn't in the same league as the Sharks player. And although Marcell Coetzee had played well on the open-side flank up till then, without Alberts he just had too many bases to cover. Pierre Spies was also invisible in that game, perhaps because, for the first time in the series, the pack wasn't advancing. But more disturbing was Morné Steyn's lack of form, though there was little Meyer could do about it. Patrick Lambie had been injured earlier in the series, and Johan Goosen had been out injured from the start of the international season.

Meyer had more time to prepare for the advent of the newly named Rugby Championship (as the Tri-Nations had been extended to include Argentina), although the full management team was still not at his disposal. Most of them were still contracted to the Bulls for the duration of the Super Rugby tournament.

The fact that Meyer still did not select Kolisi continued to attract negative comment, particularly in the Cape. But in Meyer's defence, he had included players like Kolisi in the extended squad so that they could familiarise them-selves with the Bok system.

The Boks started the Rugby Championship comfortably enough, enjoying a solid win over Argentina in Cape Town, but lost Bismarck du Plessis to a serious injury that ruled him out for the rest of the year. It was a big blow for Meyer, as Du Plessis had been his vice-captain. The robust hooker was the umpteenth experienced player to exit Meyer's plans because of injury. Schalk

Burger and Juan Smith, two stalwarts, were ruled out before the season had even started.

Losing key players to overseas clubs, Japan in particular, further depleted the pool from which Meyer could select experienced players.

"Guys like Fourie du Preez, Jaque Fourie and Danie Rossouw, who could have at least have played an important part in the initial transition period, were absent, and it made a big difference," Meyer explained.

The return Test against Argentina, in Mendoza, took place seven days after the first meeting in Cape Town, and it was a disaster. Although the Boks managed to escape with a draw, they were fortunate to even get that. And they were lambasted afterwards for their lack of inventiveness and the complete absence of a game plan. They simply looked lost, as did Meyer.

As the pack was completely ineffectual, the Boks lacked the momentum they needed to play the Sharks style of rugby, which is what the fans, the experts and some of the rugby scribes wanted them to play. In fact, they were wholly ineffectual whenever the opposition stood up to them physically, a problem that Nick Mallett, as a studio analyst for SuperSport, had picked out at the start of the year and saw as a weakness in Meyer's strategy.

Mallett, along with other experts on the sport, appealed for a more balanced approach. But things only got worse. The Boks lost to Australia in Brisbane, and this after they had won more than enough ball but kicked too much of it away. The inaccuracy of the kicking, both at goal and out of hand, obviously wasn't part of Meyer's plan, but he took intense heat for it. Morné Steyn, normally so reliable, simply seemed unable to kick the ball over the posts.

And so on to New Zealand, and a game in Dunedin that the Boks could so easily have won had it not been for Steyn's continued inaccurate place-kicking. Meyer later admitted that he had felt the pressure then, and it was a tough time for him and his family.

"I have an advantage over some of the guys who have coached the Springboks in the sense that I had a long coaching career at the top level building up to my appointment," Meyer says. "I had been assistant at the Stormers as long ago as 1999, had been head coach at the SWD Eagles and then the Bulls, and an assistant under Nick Mallett at the Boks, so I am used to talking at press conferences and answering the questions that get asked. But what I wasn't prepared for was the pressure on my family, and that is what is particularly tough."

The Bok coach has always been subject to intense scrutiny, and Meyer knew this from working for Mallett. But a significant change had occurred since the late 1990s, namely the introduction of social media. It has changed the landscape completely for Bok coaches.

As Meyer explains: "Every single kid has now got a BlackBerry or an iPhone, and every person has an opinion on the team selection or game plan. In the old days there were opinions, but they were confined to the mainstream media and the talk about rugby would be around braais and in pubs. But now it is just everywhere; every kid is texting and talking about the Boks, and it has been very tough on my children.

"I have three boys ranging in age from 12 to 16, and although they go to a good school and have wonderful friends, they have taken a lot of flak. It seems that they are in a lose-lose situation. If the Boks lose, they get crucified, and if we win, they are accused of being arrogant because they are the Bok coach's sons.

"It seems that no matter what you do, there is always trouble from some faction. I took a lot of heat for not dropping Morné [Steyn] when he was struggling last year, but then when I selected Johan Goosen and Pat Lambie ahead of him, I took flak from people for not showing the same loyalty to Morné that he had shown to me. You can't win."

Goosen made his debut in the match against Australia at Loftus, as did flanker François Louw, and both of them excelled. The media praised Meyer for finally getting his selections right and bringing a different dynamic to the team. Meyer stressed that he had not changed the game plan, and he may have been right, but no one was listening. Because the Boks had gone on a try-scoring spree in their big win, to the average Joe it simply meant that something *must* have changed. The Boks won 31-8 and scored five tries, with wing Bryan Habana notching up a hat-trick.

Meyer says that generally he can cope with the pressure; it is something that comes with the territory.

"For me, coaching has always been about trying to make a difference in people's lives, whether it was when I started out coaching at primary-school level, or when I was an assistant at South Western Districts and then right up through Currie Cup and Super Rugby. I went through the ranks, and I always saw it as my role to serve, and I really don't agree with the coach being in the limelight.

"I think that is why a lot of ex-players struggle when they first become coaches. It's unusual for them to be in a position where they have to serve others rather than be the focus of attention. So what gets to me is the knowledge of what the Springbok performances mean to the country. I feel [that] it is my duty to ensure that the team wins.

"It's not about the glory for me; I was content enough before I took [on] the job. That was why I had to do a lot of soul-searching when SARU approached me. I set high standards for myself, and I like to build teams, but I knew there wouldn't be a lot of time to prepare for each Test with the Boks.

"The new Super Rugby schedule has made it even more difficult. In Jake White's time, you used to get two, or even three weeks to prepare the team for a Test season. Now you get five days. You can get the squad together for a few Monday sessions, but you have to do a heck of a lot of begging and fighting with the Unions to get those players released."

The Boks, buoyed by the easy win over Australia in Pretoria, played well in the first half of the final Rugby Championship Test, against New Zealand at Soccer City, but Goosen was injured early on and the Boks dropped their game in the second half. New players such as Elton Jantjies made their debut, but the result was not good.

Still, the Boks had improved their international ranking from fourth to second, an improvement Meyer had overseen, and he could take some consolation from that.

"The Springboks are building and they are going to be very hard to beat," was the verdict of victorious All Black coach Steve Hansen. The coach of the World Cup champions and undisputed No. 1 side on the planet left little doubt that, in his opinion, the Boks were next best.

On the end-of-year tour, Pat Lambie played every Test at flyhalf and looked solid, and the line-outs were efficient throughout. From the first match in Dublin, where the South Africans rallied from a poor first half to win it in the second, to the last in London, the Springboks demonstrated a stubborn refusal to lose, which augurs well for this generation of players if Meyer remains the coach.

Up until the hour mark the Boks looked set for a big win against Scotland in Edinburgh, playing the Scots into the corners and squeezing them, but then they started to struggle, which is becoming a bit of a habit against Scotland. Unfortunately the last part of the game, when the Scots did most of the attacking, is what survives in the memory bank.

The win at Twickenham, however, tilted the year's results in Meyer's favour, and this with players who looked out on their feet after a long year of intense competition. It was a horrible game, and England should really have won it, with the Boks profiting from one of the weirdest tries I've ever seen. Willem Alberts went over for a try after a cruel rebound from an England kick fortuitously placed the big flank in an onside position. England dominated the forward exchanges, but the Boks defended well to win by the narrowest of margins (16-15). Of course people still criticised the Bok performance, though their attitude quickly changed when the same England team smashed the All Blacks a week later.

On the morning after the Twickenham Test, two colleagues and I had coffee with Meyer at the team hotel in Kensington. Looking out through the windows onto a London street brightened by the sun on a clear November day, Meyer spoke like someone who had just been relieved of a massive amount of pressure.

For the first time since he had become Bok coach, he said, he would have time to think about what lies ahead and plan properly. And so far in 2013 the planning has been meticulous and efficient, and certainly Meyer's strong organisational skills and attention to detail are emerging.

If the provincial unions buy into his plans and find a way to keep the top players in the country despite increasingly attractive financial offers from overseas, and the players survive the ridiculous schedule SANZAR has foisted upon them, I suspect Meyer will do well.

But I ask myself, how will he cope with the pressure going forward? If he hits a real annus horribilus such as the one Jake White suffered in 2006 and Peter de Villiers in 2010, how will he react? I've already been told that he is telling people that he's counting the days until the job is over.

My advice to Heyneke Meyer is to enjoy it for what it is. Some of the Springbok coaches I have worked with over the past 21 years may be scarred by the experiences they had, and some of them quite markedly, but there aren't many of them who look back today and don't wish that they were still there, in the moment.

27

"You can't learn from a dream start"

When Heyneke Meyer was announced as the new Springbok coach in late January 2012 in front of a big media contingent and on live television, it was a far cry from the low-key manner in which the first post-isolation coach, John Williams, had been introduced two decades earlier.

Whereas Williams had to phone the organisation then known as SARFU to confirm that he had been appointed as the coach, and then received a one-sentence letter of appointment from Danie Craven, Meyer was involved in contract negotiations that lasted for weeks. And at the press conference that followed the announcement, the questions the rugby media asked were indicative of how much the game, and the expectations, had changed since 1992. Nowadays there are questions about contracts, the appointment of the coach's own management team and the racial make-up of the squad, unlike in the days of amateur rugby, when none of the above applied.

But one thing appears to have remained the same, and it is not a positive reflection on how South African rugby is run. Up until the time Meyer was appointed, there had never been a proper handover from one coach to another. The intellectual capital accumulated during each coach's tenure has therefore gone completely to waste, and the lack of continuity from one coaching regime to another has impacted badly on the players.

It took a while for those Springboks who won the 2007 World Cup to adapt after the change in coach, which probably cost South Africa the Tri-Nations title. There was certainly enough talent in the 2008 team to win the tournament. Unlike Williams, McIntosh and many of the other coaches,

Peter de Villiers at least received an official letter informing him that he was no longer required and thanking him for his services.

De Villiers is the first to admit that he made a mistake by not retaining at least some of Jake White's management. And he was confounded when he waited throughout the late summer of 2012 for SARU to contact him about his offer to help them ensure an effective handover to the new coaching staff. No call ever came.

Some time before starting this book, I mentioned it to Joel Stransky. In response, he said that some of the coaches could have used the supposed obstacles that SARU and the politicians foisted on them as an excuse for their own mistakes. I have no doubt that he may right in some cases, so I hope I have not written a series of mini-hagiographies. I had decided to be sympathetic to the coaches from the outset, hence the title of the book, but I've also tried to be as honest as possible.

It is true that some of the coaches did not help their cause by being incapable of managing upwards. Mallett, De Villiers and White all said and did things during their tenures that caused enmity between them and their employers. In some instances, just a little bit of EQ could have avoided the escalation of a problem to the point where the coach was considered unemployable.

And why assume that SARU/SARFU were always to blame in these situations? White was guilty of appalling brinkmanship during the 2007 World Cup, one minute accusing SARU of not asking him to reapply for his job and the next saying that he wasn't available.

Rian Oberholzer was slammed for flying over to read the riot act to Mallett's team in Cardiff in 1999, but because I know what pressure he was under, I am convinced that he had no choice. Oberholzer was not universally popular, but I think even some of his biggest enemies will agree with me that in comparison to many of the leaders who followed him, he was a good administrator. His value was only recognised when he was no longer there – at least by those big enough to admit it.

But as far as I'm concerned, it is beyond any doubt that the 11 post-isolation Springbok coaches, from Williams to Meyer, have had a tougher ride than necessary. In 1992, the nation was eager to overcome its pariah status, and one way of doing so was by stamping its authority on a sport we had historically excelled at. But the nation's expectations, which were unrealistic after such a long absence from the international arena, just added to the pressure the Bok coaches would face into the future. You often get the feeling in this country that rugby has been chasing its tail trying to catch up ever since the curtain was lifted on isolation 21 years ago.

Another pressure, of course, is created by the political demands a new democracy imposes, and there is still the sense that even now, all these years later, rugby is still trying to rid itself of its reputation as the sport of the oppressor.

Having said that, the challenges may not have been so insurmountable had the sport been properly and professionally administered. Weak leadership and provincial interests continue to trip up the national team even today, much as they did in 1992, when Williams was told he couldn't assemble his Springboks until the Wednesday before the first post-isolation Test, because "Dr Luyt says he has a Currie Cup to win".

The issue of national contracting has been an ongoing saga throughout the years of professionalism. When Heyneke Meyer took over, he had grand plans for his team. But then he discovered that the players he thought would be available were not, for whatever reasons. It is no secret that Meyer had a showdown with the Sharks early in his tenure when he discovered, to his shock, that Ryan Kankowski, a player he rated highly, was being allowed to head to Japan.

With no contracting system in place, the national coaches of the future will continue to do their long-term planning blind, as the provincial unions haemorrhage players to the northern hemisphere.

Until such time as players are centrally contracted, the Springbok coach will remain relatively powerless to stop the exodus, and he will also remain toothless when it comes to determining how much rugby his key players should play in a long season.

In New Zealand, the country comes first. The franchise coaches don't survive if they don't cooperate with the national body and the All Black management, and it helps that everyone is employed by the New Zealand Rugby Union.

I don't know whether South African rugby will ever follow New Zealand's lead, but their contracting system is one of the reasons why they are leading world rugby at this point. I don't know of a Springbok coach in the 18 years of professionalism who hasn't envied the Kiwi system.

But that's not the only issue; there are many others that face the Springbok coaches of the future. Not least of these is the continued quest for that elusive Holy Grail, namely the national blueprint of how the game should be played in this country. I am not touting the same playing style for every provincial union, but rather that some core principles are adopted by all the teams so that the Springbok coach, who now has only five days to prepare for the first Test of the season (as opposed to the three weeks afforded his predecessors in the Super 12 era), has a solid foundation on which to build his strategy.

For example, how can one expect a new national coach to coach a team for the first time in such a short space of time when the provincial teams all have different defensive systems? SARU technical director Rassie Erasmus's Mobi-Unit, which is deployed to help the coaches in the various regions and across different levels, and allows the Springbok assistant coaches to convey the national team's aims to the provincial franchises, is a step in the right direction. But as André Markgraaff says, a lot of work still needs to be done.

He still laments SA Rugby's decision to disband the technical committee, which had been formed to ensure succession planning and develop the national blueprint. As he says, "South African rugby made a hell of a mistake by disbanding the technical committee, and I still say SA Rugby can't do without [it]. That committee did a lot of good work in appointing coaches. Jake was pushed into the under-20 coaching job by the technical committee. The officials said [the committee] didn't work, but if we had good succession planning in place, then the Peter de Villiers/Heyneke Meyer situation would not have happened."

Although he says that former Lions boss Jannie Ferreira was complicit in the SARU decision to disband the technical committee, McIntosh reckons he actually deserves credit for initiating the drive to develop a national blueprint.

"[Ferreira invited] me, Dawie Snyman and Dr Gerrit Pool to his office where we thrashed out a blueprint between us," recalls McIntosh. "We were the north and south pole when it came to coaching, but [Ferreira] got us to compromise and the three of us created a wonderful blueprint." McIntosh explained that the idea was not to prescribe to people what they should do, but to create a template coaches could adapt for different styles of play.

"[We] agreed there was place for Carel du Plessis' type of rugby once a certain point in play had been reached, but the consensus was that direct rugby produced the most tries. It was a brilliant idea, but unfortunately we never got it right because the national coach at the time, Harry Viljoen, didn't want anything to do with it. He scuppered it."

"Sometimes coaches don't want to be helped. But I thought Nick came close to introducing the blueprint with his style of play in 1997 and 1998, and Jake White too. Harry got it right in the game against the Barbarians at the end of 2000 in Cardiff, but then he abandoned it. [That was a] big mistake.

"Heyneke, when [he's gained enough] confidence, will [introduce] the blueprint. I am convinced of that. He will introduce a style that all the other South African coaches and teams [will want to emulate]. We must never be ashamed when people say we 'bash' too much. [Not when] that is what works. The French have moved away from their [basic style of play], and it has [eliminated some of] the things they were so good at."

If you're wondering why a blueprint is so important, consider the upheaval Springbok rugby undergoes every time a new coach comes in and tries to radically reinvent the wheel. It was a disaster with Carel du Plessis, as it was to an extent with Viljoen and even in the initial stages of Peter de Villiers' reign. At least the existence of a blueprint might prevent repeating the same old mistakes, especially when the administrators institute a proper selection process for appointing the coach and then appoint the best man for the job.

Hopefully a blueprint, as well as a grading system for coaches that makes the selection system more scientific, will usher in a new era and put an end to the roller-coaster ride Mark Andrews felt he was on during his years as a player.

As he told me, "If I can make an observation, all or most of the Springbok coaches start off by being naive and then, by the time they wise up, they are exiting the door. To be the Bok coach, you need to have a relatively big ego. So they come in feeling themselves capable of doing the job, and they have wonderful ideas and grandiose plans. Many of them start off with the intent of changing the players and the way games are going to be played.

"Then they start getting frustrated when they realise that theory differs from reality. By the time they start wising up ... they start having fights with SARU, and then they're out the door. [We] have seen this same movie many times, and believe me, as a player, I played in that movie over and over. Sadly there is no school for coaches where they can learn to become coaches."

Well, that might change if Markgraaff has anything to do with it. Although he is not involved in rugby at the moment, he says if he ever returns it will be to set up a coaching academy.

"We would solve a lot of problems in our rugby if we had a coaching institute where prospective coaches can go to learn the craft. We probably have thousands of guys in South Africa who want to be coaches, but where do you go?" Markgraaff asks. "If I got involved again, I would set something up for [prospective] coaches. It must be linked to a university with lecture halls and other infrastructure already in place. If we had a coaching institute, we [would not have] the situation where provinces appoint a guy just because they've seen him on the side of the field as the coach of a Varsity Cup team.

"There are enough coaching jobs available now to justify such an institution. The schools don't use teachers to coach any more, they go outside. There are schools that are paying their coaches up to 70 per cent of what the coaches at professional unions are getting.

"If we have a coaching institution in place, [we could introduce] a proper grading system for coaches, and then we could put proper succession planning in place. That would prevent a repeat of the Carel du Plessis situation where someone with no experience [was appointed], and it would also prevent the appointment being made on political grounds."

Markgraaff left rugby in 2005 in disgust at aspects of Brian van Rooyen's administration, but before that he was one of the few former Springbok coaches who still had some kind of influence on the Bok system. The other was Ian McIntosh.

McIntosh came back to serve a long stint with the Springboks in another capacity; he has been a national selector for nearly a decade now. After being sacked as Bok coach, he got straight back on the horse, as it were, and coached the Sharks to two more Currie Cup titles before ending his career in Wales. But what happened to the rest?

John Williams returned to Northern Transvaal for two separate stints as coach before eventually calling it a day at the end of 1997 to take over the family farm near Alldays.

"In 1995/96, after being a Springbok selector, the Bulls [approached] me and said that they wanted to establish a rugby academy at Loftus. I listened to the Bulls' proposal and agreed to help them out, but on condition that coaching wouldn't be part of my job description.

"But the Bulls were soon in the shit again, with the professional game coming in, and I took over for a while with Eugene van Wyk. I decided to call it a day when I was told that the players were unhappy [because I was] too strict. I had already decided I wanted out, and remember thinking, 'Whoa, stop this bus right here. Maybe I am just not cut out for this professional era.'

"The culture of the game had changed, and gone were the days when the team would sit in the change room afterwards like a big, happy family. The new era of players would come in from the field, strap on their Rolex watches and head out one by one. I didn't want [to be a] part of that."

Kitch Christie, battling illness, presided over a disastrous Super 12 campaign with the Lions in 1996, and was then equally unsuccessful at Northern Transvaal the following year. He died on 22 April 1998. His players' moving eulogies for their likeable mentor were reported in various newspapers.

Carel du Plessis spent a few years coaching Western Province and serving as Gert Smal's assistant at the Stormers before he parted ways with the union in 2005, following Nick Mallett's appointment as director of rugby. Although no longer involved in coaching, he still feels strongly about the game and the direction it should take.

"I want to see a bit more risk in modern rugby. I think we need an education drive, to make coaches and unions aware of the need to put on an entertaining product so that the sport can survive challenges from alternative sports, but people don't seem to care. They just want to win," he says.

Du Plessis says he would get involved again if the right opportunity presented itself, and with the degree of specialisation now required in coaching rugby, that is not impossible. Markgraaff always said Du Plessis would make an excellent attack coach, and maybe he will still get an opportunity to excel at his forte.

Jake White is coaching the Brumbies in Australia, and with great success, so South Africa's loss is definitely Australia's gain. Rudolf Straeuli is helping identify talent in his capacity as commercial manager at the Sharks, and Peter de Villiers is trying to turn the University of the Western Cape into a rugby powerhouse. Nick Mallett went on to coach Stade Francais to French and European titles before becoming Western Province director of rugby and then coach of Italy, and is now an analyst for SuperSport.

Markgraaff thinks being a TV analyst is a waste of Mallett's talent, and he makes an interesting point. "Nick is just 56 and should be in the prime of his coaching life right now. He was very young when he started; he was just 39 when he served as my assistant coach. You haven't learnt life's lessons [at that age]. I think the Springbok coaches have generally been too young. I'm a lot wiser now than I was when I was coach."

Indeed, he is in agreement with Laurie Mains, the legendary All Black coach. When SARFU axed Mallett just as he seemed to be improving his team's game during the 2000 season, Mains said: "Coaching is about learning from [your] mistakes, and unfortunately in South Africa no one gets a chance to do that."

On those points, Mallett can only agree with both Markgraaff and Mains.

"Rob van der Valk said in his book that there was a time when it was Mallett's way or no way," says Mallett. "Rob was right. I was very arrogant about the knowledge that I had. I had come from France, where at that stage coaching and strategy were more advanced. Ian Mac stood alone at the time as the only coach who really seemed to be modern, and I couldn't believe coaches in South Africa didn't even know how to defend a blindside move.

"But I've changed since then. I've become wiser. I was a different coach at Stade Francais and definitely when I coached Italy, by which time coaching was so much more advanced. And yes, you do learn from your mistakes. You never learn from a dream start, as my career with the Boks will tell you."

As it turns out, the New Zealand experience underscores these sentiments. Graham Henry was 57, one year older than Mallett is now, when he was appointed to coach the All Blacks. He blew one World Cup attempt when his team was beaten in the 2007 quarter-final in Cardiff, but against the odds was given a chance to redeem himself, and ended up winning the Webb Ellis trophy at the ripe old retirement age of 65.

I can't think of any South African coaches currently active in the professional game who are anywhere near that age. And only two of the surviving post-isolation Springbok coaches, Williams and McIntosh, are currently older than Henry was when he achieved his crowning moment as a coach.

There are too many South African coaches who are in their prime, or approaching their prime, but have given up on coaching after the system has chewed them up and spat them out. If you look across all the levels, Mallett is far from the only one to whom this has happened. In many of these cases, you could say that the system had let them down.

Hopefully that will change, for if a coaching infrastructure is introduced that incorporates a grading system, and proper succession planning is formulated around scientific measurement rather than subjective opinion, the Springbok teams of the future should be much more efficient. And it should also turn the crisis interventions of 1994, 1997 and 2006 into an amusing but largely forgotten part of South Africa's rugby history.

Post-isolation Springbok coaches' Test-match records

JOHN WILLIAMS – MAY TO DECEMBER 1992

15/08/92   **New Zealand | Johannesburg**   Lost 24-27

22/09/92   **Australia | Cape Town**   Lost 3-26

17/10/92   **France | Lille**   Won 20-15

24/10/92   **France | Paris**   Lost 16-29

14/11/92   **England | London**   Lost 16-33

PLAYED 5   WON 1   LOST 4   DRAW 0

IAN MCINTOSH – MARCH 1993 TO AUGUST 1994

26/06/93   **France | Durban**   Drew 20-20

03/07/93   **France | Johannesburg**   Lost 17-18

31/07/93   **Australia | Sydney**   Won 19-12

14/08/93   **Australia | Brisbane**   Lost 20-28

21/08/93   **Australia | Sydney**   Lost 12-19

06/11/93   **Argentina | Buenos Aires**   Won 29-26

13/11/93   **Argentina | Buenos Aires**   Won 52-23

04/06/94   **England | Pretoria**   Lost 15-32

11/06/94   **England | Cape Town**   Won 27-9

09/07/94   **New Zealand | Dunedin**   Lost 14-22

23/07/94   **New Zealand | Wellington**   Lost 9-13

06/08/94   **New Zealand | Auckland**   Drew 18-18

PLAYED 12   WON 4   LOST 6   DRAW 2

KITCH CHRISTIE | SEPT 1994 TO MARCH 1996

08/10/94   **Argentina | Port Elizabeth**   Won 42-22

15/10/94   **Argentina | Johannesburg**   Won 46-26

19/11/94   **Scotland | Edinburgh**   Won 34-10

26/11/94   **Wales | Cardiff**   Won 20-12

13/04/95   **Western Samoa | Johannesburg**   Won 60-8

25/05/95   **Australia | Cape Town**   Won 27-18   (RWC)

30/05/95   **Romania | Cape Town**   Won 21-8   (RWC)

03/06/95   **Canada | Port Elizabeth**   Won 20-0   (RWC)

10/06/95   **Western Samoa | Johannesburg**   Won 42-14   (RWC)

17/06/95   **France | Durban 17**   Won 19-15   (RWC semi-final)

24/06/95   **New Zealand | Johannesburg**   Won 15-12   (RWC final)

02/09/95   **Wales | Johannesburg**   Won 40-11

12/11/95   **Italy | Rome**   Won 40-21

18/11/95   **England | London**   Won 24-14

PLAYED 14   WON 14   LOST 0   DRAW 0

ANDRÉ MARKGRAAFF | MARCH 1996 TO FEBRUARY 1997

02/07/96   **Fiji | Pretoria**   Won 43-18

13/07/96   **Australia | Sydney**   Lost 16-21

20/07/96   **New Zealand | Christchurch**   Lost 11-15

03/08/96   **Australia | Bloemfontein**   Won 25-19

10/08/96   **New Zealand | Cape Town**   Lost 18-29

17/08/96   **New Zealand | Durban**   Lost 19-23

24/08/96   **New Zealand | Pretoria**   Lost 26-33

31/08/96   **New Zealand | Johannesburg**   Won 32-22

09/11/96   **Argentina | Buenos Aires**   Won 46-15

16/11/96   **Argentina | Buenos Aires**   Won 44-21

30/11/96   **France | Bordeaux**   Won 22-12

07/12/96   **France | Paris**   Won 13-12

15/12/96   **Wales | Cardiff**   Won 37-20

PLAYED 13   WON 8   LOST 5   DRAW 0

CAREL DU PLESSIS | MARCH 1997 TO SEPTEMBER 1997

10/06/97   **Tonga | Cape Town**   Won 74-10

21/06/97   **British and Irish Lions | Cape Town**   Lost 16-25

28/06/97   **British and Irish Lions | Durban**   Lost 15-18

05/07/97   **British and Irish Lions | Johannesburg**   Won 35-16

19/07/97 **New Zealand | Johannesburg** Lost 32-35
02/08/97 **Australia | Brisbane** Lost 20-32
09/08/97 **New Zealand | Auckland** Lost 35-55
23/08/97 **Australia | Pretoria** Won 61-22

PLAYED 8   WON 3   LOST 5   DRAW 0

NICK MALLETT | SEPTEMBER 1997 TO SEPTEMBER 2000

08/11/97 **Italy | Bologna** Won 62-31
15/11/97 **France | Lyon** Won 36-32
22/11/97 **France | Paris** Won 52-10
29/11/97 **England | London** Won 29-11
06/12/97 **Scotland | Edinburgh** Won 68-10
13/06/98 **Ireland | Bloemfontein** Won 37-13
20/06/98 **Ireland | Pretoria** Won 33-0
27/06/98 **Wales | Pretoria** Won 96-13
04/07/98 **England | Cape Town** Won 18-0
18/07/98 **Australia | Perth** Won 14-13
25/07/98 **New Zealand | Wellington** Won 13-3
15/08/98 **New Zealand | Durban** Won 24-23
22/08/98 **Australia | Johannesburg** Won 29-15
14/11/98 **Wales | London** Won 28-20
21/11/98 **Scotland | Edinburgh** Won 35-10
28/11/98 **Ireland | Dublin** Won 27-13
05/12/98 **England | London** Lost 7-13
12/06/99 **Italy | Port Elizabeth** Won 74-3
19/06/99 **Italy | Durban** Won 101-0
26/06/99 **Wales | Cardiff** Lost 19-29
10/07/99 **New Zealand | Dunedin** Lost 0-28
17/07/99 **Australia | Brisbane** Lost 6-32
07/08/99 **New Zealand | Pretoria** Lost 18-34
14/08/99 **Australia | Cape Town** Won 10-9
03/10/99 **Scotland | Edinburgh** Won 46-29 (RWC)
10/10/99 **Spain | Edinburgh** Won 47-3 (RWC)
15/10/99 **Uruguay | Glasgow** Won 39-3 (RWC)
24/10/99 **England | Paris** Won 44-21 (RWC quarterfinal)
30/10/99 **Australia | London** Lost 21-27 (RWC semi-final)
04/11/99 **New Zealand | Cardiff** Won 22-18 (RWC 3rd/4th play-off)
10/06/99 **Canada | East London** Won 51-18

17/06/00   **England | Pretoria**   Won 18-13

24/06/00   England | Bloemfontein   Lost 22-27

08/07/00   **Australia | Melbourne**   Lost 23-44

22/07/00   **New Zealand | Christchurch**   Lost 12-25

29/07/00   **Australia | Sydney**   Lost 6-26

19/09/00   **New Zealand | Johannesburg**   Won 46-40

26/09/00   **Australia | Durban**   Lost 18-19

PLAYED 38   WON 26   LOST 12   DRAW 0

HARRY VILJOEN | SEPTEMBER 2000 TO JANUARY 2002

12/11/00   **Argentina | Buenos Aires**   Won 37-33

19/11/00   **Ireland | Dublin**   Won 28-18

26/11/00   **Wales | Cardiff**   Won 23-13

02/12/00   **England | London**   Lost 17-25

16/06/01   **France | Johannesburg**   Lost 23-32

23/06/01   **France | Durban**   Won 20-15

30/06/01   **Italy | Port Elizabeth**   Won 60-14

21/07/01   **New Zealand | Cape Town**   Lost 3-12

28/07/01   **Australia | Pretoria**   Won 20-15

18/09/01   **Australia | Perth**   Drew 14-14

25/09/01   **New Zealand | Auckland**   Lost 15-26

10/11/01   **France | Paris**   Lost 10-20

17/11/01   **Italy | Genoa**   Won 54-26

24/11/01   **England | London**   Lost 9-29

01/12/01   **USA | Houston**   Won 43-20

PLAYED 15   WON 8   LOST 6   DRAW 1

RUDOLF STRAEULI | MARCH 2002 TO NOVEMBER 2003

08/06/02   **Wales | Bloemfontein**   Won 34-19

15/06/02   **Wales | Cape Town**   Won 19-8

29/06/02   **Argentina | Springs**   Won 49-29

06/07/02   **Samoa | Pretoria**   Won 60-18

20/07/02   **New Zealand | Wellington**   Lost 20-41

27/07/02   **Australia | Brisbane**   Lost 27-38

10/08/02   **New Zealand | Durban**   Lost 23-30

17/08/02   **Australia | Johannesburg**   Won 33-31

09/11/02   **France | Marseille**   Lost 10-30

16/11/02   **Scotland | Edinburgh**   Lost 6-21

23/11/02   **England | London**   Lost 3-53
07/06/03   **Scotland | Durban**   Won 29-5
14/06/03   **Scotland | Johannesburg**   Won 28-19
28/06/03   **Argentina | Port Elizabeth**   Won 26-25
12/07/03   **Australia | Cape Town**   Won 26-22
19/07/03   **New Zealand | Pretoria**   Lost 16-52
02/08/03   **Australia | Brisbane**   Lost 9-29
09/08/03   **New Zealand | Dunedin**   Lost 11-19
11/10/03   **Uruguay | Perth**   Won 72-6   (RWC)
18/10/03   **England | Perth**   Lost 6-25   (RWC)
24/10/03   **Georgia | Sydney**   Won 46-19   (RWC)
01/11/03   **Samoa | Brisbane**   Won 60-10   (RWC)
08/11/03   **New Zealand | Melbourne**   Lost 9-29   (RWC quarterfinal).

PLAYED 23   WON 12   LOST 11   DRAW 0

JAKE WHITE | FEBRUARY 2004 TO DECEMBER 2007

12/06/04   **Ireland | Bloemfontein**   Won 31-17
19/06/04   **Ireland | Cape Town**   Won 26-17
26/06/04   **Wales | Pretoria**   Won 53-18
17/07/04   **Pacific Islands | Gosford**   Won 38-24
24/07/04   **New Zealand | Christchurch**   Lost 21-23
31/07/04   **Australia | Perth**   Lost 26-30
14/08/04   **New Zealand | Johannesburg**   Won 40-26
21/08/04   **Australia | Durban**   Won 23-19
06/11/04   **Wales | Cardiff**   Won 38-36
13/11/04   **Ireland | Dublin**   Lost 12-17
20/11/04   **England | London**   Lost 16-32
27/11/04   **Scotland | Edinburgh**   Won 45-10
04/12/04   **Argentina | Buenos Aires**   Won 39-7
11/06/05   **Uruguay | East London**   Won 134-3
18/06/05   **France | Durban**   Drew 30-30
25/06/05   **France | Port Elizabeth**   Won 27-13
09/07/05   **Australia | Sydney**   Lost 12-30
23/07/05   **Australia | Johannesburg**   Won 33-20
30/07/05   **Australia | Pretoria**   Won 22-16
06/08/05   **New Zealand | Cape Town**   Won 22-16
20/08/05   **Australia | Perth** 5 Won 22-19
27/08/05   **New Zealand | Dunedin**   Lost 27-31

05/11/05   **Argentina | Buenos Aires**   Won 34-23
19/11/05   **Wales | Cardiff**   Won 33-16
26/11/05   **France | Paris**   Lost 20-26
10/06/06   **Scotland | Durban**   Won 36-16
17/06/06   **Scotland | Port Elizabeth**   Won 29-15
24/06/06   **France | Cape Town**   Lost 26-36
15/07/06   **Australia | Brisbane**   Lost 0-49
22/07/06   **New Zealand | Wellington**   Lost 17-35
05/08/06   **Australia | Sydney**   Lost 18-20
26/08/06   **New Zealand | Pretoria**   Lost 26-45
02/09/06   **New Zealand | Rustenburg**   Won 21-20
09/09/06   **Australia | Johannesburg**   Won 24-16
11/11/06   **Ireland | Dublin**   Lost 15-32
18/11/06   **England | London**   Lost 21-23
25/11/06   **England | London**   Won 25-14
26/05/07   **England | Bloemfontein**   Won 58-10
02/06/07   **England | Pretoria**   Won 55-22
09/06/07   **Samoa | Johannesburg**   Won 35-8
16/06/07   **Australia | Cape Town**   Won 22-19
23/06/07   **New Zealand | Durban**   Lost 21-26
07/07/07   **Australia | Sydney**   Lost 17-25
14/07/07   **New Zealand | Christchurch**   Lost 6-33
15/08/07   **Namibia | Cape Town**   Won 105-13
25/08/07   **Scotland | Edinburgh**   Won 27-3
09/09/07   **Samoa | Paris**   Won 59-7   (RWC)
14/09/07   **England | Paris**   Won 36-0   (RWC)
22/09/07   **Tonga | Lens**   Won 30-25   (RWC)
30/09/07   **USA | Montpellier**   Won 64-15 (RWC)
07/10/07   **Fiji | Marseille**   Won 37-20   (RWC quarterfinal)
14/10/07   **Argentina | Paris**   Won 37-13   (RWC semi-final)
20/10/07   **England | Paris**   Won 15-6   (RWC final)
24/11/07   **Wales | Cardiff**   Won 34-12

PLAYED 54   WON 36   LOST 17   DRAW 1

PETER DE VILLIERS | JANUARY 2008 TO JANUARY 2012
07/06/08   **Wales | Bloemfontein**   Won 43-17
14/06/08   **Wales | Pretoria**   Won 37-21
21/06/08   **Italy | Cape Town**   Won 26-0

05/07/08 **New Zealand | Wellington** Lost 8-19

12/07/08 **New Zealand | Dunedin** Won 30-28

19/07/08 **Australia | Perth** Lost 9-16

09/08/08 **Argentina | Johannesburg** Won 63-9

16/08/08 **New Zealand | Cape Town** Lost 0-19

23/08/08 **Australia | Durban** Lost 15-27

30/08/08 **Australia | Johannesburg** Won 53-8

08/11/08 **Wales | Cardiff** Won 20-15

15/11/08 **Scotland | Edinburgh** Won 14-10

22/11/08 **England | London** Won 42-6

20/06/09 **British and Irish Lions | Durban** Won 26-21

27/06/09 **British and Irish Lions | Pretoria** Won 28-25

04/07/09 **British and Irish Lions | Johannesburg** Lost 9-28

25/07/09 **New Zealand | Bloemfontein** Won 28-19

01/08/09 **New Zealand | Durban** Won 31-19

08/08/09 **Australia | Cape Town** Won 29-17

29/08/09 **Australia | Perth** Won 32-25

05/09/09 **Australia | Brisbane** Lost 6-21

12/09/09 **New Zealand | Hamilton** Won 32-29

13/11/09 **France | Toulouse** Lost 17-22

21/11/09 **Italy | Udine** Won 32-10

28/11/09 **Ireland | Dublin** Lost 10-15

05/05/10 **Wales | Cardiff** Won 34-31

12/06/10 **France | Cape Town** Won 42-17

19/06/10 **Italy | Witbank** Won 29-13

26/06/10 **Italy East | London** Won 55-11

10/07/10 **New Zealand | Auckland** Lost 12-32

17/07/10 **New Zealand | Wellington** Lost 17-31

24/07/10 **Australia | Brisbane** Lost 13-30

21/08/10 **New Zealand | Soweto** Lost 22-29

28/08/10 **Australia | Pretoria** Won 44-31

04/09/10 **Australia | Bloemfontein** Lost 39-41

06/11/10 **Ireland | Dublin** Won 23-21

13/11/10 **Wales | Cardiff** Won 29-25

20/11/10 **Scotland | Edinburgh** Lost 17-21

27/11/10 **England | London** Won 21-11

23/07/11 **Australia | Sydney** Lost 20-39

30/07/11 **New Zealand | Wellington** Lost 7-40

13/08/11 **Australia | Durban** Lost 9-14

20/08/11 **New Zealand | Port Elizabeth** Won 18-5

11/09/11 **Wales | Wellington** Won 16-15 (RWC)

17/09/11 **Fiji | Wellington** Won 49-3 (RWC)

22/09/11 **Namibia | North Shore** Won 87-0 (RWC)

30/09/11 **Samoa | North Shore** Won 13-5 (RWC)

09/10/11 **Australia | Wellington** Lost 9-11 (RWC quarterfinal)

PLAYED 48   WON 30   LOST 18   DRAW 0

HEYNEKE MEYER (SINCE JANUARY 2012 UNTIL 17 AUGUST 2013)

09/06/12 **England | Durban** Won 22-17

16/06/12 **England | Johannesburg** Won 36-27

23/06/12 **England | Port Elizabeth** Draw 14-14

18/08/12 **Argentina | Cape Town** Won 27-6

25/08/12 **Argentina | Mendoza** Draw 16-16

08/09/12 **Australia | Perth** Lost 19-26

15/09/12 **New Zealand | Dunedin** Lost 11-21

29/09/12 **Australia | Pretoria** Won 31-8

06/10/12 **New Zealand | Soweto** Lost 16-32

11/11/12 **Ireland | Dublin** Won 16-12

18/11/12 **Scotland | Edinburgh** Won 21-10

25/11/12 **England | London** Won 16-15

08/06/13 **Italy | Durban** Won 44-10

15/06/13 **Scotland | Nelspruit** Won 30-17

22/06/13 **Samoa | Pretoria** Won 56-23

17/08/13 **Argentina | Soweto** Won 73-13

PLAYED 16   WON 11   LOST 3   DRAW 2

References

BOOKS

De Villiers, Peter, with Gavin Rich. *Politically Incorrect: The Autobiography.*
   Cape Town: Zebra Press, 2012

FitzSimons, Peter. *The Rugby War.* Sydney: Harper Sports, 1996

Griffiths, Edward. *Kitch – Triumph of a Decent Man.* Johannesburg:
   CAB, 1997

Jones, Stephen. *Endless Winter: The Inside Story of the Rugby Revolution.*
   Edinburgh: Mainstream Publishing, 1993

Keohane, Mark. *Springbok Rugby Uncovered.* Cape Town: Zebra Press, 2004

Krige, Corné, with Peter Bills. *The Right Place at the Wrong Time.*
   Cape Town: Zebra Press, 2005

Luyt, Louis. *Walking Proud.* Cape Town: Don Nelson, 2004

Matfield, Victor, with De Jongh Borchardt. *Victor: My Journey.* Cape Town:
   Zebra Press, 2011

McCaw, Richie. *The Real McCaw.* Wellington: Aurum Press, 2012

McIntosh, Ian, with John Bishop. *Mac – the Face of Rugby.* Cape Town:
   Don Nelson, 2000

Pienaar, François, with Edward Griffiths. *Rainbow Warrior.* London:
   Collins Willow, 1999

Retief, Dan. *The Springboks and the Holy Grail.* Cape Town: Zebra Press,
   2011

Smit, John, with Mike Greenaway. *Captain in the Cauldron.* Cape Town:
   Safika, 2009

Teichmann, Gary, with Edward Griffiths. *For the Record.* Johannesburg:
   Jonathan Ball Publishers, 2000

Van der Valk, Rob, with Andy Colquhoun. *Nick and I – An Adventure in Rugby*. Cape Town: Don Nelson, 2002

White, Jake, with Craig Ray. *In Black and White – The Jake White Story*. Cape Town: Zebra Press, 2007

MAGAZINES

Rugby World and Post, Rugby Publishing Limited. Editions from 1992 and 1993

NEWSPAPERS

Cape Times
Daily News
Natal Mercury
Pretoria News
Rapport
Sunday Telegraph (London)
Sunday Tribune
The Argus
The Star
The Sunday Independent
The Sunday Times
The Sunday Times (London)
The Weekend Star
Weekend Argus

Index